S0-BBV-954

UNIVERSITY OF NOTRE DAME

Liturgical Studies

VOLUME VII

Liturgical Studies

DEPARTMENT OF THEOLOGY OF THE UNIVERSITY OF NOTRE DAME

Liturgical Piety
REV. LOUIS BOUYER (OF THE ORATORY)

Church Building and Furnishing
REV. J. B. O'CONNELL

The Bible and the Liturgy
REV. JEAN DANIELOU, S.J.

Worship: the Life of the Missions
REV. JOHANNES HOFINGER, S.J.

The Meaning of Sacred Scripture
REV. LOUIS BOUYER (OF THE ORATORY)

The Early Liturgy
REV. JOSEF A. JUNGMANN, S.J.

Rite and Man: Natural Sacredness and Christian Liturgy
REV. LOUIS BOUYER (OF THE ORATORY)

RITE AND MAN

Liturgical Studies

RITE AND MAN

Natural Sacredness and Christian Liturgy

BY

REV. LOUIS BOUYER
OF THE ORATORY

Translated by M. Joseph Costelloe, S.J.
The Creighton University

UNIVERSITY OF NOTRE DAME PRESS
1963

Imprimi Potest: Howard J. Kenna, c.s.c., *Provincial*

Nihil Obstat: Joseph Hoffman, c.s.c., *Censor Deputatus*

Imprimatur: ☦ Leo A. Pursley, D.D., L.L.D.,
Bishop of Fort Wayne-South Bend
February 19, 1963

Library of Congress Catalog Card Number 62-20224

BX
1970
.B66

BQ
4034
17

CANISIUS COLLEGE LIBRARY
BUFFALO, N. Y.

© 1963 by University of Notre Dame Press

NOTRE DAME, INDIANA

Contents

NOTE

An asterisk following a bibliographical reference in the footnotes indicates that the work is also published in a British edition.

CHAPTER I

Natural Religion
and Christian Liturgy

CHRISTIANITY is a supernatural religion: it marks a direct intervention on the part of God in the affairs of this world, in human life. To use a Biblical expression, Christian beliefs are not "thoughts risen in the heart of man." They are God's own thoughts, expressed in terms chosen directly under His inspiration. Christian institutions are not human works. In their essentials, at least, they are the realization of God's own plan, and not of any human design; and it was God Himself who personally intervened in their establishment.

But this does not mean that we are not concerned with the human aspects of Christianity. If it is the work of God, it is of a God who became man. In other words, if God has marked the whole of Christianity with His personal seal, He began by clothing Himself in our humanity so that Christianity might come into being. And yet this image of a garment does not convey the full reality of the Incarnation. God did not assume a human nature as a disguise: He was made man. In Him humanity and divinity — without being confused — became inseparable. The unity of a single person, that of the Son of God, has joined them forever.

With good reason we may insist upon the exalted yet deeply mysterious paradox of this meeting and union. And yet, no matter how far the divine nature may transcend the human, the two cannot be described as being alien to each other. And with even greater reason they may not be conceived as being opposed. In the

1

beginning, human nature was made to the image and likeness of God. Sin, it is true, disfigured this image and obscured this likeness. But the Incarnation was to restore them.

The study which we are undertaking should make these abstract truths stand forth in their reality. With the help of the modern sciences that deal with man, we intend to examine what might be described as the anthropological antecedents to Christianity. From this study, the human character of Christianity should emerge with a clarity that would otherwise be hardly suspected. But this does not mean that its divinity will be obscured. We believe that as a result of these investigations this too will shine forth with greater brilliance. Indeed, the more perfectly we know the human aspects of Christianity, the more perfectly we shall understand that part of it which is the result of divine intervention. This is not to say that the human and the divine should be found in it separated from one another. It is rather that the divine reveals itself in the transformation it effects in what is human. Nor does it subject the latter to some unnatural kind of violence. Rather, the divine restores human nature in elevating it to a supernatural life. For the latter is only the life of the transcendent model to whose image man was made, and in union with which he must be restored.

Certain discoveries which we shall make may at first disconcert us. We shall come to see what Christianity has in common with other religions, and which, perhaps, we had not suspected. Actually, as long as these common elements have not been identified and examined we cannot even imagine them. When they become, as it were, tangible, it should not be surprising that they should create some concern. If Christianity includes so many elements that are found in other religions, from what does it derive its uniqueness and its divinity?

Even more disturbing may be the fact that no matter how firmly we believe in the Incarnation, we may be astonished when we learn how much man has put of himself into his belief in the supernatural, and how much God has accepted from man so that He might give Himself to man in very truth.

A more intensive examination of these matters, however, instead of creating further confusion, should strengthen our faith by opening up far greater depths of meaning.

But we are not the first to be faced with this problem. Even the Fathers of the Church were struck by certain analogies between Christian rites and beliefs and their pagan counterparts. They reacted in different ways to these data which they were the first to gather. At times they were frankly optimistic. If there were so many things in natural religions which Christianity could consecrate, it was because from the beginning of time God had been preparing mankind for the coming of Christ. St. Justin and other early apologists maintained that in the beliefs of all peoples could be found scattered seeds, as it were, of the *Logos,* of the Divine Word which finally flowered, full and united, into the Word made Flesh. But at other times, and often in the same authors, the reaction was negative. They stoutly maintained that such analogies were a diabolical trick, a devilish caricature of the works of God our Saviour.

The same authors may present these two interpretations only a few lines or pages apart. To the casual reader this may seem to be a contradiction, but there is a profound truth behind it: the divine image in man is the occasion of his sin as it is also the foundation of any religion that he can have. The diabolical is never anything more than a counterfeit of the divine. But such a counterfeit would be impossible if there were no traces of the divine in man. And from another point of view, God will not reveal Himself to man, and in man himself through the Incarnation, by causing him to renounce his own nature. It is by a more profound discovery of himself that man is able to discover, as in an impress, the divine visage and presence. Or perhaps it would be better to say, it is only by discovering God coming to him that man solves the puzzle of his own existence. It is only in the mystery of God that light is thrown upon the mystery of man. The Fathers, moreover, extolled the deeply religious wisdom of the Delphic oracle: "Know thyself." But they unanimously repeated that God alone, who had made man, knew him and could help him to know himself perfectly. And it is only when God becomes man that He communicates this knowledge, not only of man such as he is now, but such as he should become or to which he should be restored.

The importance of the study which we are undertaking should be obvious. It furnishes us with an excellent apologetic, one that is not based on a single, but on a multiple perspective. In the nineteenth century the dominant tendency of the history of comparative religions was to reabsorb Christianity into the common religious experiences of mankind. The same "scientific" trend in psychology and in history strove to reduce all the religious aspects of life and of the human soul to what was merely human. But a fact which impresses modern scholars, even those who are not of the faith, is that neither one of these attempts has come to anything.

What is more, the natural development of the sciences dealing with man has in our day led to a real reversal of these tendencies. Without ceasing to see common features in different religions, Christianity included, historians of religion have come to rediscover in every religion the importance of certain specific data. In particular, the radical originality of Christianity, and of Judaism before it, was never brought into such sharp relief as when definite facts discovered by historians of religion were brought to bear upon it. At the same time, both psychologists and historians of religion have come to renounce explanations of the origins of religion that would reduce it to something in man that is not itself religious. The primitive and irreducible character of religion as a social fact and individual experience is all the more manifest today in that we can now describe more accurately the roots which it has in human nature.

Christian scholars thus have at their disposal a wealth of anthropological studies which can be easily adapted to a renewed presentation of Christianity to our contemporaries. They no longer need to refute from outside, as it were, and at cross purposes, the still lively prejudices that Christianity is just one among many religions, and that religion in general is a human experience comparable to, and essentially no different from, any other. The progress of the sciences dealing with man, while continuing to affirm the complete humanity of religion in general and of its varied manifestations, does not permit us to entertain any longer the illusion that religion is something secondary, reducible to other factors in man's development, nor to hold that Christianity is only one religion among many.

This immediate apologetic value of our study is not, however, its most interesting feature. The refutation of objections which modern scholars have made to religion and to Christianity in particular should not be the only product of a study of Christianity with the help of the history of comparative religion and depth psychology. What should emerge is a new understanding of our faith and of the way it should be lived.

Our vision of what is human and what is divine in Christianity, that is, of the way in which God encounters man in supernatural religion and touches him to the very quick so as to regenerate him, should be completely renewed. Our understanding of Christianity, however, with all its rites and formulas, is being constantly threatened by the same errors which in the past gave rise to the great Christological heresies. The mind has always been a prey to the danger of giving wrong answers to problems by over-simplifying them.

In antiquity there were two great errors with various ramifications concerning the Incarnation. Monophysitism so strongly emphasized the divinity of Christ that His humanity came to be absorbed in it, and even denied. Nestorianism, on the other hand, so stoutly championed the reality of this humanity that it eventually came to misunderstand it, and practically denied that it was the humanity of a divine person.

The heresies of Eutyches and Nestorius were propagated some fifteen hundred years ago, but the mental attitudes that sponsored them are common to all time. It would be quite naive to believe that they are no longer with us. As a matter of fact, in the ideological ferment of today, it is only too easy to identify them and to see them at work. The attempts to renew the liturgical life of the Church bear the mark of these same tendencies. As a consequence, it is extremely important to recognize them and to see where they lead, if we want this renewal to be solid and enduring.

Certain conservative Catholics, "liturgical integrists," could be compared with the Monophysites. To them all ecclesiastical institutions, and especially the liturgy, seem to be equally sacred, and therefore immutable. This tendency, normally associated with what we may call the "rubricist mentality," leads one to look upon Christian worship as something handed down from on high *en bloc*. The liturgy, given to us by the authority of the Church, which is itself directly assimilated to the divine authority, must be considered as wholly divine. Consequently, for one with such an attitude, the liturgy should somehow escape humanity. Any attempt to understand it in its historical development seems to discredit it by opening the way for further modifications. To suggest certain changes and adaptations would mean a disowning of the heavenly gift and the supernatural authority that presided over its organization.

An example of the above is the reaction of some to the question of a liturgical language, and, more generically, to the question of any understanding of the sacred rites and formulas by the faithful. For some the attachment to Latin to the exclusion of other languages has become a matter of principle. Why? Because it seems to them that a dead language both expresses and protects this transcendent sacred character of a worship which should be performed for men and among men, but which cannot be handed over to them, nor even really belong to them.

In such circumstances, it is not surprising that the rigorous attachment to Latin goes hand in hand with a desire to keep something mysterious and hieratic about the performance of the rites, even to the extent of making them inaccessible to the faithful. Along with the Latin, it is deemed necessary to recite certain prayers in a low voice, particularly those that are most essential. A fierce opposition is maintained to everything that could emphasize what the sacred rites have in common with simple human actions. To restore the altar to its primitive form of a table would be scandalous, as would be anything else that could stress the fact that the Mass is a meal.

In extreme instances, even simple explanatory translations are frowned upon, and, in Missals intended for private use, literal translations are avoided and are replaced with paraphrases.

In short, all that could make the liturgy a living thing, all that would help the people to share in it, is considered a profanity — as if the liturgy could only retain its sacred character by being removed from any contact with the common man.

Behind such reactions there is obviously the illusion that the liturgy is sacred, divine, for the simple reason that it is a pure product of authority, something immutably imposed from above upon men who can only receive it passively, who cannot really be concerned with or engaged in it at all. Historians of the liturgy reply in vain that the liturgy was never imposed in such a manner. They easily show how it spontaneously arose in the Christian community as the product of many individual efforts, how it was gradually elaborated by, and continually evolving within, the community from which it came. This is not the same as saying that neither divine nor merely human authority had anything to do with it. The sacraments were first instituted by Christ. Ecclesiastical authority had then to sort out, correct, and finally codify the further developments that had taken place within the community. Nevertheless, as scholars have observed, ecclesiastical authority exercised only a moderately creative influence on the development of the Christian liturgy, and even Christ Himself created nothing in it *ex nihilo*.

They tell us, moreover, that sacred meals like the Mass and purification rites like Baptism are not specifically Christian phenomena. If we limit ourselves to the "mystery religions" that were spreading through the Roman empire contemporaneously with Christianity, we find these same elements in them. And what is more significant is that we find them already tied to an idea of salvation brought to mankind through the ritual participation in the death and restoration to life of a saviour god.

It is here that the tendency we describe as Nestorian comes to the fore, in the face of, and in opposition to, the Monophysite tendency. We mean the tendency to stress the human aspects of Christianity in such a way that its individuality, along with its divinity, is in danger of disappearing.

When the history of comparative religions such as that subscribed to by the Catholic school of Maria Laach was still in an embryonic stage, it seems to have engulfed all the manifestations of essential differences in analogies that may be found almost everywhere. Thus it was admitted that the common experiences of the race could have furnished Christianity with a basic ritual, and even an interpretation for this ritual. The "mystery," which was to be found in paganism, was an efficacious rite through which one could attain salvation by re-enacting the death of a saviour god. The Mass was therefore simply an application to Christ and His work of a ritual and mythic pattern already used for Osiris, Dionysus, and many other ancient deities. These highly questionable explanations were discounted, as we shall see, by the advance of the science of comparative religion. The chimera of a single mythic and ritual pattern — to be filled out later by different religions so that with no exception for the transcendency of the Christian faith what was original in each would disappear — has been finally destroyed.

There is, however, another form of liturgical Nestorianism which we see at work today and which is no less erroneous than the preceding. It is a reaction against a patent confusion of what is sacred in Christianity with what is naturally sacred, but it is an unfortunate reaction. It also strives to secure what is human in Christianity, but while taking care not to confuse it with other religions, it attempts to present Christianity as a radically new religion precisely because it rejects all sacrality in the ordinary, pre-Christian meaning of the word. According to this view, the Incarnation consecrated humanity as such, and not some particular area of human activity, or some part of man that could be defined as sacred: the whole of humanity just as it is, was — if it may be said — consecrated "in its very profaneness." If in pre-Christian natural religions the sacred was that which was "set apart" from the profane, in the religion of Christ the "sacred" would be nothing else than the "profane" seen in the light of the Incarnation.

According to this view, Christianity not only could not have, and should not have, accepted anything of the sacred rituals of non-Christian religions for its own liturgical uses, but on principle its only rites were common human actions simply consecrated through the presence of Christ. Thus, in place of the ritual sacrifices of the ancient religions, Christ was put to death upon the Cross (a death which was in no sense hieratic, nor even sacred from the viewpoint of religious ritual, whether it be that of Judaism or some form of paganism); and thus, too, for the more or less formal liturgies, He substituted a common meal that was simply illumined and consecrated by His presence in the midst of His followers.

Later, to be sure, the natural tendency of the human mind contributed to dressing up the simple and direct actions of the Last Supper in a ritualistic and sacred attire. Highly elaborate liturgies for the Eucharist came into being, but the evangelical ideal of Christian worship, to which the Church must constantly strive to return, should as far as possible set aside all these artificial trappings which veil the true nature of the Eucharist as conceived and instituted by Christ. We should always rediscover the primitive Supper in the Mass, and to do this, all that is archaic or hieratic should be discarded, and the Eucharist should take on as far as possible the appearance of a meal taken in common among friends. The readings from Scripture and comments upon them and the accompanying prayers should recall as far as possible a friendly gathering about the family table in which the head of the household tells his children of his plans for each and all of them. The celebration of the Mass and particularly of the Communion should take on the appearance of a festive banquet. Men will thus come to realize that the originality of Christianity consists in consecrating their everyday lives through the Incarnation, and not in attempting to live in a world that is supposed to be holy but which is in fact artificial and out of contact with reality.

If we adopt this point of view, we arrive at the exact antithesis of the Monophysite tendency described above. According to the Monophysite concept of Christianity, the Mass can only be the Mass by being something entirely different from ordinary life and completely separate from it. The altar should not look like a table, the reception of Holy Communion should not resemble a meal, nor should the vernacular be used at Mass. According to the Nestorian concept, however, everything about the Mass should recall a profane meal, even to the inclusion of mundane conversations. It is only a new spirit, the shining forth of the divine presence, that should consecrate that which is profane, but without changing or rejecting it.

If Nestorianism tends simply to superimpose what is divine upon what is human, it may be said that it here enjoys a free hand. It is true that such people maintain that all of human life should be permeated with the presence of Christ. But they do not admit that in this "all" anything could be set aside in order to manifest its special consecration to God. Everything should belong to God in a sense, but it should also remain human with the common humanity of man, not only unchanged, but stripped of all that which could affirm in man the transcendence, the unique personality of God made man.

The ultraconservative liturgists, of the type that can be described as "integrists," are rightly anxious to maintain this transcendence and the sovereign authority of the Saviour's unique personality. But they are mistaken in their desire to see the liturgy dehumanized on this account. Their extremist opponents, looking for reforms and innovations, strive to preserve the human character of the liturgy and of the whole of Christ's religion in the name of the Gospel. They are right in their aim, but they are wrong in believing that a salvation of humanity means to leave it as it is, and even to wipe out all distinctions between the sacred and the profane in order to allow it to be simply itself while belonging wholly to God in Christ. The "Law of the Incarnation" which they advance is not actually what they believe it to be, that is, the assumption of profane humanity *en bloc* so as to consecrate it with no other change than an illumination of its profound nature through grace. Quite the contrary, the "Law of the Incarnation" consists in producing a new sacrality, a renewed consecration, by the setting aside of a humanity which, in order to belong wholly to God, does not at all belong to itself. Such is in fact the humanity of the God made man, and it is because of this that it can save us. In this way, and only in this way, as St. Paul declares, is there prepared a final consecration of the whole of humanity in the body of Christ. Yet this saved humanity will also have to renounce itself in a certain way to be united with Christ. It is only by sharing in the Cross of Christ that it will be integrated through a new birth into His Mystical Body.

Depth psychology can be of great help to us in destroying this chimera of a humanity that could be true to itself only in as far as it would reject what is sacred and thus so possess itself that nothing, either in itself or in the world, would be acknowledged as God's exclusive possession. Actually it shows us that the concept and reality of the sacred, of something being put aside for God and belonging wholly to Him, cannot be eliminated or neglected. Modern man, who thinks that he has succeeded in doing this, is on that account only less a man. An analysis of his dreams, and the highest reaches of his poetry are proof of the fact that man, in spite of himself, cannot live without that which is sacred. When he is locked up in himself and shut off from the presence of God in time and space, he is stifled. If this presence is not given to him, he must shamefully make for himself a wretched substitute. Otherwise he will die, spiritually asphyxiated.

Christianity, therefore, far from encouraging this deadly atrophy in him, alone satisfies his endless longing for a sacrality that is not deceptive. For the sacredness of the Gospel is not an arbitrary sacredness that burdens man as it fills him with illusions. It is the only sacredness that is at once completely real and liberating. It is the sacredness of the sovereign God, but of a God who is also the Father, and who does not break into the closed world of His rebellious creatures except to endow them with their native destiny of "sons," by handing them over in the only Son made flesh to the love of the eternal Father.

The Incarnation therefore does not efface or render useless or outmoded the primitive notion of the sacred — of a domain "set apart," as the word indicates, in the life of man, to belong wholly to God and God alone. How could it do this without abolishing even man's sense of God as of a being distinct from man, independent of him, but sovereign alike over him and all things? But the signs of what is sacred, those spontaneous signs which are consequent to man's primitive and basic experience of his utter dependence upon a God who is both distinct and transcendent, become charged with a new sense. They are no longer the signs of a remote, hidden, and even strange God. Assumed by the God who reveals Himself, who becomes man, they become the signs of His revelation and of His coming.

They thus lose their puzzling and at times ambiguous appearance, but it would be completely wrong to conclude from this that they are no longer mysterious. They are still mysterious, even more so, but in a different way. For the God of revelation, in a certain sense, reveals himself precisely as the hidden God, that is, as the Being wholly different from anything that we can know from natural reason or even from imagination. If His love brings Him infinitely close to us, the revelation of what this love is raises Him much farther above us than any elemental concept could have done.

The Incarnation, therefore, does not lead to the disappearance of natural sacredness but to its metamorphosis. This sacredness, in spite of all its deficiencies and even its distortions, remains in man as the stepping-stone to the Incarnation. To eliminate it would be to make the Incarnation impossible by shutting off in man every possible approach to God. Just as the Incarnation would have no meaning for us if it had taken place in flesh other than our own, so the new sacredness coming from it would not be accessible to us if it did not flow into us through the channels of natural sacredness. This is certainly the truth that lies beneath oversimplified solutions of certain analogies, such as those proposed by the school of Maria Laach. The same God who became incarnate is He who has never ceased to leave to man, and even to those that are most degraded, some evidence of His existence, His presence, and His rule. Once again, without these traces, the

Incarnation would not have been possible. With a being which no longer had in itself, in its own world, a recognizable place for God — were it only the void which the divine absence has left — a renewed contact would no longer be possible. For such a being, a fall would already be an irremediable damnation, as it was for the fallen angels.

Finally, it is equally chimerical to try to find in the Incarnation a wholly new sacredness, of such a kind that it would appear to have come down entirely from heaven, or no longer to desire any special sacredness under the pretext that everything should now be assumed into the sacredness of the Incarnation. The first error amounts to a wish that the flesh of the Incarnation should have itself descended from heaven, which is in effect to deny the reality of the Incarnation. The second amounts to confusing the flesh of the Saviour with all flesh indiscriminately, which ultimately means that He had no flesh of His own.

Entirely different from this last error is the profound truth which lends it a semblance of justification. It is indeed true that the Incarnation should tend to consecrate all flesh, but by this, as we shall see, it merely tends to restore the primitive, original form of natural sacredness, while transfiguring it; for everything without exception was originally conceived as pertaining to the divine domain. But it tends to this end effectively only because it starts from the unique sacredness of the flesh of the Son of God made man, which, as we shall also see, far from abolishing the process of segregation which was at the heart of Jewish sacredness, brings it to its completion, just as the latter, far from abrogating the segregations of natural sacredness, had already perfected them.

Actually, the typical error of our contemporaries is to believe that humanity, whether it is found among Christians, pagans, or Jews, should remain or become profane in order to be "real" or "true." This is the prime error of those who are overcivilized. It is the illusion which threatens every civilization. As a matter of fact, natural man is not at all a profane man. Among men there is nothing more artificial, nothing less natural than the purely profane man. As we are discovering today, sacredness is not some secondary, artificial adjunct to humanity as such. There is no humanity that does not, at least remotely, proceed from it.

Because of its natural sacredness, a fully *human* humanity — such as that of Christianity should be — cannot be desecrated. A desecrated humanity would find it impossible to become Christian solely because it would have ceased to be human. The humanity of Christianity should be a humanity in which the appreciation for what is sacred, which is its prerogative as a creature, should be recovered, saved, and transfigured in the redemptive Incarnation.

Then without doubt, beginning with that which is supremely sacred, withdrawn from man, and wholly restored to God and to God alone — the humanity of Christ — all mankind and all the world will be effectively called to become sacred again in the same way and even more perfectly than it all was at the beginning when it left the divine hands. But again, this will only be brought about by following the way of the Incarnation, the way which, far from avoiding the ancient ways of God with man and the world, would restore and illumine their imperishable traces.

As a conclusion to this introduction, there is no need to emphasize the special importance of our study in the face of the missionary problems that confront us. Whether it is a question of missionary activity in pagan lands which must replace false and imperfect religions by the one true faith, or whether it is a question of missionary activity to a de-Christianized world, the value of such a study should be obvious. Without it, in the first instance, we shall not be able to avoid either confused amalgams in which the originality of Christianity would be lost, or a Christianity superficially applied to humanity, since we shall miss those stepping-stones without which man would never become one with the faith proposed to him. But, in the second instance, without the same study, the necessary adaptation would be equally destructive or impossible. To pretend to consecrate a profane world by leaving it to its profane character is to attempt a contradiction. There are obscure threads, particularly difficult to trace today, which do not cease to direct man, even when he does not understand them, toward the God who is looking for him. But under the weight of the indifference that encumbers men who have been literally "profaned," how and where are these threads to be found, so that they may lead them to the full light of the Gospel? The answer which we may be able to give to such an urgent question should not be the least advantage of our study.

CHAPTER II

Recent Developments
in the History of Religions

A GOOD ACCOUNT of the history of religions would provide an
excellent indication of the progress of the human mind in modern
times. Unfortunately, such an account exists in only a rather fragmentary and superficial form. If it were to be written as it should,
there would be need of numerous studies such as that which Henri
de Lubac has dedicated to the discovery of Buddhism by the
West.[1] A glance at the history of religions is sufficient to show
that the human mind has not experienced that steady progress it
has claimed in freeing itself from prejudices. Here perhaps less
than anywhere else we witness the advance of mere facts in the
light of pure reason. It almost seems that scholars have been busily
engaged in fitting themselves with glasses to hide the facts from
their view or to reveal only those colored by their own particular
prejudices. Only in recent times has the pressure of the facts become so strong that it has imposed an objective methodology. All
at once the circle of ambitious theories which had been steadily
growing was broken to bits and relegated to the limbo of dead
ideas, while the profound reality which never ceased to animate
the apparently dead religious myths was rediscovered.[2]

[1] H. de Lubac, *La rencontre du Bouddhisme et de l'Occident* (Paris,
1950).*

[2] Arthur Koestler's interesting work, *The Sleepwalkers* (New York,
1959),* shows how the history of modern science is quite different from
this edifying plan.

14

The science of comparative religion is of fairly recent date, but like all the other sciences it has antecedents in the distant past. These are of particular interest since of all the sciences that of comparative religion has experienced the most difficulties in its development.[3]

There is still much to be gleaned from the gossip of Herodotus, who was already dominated by an Egyptomania that was to reappear in a number of his successors. Pausanias is a richer source and, what is more, more accurate, thanks to his indefatigable curiosity as an antiquarian.[4] The different religious syncretists at the beginning of our own era rival him in this but do not match him. They were the first to exhibit the tendency to identify things on the basis of a common resemblance or at least to reach the conclusion that analogous features indicate the dependence of one thing upon another.

The first to sense the presence of certain irreducible factors behind the most disturbing similarities were the Christians of the Patristic Age. But they were to an extent the victims of another temptation that besets historians of religions, that is, a preference for the written document, even to the point of neglecting obvious facts. The Apologists never lack for words when they discuss the religion of Homer, although it was no longer extant in their own day; but they show surprisingly little interest in the religion of their contemporaries, to which they had once themselves subscribed. Clement of Alexandria, who had perhaps himself been initiated into the pagan mysteries before becoming a Christian, is undoubtedly the prime example of this attitude.[5] He discusses at great length the myths which had only a literary survival in his day, but it is rather questionable if he ever really opened his eyes to the religious practices that were being carried on next to his very classroom.

If this was true of the Fathers of the Church, who could still see paganism flourishing under their very eyes, and who had frequently been pagans themselves before their conversion to Christianity,

[3] A résumé may be found at the beginning of *Studies in Comparative Religions*, edit. E. C. Messenger, 5 vols. (London, 1935).

[4] See Sir James Frazer's moving essay, *Pausanias, and Other Greek Sketches* (New York, 1900).

[5] See the whole of his *Protrepticus* in *Sources Chrétiennes*, II, French trans. by Mondésert (Paris, 1943).

it should not be surprising that the Middle Ages, which had to draw its information about pagan worship from written sources, particularly Ovid and Virgil, should have had a very imperfect knowledge of it.[6]

Cardinal Nicolas of Cusa was perhaps the first to attempt a first-hand study of a non-Christian religion, and one in which some general sympathy was combined with a critical attitude.[7] Though something of a bookworm himself, he nonetheless went straight to the Koran to learn about Islam. That irenicism which manifests itself in his *De pace fidei,* and the feeling for irreducible differences expressed in his *Cribratio Alcorani,* are traits that can already be noticed in some of the writings of the Fathers of the Church. Justin was able to recognize in the most diverse philosophies seeds of the Word which would become flesh, and at the same time to set the God of the Bible up against pagan idols, the "logical" sacrifice against the bloody sacrifices.[8] Clement in turn was fascinated by the evocations, or promises involved in the ancient myths, though he was critical of their substance. But no ancient Christian pushed the examination of possible points of agreement and insurmountable obstacles so far or so systematically.[9]

But it is among the Platonists of the Renaissance, and especially in Marsilio Ficino, that a genuine enthusiasm for foreign ideas studied at their source is for the first time found among Christians.[10] They were, moreover, more interested in a religious philosophy, such as Neo-Platonism, or in a philosophical religion, such as Hermetism, than in religions as such. And it is quite certain that they did not hesitate to distort these ideas into the framework of their own Christianity, even though they were more aware of the limitations to possible assimilations than their dithyrambic

[6] See E. R. Curtius, *European Literature and the Latin Middle Ages,* trans. W. R. Trask (New York, 1953),* pp. 3 ff.

[7] See in particular the study of E. Vansteenberghe, *Le cardinal Nicolas de Cues* (Paris, 1920).

[8] See my *Spiritualité du Nouveau Testament et des Pères* (Paris, 1960), p. 268. (This book will appear in English as *The Spirituality of the New Testament and the Fathers.*)

[9] See especially the beginning of the *Protrepticus,* with our commentary, *op. cit.,* pp. 323 ff.

[10] See Raymond Marcel's book, *Marsile Ficin* (Paris, 1958).

formulas or the syncretistic atmosphere of their preferred authors would lead us to believe.[11]

Ficino was the first of the moderns to perceive the heights which the mysticism of Plotinus had been able to attain, and he was the first also to have at least had a presentiment of the historical importance of the mystery religions. But his approach to them helped to create a lasting confusion between the mystery religions themselves and the use which Hermetism and late Neo-Platonism made of their symbols.[12]

Quite similar to this, both for better and for worse, was the rediscovery at about this time of the Jewish mystical traditions, especially that of the Cabala by Gilles ⌐f Viterbo, Pico della Mirandola, and Johannes Reuchlin.[13]

A little later, the expansion of Christian missions in Africa and Asia, and then in America, quickly renewed the knowledge of non-Christian religions. The flood of reports from eyewitnesses remained for a long time badly mixed up. Genuine but scattered and fragmentary information was buried in fairy tales or in an apologetic even more hasty than that of the Platonists of Florence.[14] Montaigne's famous *Essay on the Cannibals* reveals this state of affairs. He was also one of the first to betray the relativistic reaction which was soon to become popular. Missionaries too easily convinced of their success were overly optimistic in interpreting their discoveries. These impressions were soon supplanted by an idea that was at first vague and fluctuating, as in Montaigne, but which was shortly organized into a system that proved to be more influential than the Jansenistic or semi-Jansenistic pessimism so popular during the second phase of the debate over the "Chinese rites."[15] This was that all religions, diverse as they may be, are basically the same, and consequently it is better to hold on to what is found in the cradle, though not exclusively.[16]

[11] R. Marcel, *op. cit.,* pp. 647 ff.

[12] R. Marcel, *op. cit.,* pp. 486 ff.

[13] See the works of F. Secret, particularly on the first of these authors.

[14] Paul Hazard in his *Crise de la conscience européenne* (Paris, 1935),* has noted the influence of these romanticized tales.

[15] For a careful study of this problem, see H. Bernard-Maître, *Sagesse chinoise et philosophie chrétienne* (Paris, 1935).

[16] See the conclusion of his *Essay on the Cannibals.*

During the course of the seventeenth century, under the influence of the new materialism or of the common rationalistic outlook, there was an easy transfer to the opposite position: religions are nothing but priestly inventions and are all equally devoid of foundations. At least from the beginning of the eighteenth century, it was thought that one could see in religion nothing but the first childish, and now obsolete, advances of the human mind in its discovery and interpretation of the world.[17]

It may be said that the science of the history of religions, which was originally pointed in the first direction, was soon fixed upon the second. Only recently has it escaped from this alternative. This is why it was so long taken up with, and centered about, a false problem, that of the origin of religion, understood in the sense of something that was, and could only be, a transitory phenomenon and quite accidental. From this came the endless search of the nineteenth century for an element in itself non-religious which could have been the origin of religion through some accident or fraud.

At the end of the eighteenth century, the beginnings of this quest for the origin of religion may be seen in the work of the polygraph Dupuis entitled *The Origin of All Cults*.[18] According to him, religion may be traced to astrology, that is, to the conviction that the course of the stars controls the progress of man's life and the universe. It was an idea that was destined to have a lasting influence and numerous revivals.

The history of religions, however, did not begin to take on the character of a science until after a preliminary study of the great religious books of the East had been made. This was undertaken by Friedrich von Schlegel at the beginning of the nineteenth century.[19] Herder had prepared the way with his studies of Hebrew poetry and of the other newly discovered types of religious poetry of the East.[20] Over and above the vaguely romantic but fruitful theories about the soul of the people gaining an awareness of itself in the great myths of humanity, the linguist Max Müller

[17] This is the underlying thesis of the *Encyclopédie* of Diderot and d'Alembert.

[18] *De l'origine de tous les cultes* (Paris, 1795).

[19] His lectures on the sacred books of India date from 1808.

[20] His studies on Hebrew poetry date from 1770.

succeeded in the second half of the century in proposing the first really scientific explanation of religious phenomena.[21]

According to him, religion is intimately connected with an elementary stage in the development of every language. Man can only formulate his impressions of the universe in a language invented to express his own sentiments about his own actions. This is why he attributes a personal character to the phenomena of nature. In short, the gods are nothing more than metaphors, inevitable in the first stage of a language, but taken literally by mankind in its infancy stage.

Preoccupation with the origins of religion led to an ever-increasing interest in primitive peoples. From this came the increasing importance attached to the study of extant religions of this type in Africa and, perhaps even more so, on the islands of the South Pacific. New theories arose alongside that of Max Müller, though they still retained his basic premise that religion belongs properly to an elementary stage of human development. Among these theories were two that marked particularly significant advance.

The first, animism, was expounded by Tylor in his *Primitive Culture*.[22] According to this theory, every religion has its origin in an idea of the soul, a counterpart of the material man, whose activity, as it seems to him, surpasses that of his body, to the extent of being able to survive even after the death of the latter. Thus is derived, by the same process of projection, a general explanation of the activity apparent in the world, by making it depend upon souls with which all things are believed to be endowed.

The second theory was that of the French sociological school of Durkheim and Lévy-Bruhl. It differs from Tylor's in that it insists upon the eminently social character of all religion, even to the point of failing to see anything else in it. The totem rather than the soul is now regarded as being the origin of all religion. Among certain Indian tribes, such as the Algonquins, this word indicates a legendary animal that is supposed to be the ancestor of a human group. According to Durkheim, in *The Elementary Forms of the Religious Life*,[23] the collective conscience of the primitives tends

[21] *Comparative Mythology* appeared in 1856, *Introduction to the Science of Religion* in 1870, and *Origin and Growth of Religious Ideas* in 1878.

[22] E. B. Tylor, *Primitive Culture*, 4th ed., 2 vols. (London, 1903).

[23] Trans. J. W. Swain (New York, 1926).*

to represent itself under the form of an ancestor, a kind of super-man depicted under the form of an animal, the totem. Since it is thought to survive in all its members, this totem is a sort of collective soul of the group. Religion would therefore be only the prevailing collective consciousness in a society where the individual has not yet attained a clear recognition of his own autonomy with respect to the group. Lévy-Bruhl, in his study *Primitive Mentality,* defines it more precisely as the product of a prelogical mentality accompanying this original immersion of the individual consciousness in that of the group.[24]

Among other theories proposed were those of Andrew Lang[25] and Sir James Frazer,[26] who placed the origin of religion in magic, and those of the anthropologists such as Codrington[27] who derived it from "mana," a kind of mysterious fluid, conceived in a quasi-physical, impersonal fashion, which the primitive believed to be proper to certain beings and certain objects. But they all enter into the framework of an evolutionary concept of the human mind that was best expressed by Auguste Comte.[28]

According to Comte, man, in the process of coming to know the world, passes through three successive stages. He called the first of these the theological stage, one in which religion dominates man's vision of the world. In his efforts to explain the various phenomena of the world, man posits personalities behind them naively conceived as being like his own. He later reaches a metaphysical stage where these elementary representations are replaced by impersonal abstractions. But this is no more than a bridge to the final, positive state, that of the adult intelligence. At this stage, man is at last content with an observation of facts, and from these he deduces the laws of nature by simply applying his reason to the data of experience. Divine images and metaphysical concepts disappear, since they are useless and without validity.

The different theories of religion which the nineteenth century elaborated are no more than so many different attempts to fit the

---

[24] Trans. L. A. Clare (New York, 1923).

[25] *The Making of Religion* (London, 1899), and *Magic and Religion* (London, 1901).

[26] Especially *The Golden Bough,* 3rd ed., 12 vols. (London, 1911-1914).

[27] R. H. Codrington, *The Melanesians* (Oxford, 1891).

[28] See the introduction to his *Cours de philosophie positive.*

history of religions into a plan of this kind. If Müller, Tylor, Durkheim, and Frazer in particular, with their different theories have brought about at least a partial ordering and clarification of an ever-increasing multitude of details, their repeated efforts to systematize the whole betray the inability of any one of these theories to embrace them all. Along with the presupposition that religion is a transitory, irrational phenomenon that can be reduced to something else, they share the common defect of being unable to point out what is essential to it. Only the appearance of a new scientific philosophy could free the history of religions from the radical inability of the Positivistic mentality to grasp the whole of reality.

This is exactly what happened in the course of the last half-century with the appearance of phenomenology. As elaborated by Husserl, phenomenology is not a restoration of either the metaphysics or the theology decried by Auguste Comte and the other Positivists.[29] It has, however, perhaps laid the groundwork for their rehabilitation within the framework of the modern scientific mind. Without actually discussing the existence or nonexistence of metaphysical or theological entities, it has re-established the fundamental importance of the object (with which human activity is engaged or about which human thought is oriented) for the understanding of all human activity, and particularly that of thought. This is their intentionality, without which they remain incomprehensible. As a consequence, a study of religion in which the religious object is considered as being secondary or even insignificant, and where the attention is systematically directed to something else is seen to be ridiculous. On the other hand, it becomes obvious that the science of religions should concern itself particularly with what is specifically religious in the object. Even if it is true, and this cannot be clearly demonstrated, that the religious object has been historically derived from the metaphors of primitive language, from a shadowy concept of the soul, from the rude figure of the totem, or from anything else of the sort, the formal study of religion begins to advance only when it investi-

[29] E. Husserl, *Logische Untersuchungen,* 3rd ed. (Halle, 1922). See the article by Herbert Spiegelberg, "Der Begriff der Intentionalität der Scholastik bei Brentano und bei Husserl," in *Philosophische Hefte,* V, 1/2 (1936), 75 ff., and for a more general treatment, Stanislas Breton, *Conscience et Intentionnalité* (Lyon, 1956).

gates the religious object as such, distinguishing it from every-thing that is antecedent to, or contemporary with, it.

The influence of phenomenology in this area has been augmen-ted by the appearance of the so-called philosophy of emergence in Anglo-Saxon countries, and particularly in America, where the progress of the history of religions during the last decades has been quite remarkable.[30] Surprisingly little known in Latin coun-tries, this scientific philosophy, associated with the names of Whitehead, Webb, and Dewey, represents an effort of modern philosophical thought to follow the developments of science itself since the nineteenth century.[31]

The science of the 1850's developed within a mental frame-work which could be described as being naively materialistic. As a consequence of this, a fundamental principle of the Positivism of Comte and his contemporaries was that reality ("facts") could only be of a material nature. From this *a priori* assumption came the necessity of reducing all phenomena which appear to be im-material, including that of religion, to material processes.

The progress of the physical sciences, of physics and chemistry in particular, has broken through this prejudice by radically modi-fying, and even demolishing, the apparently simple and obvious concept that nineteenth-century science had of matter. In the hands of modern physicists, matter, which was formerly so neatly distinct from the mind as to be opposed to it, has been resolved into elementary data where its former characteristics such as mass, extent, and immutability have disappeared. In its place, we now have a reality which can only be defined in terms of belonging rather to that which was formerly opposed to it. Unwittingly, men have returned to a definition of matter given by one of the Fathers of the Church, Gregory of Nyssa: a complex of intelligible quali-ties, of mathematical relations between forces that are themselves immaterial, considered in abstraction from the mind that thinks of them.[32]

[30] See *History of Religions: Essays in Methodology,* ed. Mircea Eliade (Chicago, 1959).

[31] See especially A. N. Whitehead, *Process and Reality: An Essay in Cosmology* (Cambridge, 1929).

[32] See Hans Urs von Balthasar, *Présence et Pensée* (Paris, 1942), pp. 19 ff.

The evolving framework within which nineteenth-century science tended to limit the vision of the world has thus been radically changed, though it has not completely disappeared. And it is this change which the philosophy of emergence is striving to follow. In place of an evolution conceived as if the higher realities issue continuously from the lower in the sense that the former would have been contained in, and could be reduced to, the latter — which is in itself a confused and contradictory concept — a theory of a kind of creative evolution, or perhaps better, of an evolving creation, has made its appearance. In this new philosophy the definite stages in the process of evolution are as important as its continuity. From inanimate matter to living matter, from living matter to man, and from man to his elevation to the supernatural order, there is an unbroken continuity. But instead of any higher stage being reducible to the lower, like the parts of a telescope, it is only the higher stages that reveal all the potentialities of the lower, for it is only then that these potentialities emerge fully activated. Consequently, instead of mind becoming understood by a reduction to matter, it is mind that makes matter really intelligible. The reduction of one phase to that which precedes it is never possible. On the contrary, each essentially new link in the evolutionary process is necessary for a reflex knowledge of the preceding one. In other words, no preparatory factor is really explicable until the appearance of the ultimate reality.

The striking progress made in psychology in the twentieth century was bound to prove the fruitfulness of these philosophical views. It can even be said that they have conclusively foiled the attempts made to explain the human mind in terms which would gloss over, or deny, its autonomous reality. However, the human mind as it has reappeared through the philosophy of emergence and developments in depth psychology, can no longer be set apart from the physical world. Rather, this mind is now seen to embrace the physical world itself: it does not deny matter but assumes it into a higher and wider reality. Consequently, we can no longer expect to discover the divine by means of abstraction and by the deliberate cutting-off of all that is human. It is in the whole human experience, that of the whole man, body and soul, that we are to discover it.

Within this new intellectual context we can understand the recent developments in the history of religions, and at the same time understand how they are linked to the permanent acquisitions of the past, though no longer restricted by its unwarranted prejudices.

Father Wilhelm Schmidt, an Austrian missionary of the Society of the Divine Word, started the new trend of thought with his important work *The Origin of the Idea of God*.[33] The title might seem to indicate that he was preoccupied with the ideas about religion current in the last century, but, as a matter of fact, his aim was to oppose them. Though his conclusions, or perhaps rather the way in which they were formulated, are questionable, Father Schmidt has defined more clearly than anyone else the effects of cultural environment on every type of religion. He has drawn a parallel between the different types of religion and the different stages of cultural development. Each one of these types corresponds to a certain attitude of man toward the world which conditions his whole existence. The different divinities which he invokes reflect those aspects of reality upon which his well-being depends in the particular circumstances in which he finds himself.

However, as Father Schmidt insisted — on the basis of a great deal of evidence — no matter out of what cultural milieu man has fashioned his images of the divinity, there is always present in his religious consciousness a belief in a "great God," the source of all things, source even of all the other "gods" — those that are being invoked at the moment as well as the rest. Everything occurs as if nobody knew how to reach this "great God," or how to address him any more.

But actually, according to Father Schmidt's belief, this "great God" is the only one known in the most primitive cultures, that is, in those which do not as yet have a knowledge of agriculture or of the care of flocks, nor even of the chase, but where men live solely from what they can gather of the fruits of the earth without doing anything on their part to develop them. It is to this God that they direct their prayers and their various forms of worship. From this, Father Schmidt concluded that man is naturally mono-

---

[33] The German title of this work is *Der Ursprung der Gottesidee*,* I, 1st ed. (Münster, 1912), 2nd ed. (1926); II(1929); III(1931). See also *The Origin and Growth of Religion*, trans. H. J. Rose (New York, 1935). Many of Father Schmidt's earlier ideas have been incorporated into this work.

theistic. Because of his increasing involvement with the world, man drives this singular image of the divinity into the background of his consciousness, but he never completely obliterates it.

Father Schmidt believed that in this way the thesis current at the end of the nineteenth century, according to which monotheism developed from tribal henotheism, could be refuted. According to this theory, a god that was recognized as the protector of a tribe ended up by dominating over the other deities, practically absorbing everything else that was divine. Contrary to this, Father Schmidt held that monotheism alone is truly primitive.

Contemporary historians of religion are of the opinion that both systems are vitiated by *a priori* assumptions.[34] What Father Schmidt has certainly shown, however, is that one cannot properly speak about a genesis of the idea of God. This idea is found in the most elementary manifestations of a religious consciousness, and it persists, even though partially concealed, in its most corrupt forms. What we call monotheism is actually neither the beginning nor the end of man's religious experiences. It is a notion of the divinity which man obtains by reflecting on that perception of the divine which is at once immanent and transcendent to the most diverse representations which he can make of it.

This has been shown with remarkable insight by another historian of the philosophy of religion, Rudolf Otto, in his work, *The Idea of the Holy,* which appeared in 1917.[35]

Otto took as his point of departure the elemental and rudimentary sacredness known as "mana," a kind of mysterious energy, proper to certain beings, certain objects, and certain places. At first, this energy seems to be impersonal, "physical," like a kind of electricity, or like that force which struck the Israelite foolish enough to touch the Ark of the Lord.[36] But Otto had little difficulty in showing how this is a superficial analysis, neglecting what

[34] The reader will get a good idea of the positions generally taken today by reading W. F. Albright, *From the Stone Age to Christianity,* 2nd ed. (Baltimore, 1946),* pp. 124 ff., or E. O. James, *The Old Testament in the Light of Anthropology* (London, 1934), pp. 83 ff.

[35] Rudolf Otto, *The Idea of the Holy: An Inquiry into the Non-Rational in an Idea of the Divine and its Relation to the Rational,* trans. from the 9th German edition by J. W. Harvey (London, 1936).

[36] *II Sam.* 6:6-8.

is most important and significant, since it is based on a desire to reduce the sacred to the profane.

Without doubt the sacred first betrays its presence by a fear, and this fear spontaneously arising in a primitive can easily be confused with the purely physical fear of a material object. But a more careful study of the earliest developments of the religious consciousness reveals other elements so different from this fear that their very presence seems paradoxical.

In the first place, the fear of what is sacred is always accompanied by an attraction which can even develop into a fascination. The sacred is at once a *mysterium tremendum* and a *mysterium fascinans* — a fearful and a fascinating mystery. And certainly, attraction, like fear, is usually bound up with a hope for material advantages such as success in the hunt or an abundance of crops. But this explanation of the sacred is no more satisfactory than the other. Over and above being a source of fear and attraction, the sacred is immediately felt to be something other than the immediate but nonetheless secondary objects of these feelings. It is something entirely different from them, entirely different in fact from anything else in the world, though present everywhere. At the very outset this transcendent quality is felt as being present in both the fear and the attraction. It is not any *tremendum* that could paradoxically, if somewhat irrationally, be also *fascinans*. Rather it is that the *mysterium* has been uniquely experienced as being both *fascinans* and *tremendum* in a way that is ultimately ineffable.

When subjected to a reasoning process, this "entirely different" reality appears as sovereign, and even as omnipotent. And it is at this stage that the monotheistic formulas make their appearance. But it is not this more or less rationally expressed and justified uniqueness that leads to a belief in one God. Quite to the contrary, this belief has arisen from an immediate unicity of the sacred which preceded the ulterior rationalizations of monotheism, and will never be really exhausted by them. Hence, the more self-conscious monotheism becomes, the more, strangely enough, it feels the need of completing itself by maintaining that the one God is actually as far beyond rational unity as He is beyond multiplicity. The last word that can be said comes back to the very first impression: God is ineffable.[37]

[37] See VI. Lossky, *Essai sur la Théologie mystique de l'Église d'Orient* (Paris, 1944), pp. 28 ff.

Otto's separation of what is irreducible in man's religious experience from every other experience which he can have did not lead him to discount the importance of other factors in religion, whether rational, ethical, aesthetical, or simply utilitarian. He was the first to warn others of the danger of looking for the sacred in a pure state. The sacred is not so much a part of human experience as an aspect under which its entirety may be seen. But he maintained with equal vigor that all the other human realities cannot produce the sacred: it is rather the sacred which modifies and changes all of them in an absolutely unique fashion from the moment of its appearance.

This exact and carefully shaded view of the matter led Otto to issue a very pertinent warning against making comparisons in which different experiences are matched step by step in an attempt to reduce one to another without taking into consideration the whole of the experience in which each step has its own place. The unicity of the sacred does not mean a confusion of religious experiences, just as these latter cannot be reduced to any other human experience.

Otto, using these insights in another book, *Mysticism East and West*,[38] made a comparative study of Meister Eckhart, the great Rhenish mystic, and of Sankara, one of the greatest contemplatives of India. To any historian preoccupied with simplifying problems and reducing them all to the least common denominator, this would seem to be an easy means of illustrating the ultimate indistinction of the higher religious experiences. Both the Christian and the Hindu, in fact, employ the same personalist and impersonalist expressions, sometimes separately, sometimes in conjunction with each other, that presuppose either a radical and absolute otherness between the adorer and the object of his adoration, or a mutual fusion and absorption in one another. But the more refined analysis of Otto, by carefully distinguishing the proper intentionality of each experience under consideration, dispels this first impression. With Eckhart the focal point of the experience lies in the personal meeting, and the apparently impersonalist expressions as he uses them are subordinate to this fundamental conviction. With Sankara, the exact opposite is true. Their most

[38] Trans. B. F. Bracey and R. C. Payne (New York, 1932); see also, R. C. Zaehner, *Mysticism Sacred and Profane* (Oxford, 1957).

astonishing verbal similarities should therefore not be interpreted as a proof of any real agreement in thought or experience but rather as the crossing of two paths so little confused that they actually run counter to each other.

The work of Otto revealed how the use of phenomenological methods could give entirely new perspectives to the science of religions. But it was Gerard van der Leeuw who succeeded in making a systematic application of these methods to the vast treasury of data gathered during the course of a century by anthropologists and students of comparative religion. It was he who was able to show that what Lévy-Bruhl called a prelogical mentality is in reality a metalogical mentality. The religious apprehension of the data of human experience is not at all an embryonic form of thought to be succeeded by a rational apprehension which should mark the death of the earlier mode of knowledge. In every kind of thought, whether primitive or otherwise, the two are united or at least juxtaposed. The primitive who invokes his gods and has recourse to an elaborate ritual when he builds a boat does not act in this way because he is as yet unable to make use of a reasoned technique, the fruit of experience. His technique, as a matter of fact, could be so perfect that an educated man would have great difficulty in imitating it. He knows perfectly well the best shape for his craft for its intended purposes. He knows what type of construction will guarantee him the desired strength and lightness. And this, as is obvious, is not the effect of blind instinct but of judicious observation. But for the primitive, this aspect of reality does not at all nullify a complementary aspect to which his beliefs and rites are directed. After making these observations, Van der Leeuw limits himself to insinuating that conversely, in a scientific, technical civilization such as ours, no matter how atheistic it may claim to be, there subsists a good deal more of the primitive than is supposed. And since then, depth psychologists have furnished abundant proof of this.[39]

These latter authors have finally broken the impasse into which the science of comparative religion had fallen. It now goes straight to the heart of religion, to religion as such, without further delay in vainly seeking to break it down or absorb it into something else.

---

[39] See his article "La Structure de la mentalité primitive," in *Revue d'Histoire et de philosophie religieuses,* VII (1928), 1-31.

Van der Leeuw took up the task of describing the relation between the subject and object of religion and of examining in detail the connections between the two. His work, *Religion in Essence and Manifestation,* with its subtitle of *A Study in Phenomenology,*[40] takes up in turn the representations of the religious object and the awareness which the religious subject (simple believer, priest, isolated or in a community) gets of himself through his religious life, in order to concentrate on the different modes of that life and the different means it sets in operation.

In his descriptions and analyses of religious activity, Van der Leeuw has been particularly successful in showing how it is manifested in prayer formulas and in rituals. With that objective sympathy which is the ideal of phenomenology, Mircea Eliade has gone on to deepen our appreciation of those representations that are basic to all religions.[41]

More effectively than anyone else, Eliade has helped us to understand that the religious attitude is not merely a primitive attitude of man in the face of reality. It is a permanent attitude. For it is the relation of man to his whole experience. Through that relation man discovers the world as a totality which is also a unity, and a unity perceived as being at once both immanent and transcendent. This discovery finds its concrete expression in a group of representations which Mircea Eliade happily calls "hierophanies." These are found lying beneath the most diverse forms of religion, though the interpretation given to them and the value set upon them is highly flexible.[42]

The most fundamental of these seems to be that of the heaven, through which man comes to know the divine as ruling, embracing, and at the same time surpassing all things. Next is the sun, which manifests the divine as the source of life, but a source which gushes forth from a changeless eternity. On the contrary, the moon, always connected with waters, expresses the sacredness of becoming, of the alterations of progress and decline, of life and death. The waters are especially connected with birth and death:

[40] Trans. J. E. Turner (London, 1938).

[41] See especially his *Patterns in Comparative Religion,* trans. Rosemary Sheed (New York, 1958).*

[42] See Eliade, *op. cit.,* pp. 323 ff. Cf. his *Mythes, rêves et mystères* (Paris, 1957).*

they represent creation as one of the cosmic catastrophes in which the universe was swallowed up, only to be reborn. The earth itself is a hierophany, but decidedly secondary in the sense that if the image of the heaven is paternal, that of the earth is eminently maternal. From this mother, the creations of the father are drawn, and in her they have had a mysterious pre-existence. We should here add that the wind and also the breath of life appear as very special hierophanies through which the divine immanence is manifested in the world and in man himself, but in a way that is incomprehensible and which preserves the divine transcendence.

A connection must be established between these hierophanies and certain dynamic patterns which seem to lie beneath all ritual, and in which the divine is apprehended in a sacred action as being something timeless and yet somehow sharing in human time, a fact which is, as we shall see, the distinctive element in ritual action. The most fundamental of these is the creative pattern, which cannot be separated from a pattern of salvation: God is the origin of all things by a generative act, but he is also the constant recreator or regenerator of all things, particularly at the return of each year.

On this fundamental ritual and mythic pattern, others are grafted. Among these we have the theme of paradise lost, of the fall which drove man out of it (or made this blessed abode disappear or withdraw from man), and the hope of a return. No less important than this theme of the fall, with which it is connected and more or less confused, is that of divine loves which involve the gods in an alliance with their work (and perhaps in the fall of it), and which lead them to restore or regenerate it, though at the price of their own death.

All of these hierophanies and many others, like their ritualistic or mythical dramatizations, can be interpreted in an almost limitless variety of ways. But their constancy, and the constancy of the themes they represent, is universal. There is no religion which can do without their help, just as there is no man, even among those who claim to have no religion, who really escapes their influence.[43]

Joachim Wach, a recently deceased expert in the history of religions, taking into account these latest developments, was able to leave as a kind of testament a work in which he drew up the fol-

---

[43] See my comments on the work of C. G. Jung, in the following chapter.

lowing four criteria for determining the specific character of a religious experience:

1) It is man's response to the final reality behind all things, which he apprehends as a sovereign Being who is transcendent but with whom he can enter into some relationship.

2) Any approach of this Being demands a total response from man, and one in which his own whole being, including mind, body, and emotions, is involved.

3) The intensity and the completeness of the resulting experience which results from this not only embraces the whole man but it appears to him as something that cannot be compared qualitatively with anything else.

4) This experience cannot leave a man as it found him: it is a radically creative experience that tends to transform him altogether."

If some conclusion is to be drawn from this exposition, it is that the history of comparative religions has had to recognize the fact that religion is a permanent, irreducible, and generally dominating element in all human experience. But it arrived at this conclusion only after it had exhausted itself attempting to reduce religion to other human experiences and had tried vainly to show that it was a childish illusion which the human mind should of its own accord abandon and confidently explain away. To look for some accidental origin of it in man's infancy is futile. Religion is the spontaneous response which man's existential situation elicits as soon as this latter is fully accepted in its reality.

Nevertheless, we should also mention two other explanations of religion that are popular today. Both claim to be scientific, but they are actually only the relics of an outmoded scientism. Their seductive influence lies in the prestige of a mythological science that is really dead as a science, although it persists in the popular imagination through works written for the general public based on principles that are no longer acceptable.

These theories are not, however, without interest, for their explanation of religion is in fact an explanation of the character it assumes when it begins to degenerate. We are referring to the theories proposed by Marx and Freud.

" Joachim Wach, *Comparative Study of Religions* (New York, 1958), conclusion.

According to Marx there is no human reality that is not basically economic. In an oppressed class, failure to attain essential goods releases a compensatory balm in the form of a collective dream of "another world," a "paradise" which will succeed the present world and where one will enjoy the pleasures that have been here denied. The proprietary class, seeking the advantage to be derived from this dream for checking the instinct of revolt among those whom they exploit, promotes this consoling but deadening illusion. From it have come both priests and organized religions, the "opium of the people," secreted by the people themselves but subsequently refined by their exploiters.[45]

The analyses which Bergson has made of an open, creative religion, which breaks down the social barriers and the various compartments into which humanity settles, in contrast to a closed religion that only hardens a society in its existing state, is the best answer that can be furnished to the Marxist view of religion. At the same time that it makes us realize how Marxism misses the real problem of religion, it helps us recognize the fact that there is some truth in it. If the Marxist description is not applicable to a living religion, it is certainly applicable to what the ruling classes may have made of religion, especially in the nineteenth century. The unbelieving bourgeois who claimed that there had to be a religion for the people, and the materialistic state which subsidized the Church because it regarded it as a kind of check on the proletariat's mind, fit only too well into the picture of religion drawn by Marx. This is but one example of how certain alliances which at first seem to be a boon to religion can be its ruin.[46]

Freud in his turn reduced, or at least tended to reduce, all human activity to sex. In such circumstances a religious object would only be an illusion which the unsatisfied sexual appetite creates for itself and upon which it disguisedly projects its repressed drives. This is the reason, we are told, for the importance of sexual asceticism in the higher religions.[47]

[45] The different articles on religious subjects in the *Sovietic Encyclopedia* give what may be called the classic popularization of this theory.

[46] Henri Bergson, *The Two Sources of Morality and Religion*, trans. R. Z. Audra, C. Brereton, W. H. Carter (London, 1935).

[47] See, with Sigmund Freud, *The Future of an Illusion*, trans. W. D. Robson-Scott (London, 1928), the study by Zillboorg, "L'Amour et Dieu chez Freud," in *Supplément de la Vie Spirituelle*, XXIV (1953), 5 ff.

Here again, but more profoundly than in the explanation proposed by Marx, we run across a penetrating description of certain characteristics of a degenerate religion that have been confused with religion itself. Actually, there is a tendency among all false mystics to camouflage self-complacent dreams of an unsatisfied eroticism behind ardent longings of the soul.[48]

Behind Freud's mistake is the ambiguity of his concept of sublimation. As we shall have to repeat, Freud was certainly right in postulating sex as a center of gravity for all of man's physical and psychical energies. The whole question is to know if these latter can only disguise this primary organization, while pretending to surpass it, or whether they can truly dominate and transcend it, which is not the same as saying that they annihilate it. That love furnishes a spontaneous language for the loftiest aspirations of the soul does not necessarily mean that this language can never be understood except in a strictly literal sense.[49]

Recent developments in the history of religions, however, have done more than confirm the originality of the religious experience in general: they have shed further light on the originality of Christianity itself. Just as the science of the last century strove to reduce religion to something that was not religious, so it endeavored to reduce Christianity to the status of other religions. The attempt was fruitful, but the effects produced were the very opposite to what had been expected. The transcendency of Christianity has never been so manifest as it is today, for the simple reason that its insertion into the course of human events has never before been made so clear.

What was known in Germany as "the school of the history of comparative religions" made valiant efforts to bring primitive Christianity into the general framework of the religions of the Near East, and especially the mystery religions, that were contemporary with it. Isaac Casaubon pioneered this work in his *Exercitationes de rebus sacris.*[50] He tried to show that the sacramental system of the early Christians was simply an imitation of concepts and practices found in the ancient mystery religions.

[48] See Roland Dalbiez, *La méthode psychanalytique et la doctrine freudienne,* II (Paris, 1949), 369 ff.

[49] See Charles Baudouin, *L'Ame et l'Action* (Geneva, 1944), pp. 162 ff.

[50] Geneva, 1655.

Later this theory was pushed farther to include all the essential dogmas of the New Testament. Richard Reitzenstein's *Die hellenistische Mysterienreligionen* and Wilhelm Bousset's *Kyrios Christos* expounded it in a thoroughly scientific fashion.[51] According to Bousset, Christianity was cast in the common mold of the mystery religions, which consisted in a sacred action representing the death and return to life of a saviour god. According to Reitzenstein, there was behind all this an Iranian myth narrating the story of a primitive man fallen from heaven into a wicked and material world from which he would finally escape so as to redeem those who would cleave to him by faith and ritual.

These ideas were popularized in France by the work of Alfred Loisy, *Les mystères païens et le mystère chrétien*.[52] His bias is rather surprising. On practically every page he first describes and explains the mysteries in Christian terms, though these terms were not used in the mysteries themselves. From this it was only too easy for him to conclude that there is nothing in Christianity that was not first to be found in the mystery religions. This continued twisting of the facts only adds more weight to Loisy's incidental remarks, who was too clearheaded and too honest not to recognize the real gap in his comparisons.

Under the leadership of Dom Casel there came into existence an intrepid school of Christian scholars who accepted in general the description of the facts as given by Bousset and Reitzenstein but interpreted them in an opposite way.[53] According to them, Christianity was indeed laid on a bed that had been prepared by the mystery cults of the pre-Christian religions. But these should be regarded as having been a providential preparation for Christianity. Casel's position was something like that taken by Clement of Alexandria, who looked upon the religious philosophy of the Greeks as a kind of second Old Testament. Without having recourse to the radical denials of Albert Schweitzer[54] or Karl

[51] The first edition of Reitzenstein's work was published at Leipzig in 1910, and the revised edition in 1927. Bousset's second edition was published at Göttingen in 1921.

[52] 2nd edition (Paris, 1930).

[53] Odo Casel, *The Mystery of Christian Worship and Other Writings,* ed. B. Neunheuser, trans. I. T. Hale (Westminster, Md., 1962).*

[54] *The Mysticism of Paul the Apostle,* trans. Wm. Montgomery (New York, 1931).*

Prümm,[55] and without rejecting all possible points of contact between Christianity and the mysteries, it must be confessed that the views of the school of the history of religions do not stand up to a critical evaluation of the facts. The conclusions of the school of Maria Laach must, therefore, also be rejected to the extent that they are based on the false premises of the other.

Later on in this work we shall have to examine this question in more detail. For the present it should suffice to give some of the more general conclusions that have been gaining ground with scholars. In the first place, when the separate terms of the comparison have not been confused at the outset, they assume more just proportions, though some analogies certainly remain. This is true not only when Christianity is compared with the different mystery religions, but also, though less so, when these are compared among themselves. The common traits are not perhaps quite so common as was first imagined, and the differences are unmistakable. This is what comes out of every purely objective, unbiased study such as Franz Cumont's *Oriental Religions in Roman Paganism.*[56]

At any rate, if there is anything common to all non-Christian mystery religions, it is their origin in agrarian cults. Their mythic and ritual development is inscribed within the closed circle of the forces of nature that are constantly changing winter's death to spring's rebirth. In opposition to these cosmic cults, never freed from the cyclic setting of an eternal return, the worship of the Christians is directed toward a saviour god who, though He transcends the world, once and for all descends into human history to transform it, and at the same time, in an irreversible manner, the whole course of the cosmos.[57] No matter how many common features or superficial resemblances there may be between the mystery religions and Christianity, their respective frameworks are entirely different. This is what is becoming clearer every day as

[55] See his article "Mystère" in *Supplément du Dictionnaire de la Bible,* VI (1957), 1-225.

[56] Authorized translation (Chicago, 1911).* A fourth French edition of this work is available, *Les religions orientales dans le paganisme romain* (Paris, 1929).

[57] See my study on "Le salut dans les religions à mystères et le christianisme," *Revue des Sciences religieuses,* XXXI (Strasbourg, 1952).

Bruce Metzger has aptly shown in his "Considerations of Method in the Study of Mystery Religions."[58]

As a matter of fact, in recent years historians of religions have been almost unanimous in recognizing and denouncing the false reasoning which maintains that a sufficient number of detailed comparisons between two religious systems indicates an historical dependence of one upon the other. Thus, since the alleged continuity of all the great myths disappears, any attempt, like Sir James Frazer's, in his *Golden Bough,* to reduce the higher to the lower becomes meaningless.

M. Dumézil, in particular, has shown how the fundamental structures of the myths are everywhere the same, a discovery which was to be elaborated and deepened by Mircea Eliade. Since this is so, even in cases where there is no possibility of external influences, there is no way of concluding from the presence of similar traits to a kind of filiation. Man actually has at his disposal only a limited number of ideas, ritual forms, and religious images. That they are found perceptibly the same in religions that are near to one another in time and space should not deceive us: they are also found the same in religions between which it would be fantastic to postulate any historical connection. But what is essential to each is not in this material but in the way it is arranged.[59]

The fact that a number of different architects have made use of the same stones does not make them pupils of each other. But if they work in the same style, even though with different materials, some connection is certainly indicated. Similarly, the presence of a common series of elements, A, B, C, and D, however extended it may be, does not necessarily indicate the influence of one religion upon another. What would indicate such an influence would be the same relationships existing between the same elements. Even then there is danger of going astray unless we can see the ideological relations translated into lexicographical relations: that is, unless the language itself bears traces of the transfers of which it must have been the medium.[60]

[58] *Harvard Theological Review,* XLVII (1955), 1 ff.

[59] See especially M. Dumézil, *Mithra-Varuna* (Paris, 1940).

[60] This has been the great merit of the school founded by Msgr. Cerfaux.

Thus we shall see that the Hebrew religion represents a first and decisive creative change in the use it made of mythical images and ritual customs that were more or less common to the people living about the Mediterranean. Later, Christianity, while taking shape in the Jewish framework, caused another and even more decisive change. And later still it was to prove that it could reinterpret and refashion in an entirely new way everything which it appropriated for itself from the manifold treasures of natural religion.

CHAPTER III

Recent Developments
in Psychology

RECENT developments in the history of religions have already engaged us in an exploration of the human soul in some of its most fundamental and constant layers, something like the depths of the seas untouched by the disturbances on the surface. On the other hand, the first systematic exploration of the depths of the soul has been one of the most remarkable psychological attainments of the last half-century. The result of this has been an agreement between the findings of historians of religion such as Mircea Eliade, and of psychologists such as Carl Gustav Jung. In his *Mythes, rêves et mystères,* Mircea Eliade has himself emphasized this convergence, though he has at the same time marked its limits.[1]

The discovery of the underground recesses of the soul lying beneath the upheavals on the surface has revealed, even against its own will, how fundamentally religious that soul is. Still, the growth of religion should not on this account be reduced to the emergence of the unconscious structures of the psyche any more than to any other metamorphosis. But it is certain that the full humanity of religion, as well as the ineradicably religious character of man, emerges with this discovery.

In the nineteenth century, even those scholars who did not attempt to deny with Auguste Comte the possibility of a science of

[1] See the first chapter of this volume.

psychology, were strongly inclined through the influence of Positivism to reduce psychology to a simple appendage of physiology. Psychological phenomena were reduced, or it was thought that they should be reduced, to simple epiphenomena, that is to say, to secondary manifestations that were impotent since they were deprived of any proper consistency. This found expression in the famous sally: "The brain secretes thought as the liver secretes bile." [2] What were called psychological experiences and had formerly been attributed to the soul could be nothing but a kind of activity of the brain or of the nervous system in general.

It may be said that the last and most radical effect of this tendency, when it is not checked by the complete rejection of Comte, is "Behaviorism." This term, derived from the word "behavior" in the sense of a way of acting, has been applied to a school of psychology that systematically excludes the contents of psychological phenomena in order to limit itself to the study of the conduct, or the exteriorly ascertainable ways of acting, that accompanies these phenomena. This psychology on principle puts the "psyche" in parentheses, since it cannot simply deny it. The only question it deems worthy of a scientific answer is how a man will react externally to different stimuli to his psychic make-up. What his internal reactions may be are of no concern to it. [3]

The fact, however, that such a purely materialistic approach has been unable to cure certain psychological disorders has been a check to it. Actually, it proved quite impossible to treat these troubles by some action on the brain or nervous system, since no lesion in these organs was ascertainable. On the other hand, experience was to show that a purely psychological treatment could be efficacious, as soon as the source of the trouble was recognized as a psychic and not a physical trauma.

The false claim of Positivism, to limit itself to facts alone while on principle excluding the possibility of any that are not purely physical, is here particularly apparent. The obstinacy of certain scholars in their absolute refusal to conduct any research in an

[2] It is the wish of every materialist to reduce thought to a kind of chemical secretion of the brain, but this is something quite different from anything that science can establish.

[3] In Gilbert Ryle, *The Concept of Mind* (London, 1949), behaviorism may be found in its most highly developed form.

area from which they have voluntarily excluded themselves, and their still more stubborn refusal to recognize the conclusions of such research proved by experimentation, is almost unbelievable. As a consequence of its own sterile dogmatism, psychological psychiatry, especially in France, has been consistently outlawed by official science. As a result, when the pressure of the facts has been too strong to withstand, it has engulfed everything in a hopelessly confused flood. For a science blind on principle runs the risk of being followed by a demi-science where fancy and charlatanism are mixed in with definite and extremely valuable discoveries.[4]

Consequently, it cannot be concealed that these new investigations had to make their way through a questionable empiricism, but one which has had at least the merit of having made intolerable a science that refused to face the facts. In his attempts to treat hysteria with hypnosis, Charcot was the first to bring the study of nervous disorders back to an examination of their psychological causes. By passionately following these early gropings, Freud was led to his own surest discoveries. His experiences at La Salpêtrière enabled him to lay bare the psychological origins of neuroses, and this in turn enlarged and renewed our understanding of the human soul.[5] Freud discovered that neuroses, while they are undoubtedly psychological, have their origin in a mental trauma which is no longer present to the patient's consciousness, and which perhaps was never completely there. It is by the resurgence of this trauma, by its first complete emergence indeed, that these neuroses can be dissipated.

For the first time attention was drawn to what was then called the subconscious, as a kind of mere penumbral halo of the conscious, but which soon came to be known simply as the unconscious, a dark cone with infinite prolongations stretching out from the luminous apex of the conscious.[6]

---

[4] See A. Farau, H. Schaeffer, *La Psychologie des Profondeurs* (Paris, 1960).

[5] See Sigmund Freud, *Autobiography,* trans. James Strachey (New York, 1935).*

[6] See especially Sigmund Freud, *A General Introduction to Psychoanalysis,* trans. Joan Riviere (New York, 1920).*

This is not to say that no notice had ever been taken of the fact that the conscious has its roots in the unconscious. In antiquity Plato maintained that our current knowledge is due to the dark treasury of a memory which we constantly draw upon, but which we cannot at a single stroke bring completely to the fore. He was so convinced of this that he postulated a former life where we would have had an immediate vision of truths now hidden in a soul weighed down and dulled by its union with a body. Thus, according to him, all our apparent discoveries are nothing but recollections that have been stirred up in us by the images of the eternal ideas which we encounter in the sensible world.[7]

Leibniz, in an entirely different and much more positive way also appealed to the unconscious to explain the conscious. According to him, we only arrive at a fully conscious apperception at the end of a process where isolated and completely unconscious perceptions have been added until they break through the confused perception, which is only the threshold of the conscious.[8]

But, as Freud himself observed, it is perhaps Jean Jacques Rousseau who made and recorded the first psychological observation that contains in germ the whole initial discovery of Freud. Rousseau tells us how he once noticed that he had turned at a street sooner than usual, though he was in the habit of taking his daily walk along a set route. Surprised, he asked himself why he had done so. He then remembered that the day before he had been upset by a particularly unpleasant beggar he had met on the way. He had apparently forgotten the incident. It certainly had not changed his plans for the future. But it had somehow been engraved on his mind, and this had been enough to provoke, without any immediate awareness on his part, a change in his regular habits.[9]

This is just what Freud, under the name of a "repression," later analyzed and showed to be at the root of a neurosis. Apparently transient impressions, which the conscious mind neither retains nor recognizes, stir up unavowed desires in the soul. Secretly lurking under what is judged to be a normal consciousness, they can lay

[7] See *Meno* 80d-86c; *Theaetetus* 149a-150d; *Phaedo* 72e-77a; *Phaedrus* 249c-250a.

[8] See the preface of the *Nouveaux Essais* (published in 1703).

[9] The narrative and the analysis are given at the beginning of the sixth *Rêverie d'un promeneur solitaire*.

the ground for a complete nervous breakdown if they are not recognized and admitted.

A truer appreciation of the role of the unconscious in the psychological life of an individual was bound to lead to a discovery of the complexes. Freud gave this name to a knot of desires repressed by the conscious mind because of moral or other prohibitions, but which still are not completely suppressed. Their accumulated force within the unconscious is revealed through a neurosis that cripples consciousness itself. According to Freud the basic means of correcting these disorders is to bring the repressions to the surface so that they can be assimilated within the conscious mind which will destroy them by means of a frank avowal hitherto, unfortunately, denied them.[10]

It was in this context that Freud came to discover the meaning and importance of dreams. They are a kind of undisguised projection of desires in the conscious life seeking satisfaction in the imagination.[11]

The most important and, at the same time, the most controversial factor in Freudian psychoanalysis is the identification of the repressed desires. According to Freud himself, they are essentially of a sexual nature. The neuroses which Freud studied and which he sought to cure, often with complete success, showed him that the origin of the trouble was actually in a traumatic sexual experience. Because the remembrance of such an experience arouses a storm of intense feelings that frighten the subject, it is repressed. But this very repression crystallizes the complex which later reappears in a seemingly inexplicable form.

Freud soon came to look upon what he called the "Oedipus complex" as something particularly important in a man's psychological development. According to him, every male naturally experiences a precocious attachment to his mother which is accompanied by a feeling of hostility for his father. If this complex is not recognized

[10] See along with his *General Introduction to Psychoanalysis,* the study of Dalbiez, *op. cit.,* I, pp. 240 ff.*

[11] *The Interpretation of Dreams,* trans. by A. A. Brill, completely revised edition (New York, 1937).*

in time and resolved by being brought to conscious light, the individual's whole psychological balance will be upset.[12]

It is obvious that Freud here made the same mistake that many others have made who have discovered something of capital import. He soon tended to explain everything in the light of the discovery which he had been the first to make. This is what is behind his pansexualism which reabsorbs every type of psychological activity into a search for unavowed satisfactions by a sexuality checked by circumstances and especially by prohibitions of a moral or social order. There is no doubt that Freud, and, especially, his strict interpreters, in their search for a unified reconstruction of our inner life, were led to overemphasize the role of sex, dragging it in almost everywhere. In these systematic misunderstandings about the place of sex in human life, an essential part was played by the ambiguous meaning of sublimation, in which the Freudians could not, or would not, distinguish between a simple camouflage and a real transposition or outgrowth.

It is nonetheless true that Freud's work is of great importance, not only because of his discovery of the unconscious and the complexes, their effects and possible resolutions, but also because of the attention which he brought to bear upon the place of sex in man's psychological life. If a thorough study of the evidence shows that the exclusive reduction of the latter to the former must be rejected, Freud's recognition of the central place and meaning of the sexual instinct, far more extensive than civilized man would be inclined to admit, is on the contrary a permanent acquisition. On the one hand, there is no doubt that the sex instinct in man is not simply one among many others. It is a basic drive and one which synthesizes the psychological life. On the other hand, the discovery of this Jewish physician with his narrowly scientific and materialistic outlook has proved to be a surprising, yet decisive justification of an essentially Christian proposition, despite all the confusion that it has also created. Indeed, because of Freud, it is no longer possible to say that sex can, without endangering the whole human equilibrium, be reduced to a search for an isolated physical pleasure. On the contrary, it must be recognized as being

[12] *Three Contributions to the Theory of Sex,* 4th ed., trans. by A. A. Brill (New York, 1930).*

tied, even in its apparently purely physical manifestations, to the wellsprings of one's personality and whole development.[13]

Here we should mention another of Freud's discoveries. Although he was not able himself to develop it fully, we have come to realize its significance. It concerns the strange connection that seems to exist between the unfolding of the sex instinct and the development of an instinct for death.[14] We shall have to refer again to this troubling fact, for the longing of life for its own fecundity is mysteriously united with a fascination for death in all the religious representations which man makes of his destiny.

However this may be, we must for the present keep well in mind how Freud has enlarged our vision of the psyche, or human soul, in whatever way we now conceive it. As the result of his studies, the conscious appears as an intermediary between what he called the "id," an underlying area with indefinite extensions (something like a neuter "ego," in the sense of being impersonal and having no responsibility), and that which he called the "superego," which he maintained is an essentially social projection by means of which the ego sketches an ideal towards which it tends or is simply directed.[15]

It is over the question of the place to be given to the sex instinct in the analysis of the unconscious that Freud's two greatest disciples, Adler and Jung, left him to set up their own rival schools.

Through his early interest in the problem of juvenile delinquency Alfred Adler was able to add what he called the "inferiority complex" to the Oedipus complex as a source of psychological deviations.[16] He thus showed the importance of aggressive drives, which he thought were even stronger than those of sex. Adler asserts that this complex has its origin in the inferiorities, first of all physiological, to which everyone is more or less subject, since no human being enjoys a perfectly harmonious physical integrity. A deficiency of this kind tends to seek its compensation in an ag-

[13] The idea that Freudian psychoanalysis would of itself lead to the mere satisfaction of the instincts is not only a caricature, but a false interpretation, even though more than one disciple of the Viennese master may have leaned toward it.

[14] See *Collected Papers,* trans. under the supervision of Joan Riviere, II (New York, 1959), 255 ff.*

[15] *Ibid.,* II, 250 ff.

[16] See the chapter devoted to him in Farau and Schaeffer, *op. cit.*

gressiveness modeled after what is felt to be lacking. The fundamental problem of all psychological growth will be to establish a balance by becoming clearly aware of one's own individual problem under the particular form it takes in each.[17]

The value of Adler's work is that it opens up the way to a superior kind of pedagogy which should enable everyone to develop his own personality by building upon his own original weaknesses once these have been recognized and positively surmounted.[18]

Jung's work is far more varied and more directly concerned with religious psychology than any other.[19] He has studied the religious instinct with increasing sympathy and great attention, and has striven to draw every possible advantage from it. Though at first view Jung's theories are more acceptable to Christians and others who believe in the existence of the soul than those of Freud, they contain hidden ambiguities which are no less dangerous than the obvious ones in Freud. Despite his interest in spirituality, especially that of the Catholic Church, Jung constantly seems to be attempting to naturalize the supernatural and to reduce all religious symbols to simple projections of the immanent content of the human soul. We have here a particularly disturbing example of what Mircea Eliade has described as a tendency among many psychologists to reduce religion to their own speciality. But if one is on his guard against this tendency in Jung, one will find that his studies contain priceless data for the understanding of the religious fact in general and for the particular forms in which it appears.[20]

The principal point of disagreement between Jung and Freud was the nature of the fundamental instinct which constitutes the

[17] See Alfred Adler, *The Neurotic Constitution: Outline of a Comparative Individualistic Psychology and Psychotherapy*, trans. B. Glueck and E. Lind (New York, 1917).*

[18] Many examples of this may be found in Farau and Schaeffer, *op. cit.*

[19] A good idea of Jung's trend of thought may be obtained from his two works, *Modern Man in Search of His Soul*, trans. W. S. Dill and C. F. Baynes (New York, 1933), and *Seelenprobleme der Gegenwart* (Zurich, 1931).*

[20] Without doubt the two best studies on Jung and religion are those by Fathers Victor White, *God and the Unconscious* (London, 1952), and Raymond Hostie, S. J., *Religion and the Psychology of Jung*, trans. G. R. Lamb (New York, 1957).*

source of the whole psychological life. Jung, following the lead of his teacher, continued to call it the *libido,* but he gave the term a new meaning.[21] He no longer regarded it as a sexual drive but as an indifferentiated vital instinct which could manifest itself under the most diverse forms, of sex, of Adlerian aggressiveness, or in some other way, none of which enjoyed a privileged position. The problem of all human life for Jung as for Adler was that which furnished him with a title for one of his most important works: individuation, or the integration of personality.[22] But Jung was no longer concerned simply with the adaptation of the sexual desire to its object, or even, like Adler, with the integration of one's affirmation of oneself in the life of the community. He was more interested in the unique and total integration of the ego through its experience of the world. From this, Jung's attention turned to the problem of religion as defined by contemporary historians of religion such as Wach or Eliade. According to Jung, an individual has not reached his full stature until he has personally confronted this problem of man in the universe, of man who only attains full consciousness of self by measuring himself with the whole of reality, as recognized in that unity underlying all things, which is the unity of the sacred.[23]

Just as Jung denied Freud's claim that sex and its elementary manifestations is *the* problem of man, so he disagreed with him over what is to be considered the decisive period of an individual's life. Freud maintained that it is to be found in the first years, before the attainment of speech, at a time when the complexes, and especially the Oedipus complex, make their appearance. Jung, on the other hand, holds that the decisive period is rather what he calls the "middle of life," a period at about the age of forty when a man who has passed through childhood with its adaptations to parental influences, adolescence with its adaptation to developed

---

[21] See C. G. Jung, *Psychology of the Unconscious: A Study of the Transformation and Symbolisms of the Libido,* trans. B. M. Hinkle (New York, 1925), pp. 127 ff.

[22] *The Integration of the Personality,* trans. S. M. Dell (New York, 1939).

[23] In this connection, Jung's last statements are interesting. He made them to the journalist Frederick Sands some days before his death, which occurred on June 6, 1961. They were printed in *Le Nouveau Candide* (June), 15-22.

sexuality, adulthood with its problems of marriage, professional occupation, and the education of children, for the first time finds himself alone before the crucial problem of his success or failure as an individual. All the protective screens afforded by former social relations have given way. He is at last alone with himself and confronted with the great and unique problem of the meaning of existence and of the world into which he has been plunged.

Jung, who placed no less importance than Freud on dreams, has emphasized the special significance of those that occur at this time, like that of the bridge crossed in great haste which collapses when it has scarcely been cleared. They are more interesting for their lessons and warnings for the future than they are as a recall of repressed memories. And he sees them as heralding the inevitable dissolution of a transitory past and the establishment of a new, supreme, and definitive reality.[24]

The great difficulty which modern man experiences in reaching the necessary maturity at this stage, his confusion and frequent inner dejection before the prospect of retirement strikes Jung as evidence of the collective neurosis of our age.

Our technical civilization, with its almost exclusive exploitation of the external world and of the purely material resources of the universe, leaves us unprotected when we are compelled by the passage of time to make a spiritual conquest of ourselves or lapse into nothingness. Our conscious self has been built up with the sole view of making a purely material use of reality. In the same or even greater degree than it has given us all that we could expect from it in this regard, it leaves us with a sense of utter frustration, and, what is more serious, it deprives us of the ability to find in the world what we have not been in the habit of seeking but which we cannot, for all that, do without.

> The more engaged I have been with these problems during the course of the years [Jung writes] the more I have been impressed by the fact that our modern education is slanted in one sickly direction. Certainly it is wise to open the eyes and the ears of youth to the perspectives of the vast world, but it is foolish to believe that this sufficiently prepares young people for life! This education simply gives to youth an ex-

[24] C. G. Jung, *The Integration of the Personality,* pp. 96 ff.

ternal adaptation to the realities of the world, but no care is given to an adaptation to oneself.[25]

A man who is concerned only with his hold on the world sees it slip from his grasp and can no longer recognize himself in it when the true reality lays hold of him. In this loss of his soul is, however, his true salvation if he but knows how to seize it.

This is the one whom Jungian psychology aims to assist by making him rediscover the true dimensions of a soul that has become atrophied by its very conquest of the world, illusory as it is.

Jung's view of the unconscious is actually much more extensive than that of Freud. As we have already seen, the unconscious for Freud consisted in those early experiences, in a consciousness then just awakening, of conflicts which we do not habitually recall, but which can be recalled with effort and must be resolved if they are not to burden one's whole existence. For Jung, however, it goes beyond the global experience of conscious life and is dominated by a mysterious gathering of the sum total of human experience, or in other words, by the perennial problems of the race from which we have sprung. Our own individual problems are seen gathered in the train of the larger problems which engulf us, which we can hide from ourselves and apparently discard for a time, but from which we can never really escape.

As civilized beings, no matter what view we may take of the conscious world, our soul remains dominated by certain changeless archetypes. These are like a fabric on which have been embroidered all the great religious myths. This explains the surprising analogies that have been discovered by historians of religions but which have no historical connections. The pre-Columbian religions in America, for example, made use of the same symbolic patterns as were to be found in the Near East. The dreams of the cultured engineer who is, or wants to be, a materialistic atheist betray the fact that his soul is cast in the same mold as that of the primitive whom he foolishly ridicules, not realizing how closely he himself resembles him, his brother. And the great poetry of all times, whether of Walt Whitman or of Maiakovsky, whether it chants the praises of America or Marxism or is the work of the authors of the Vedas, is nothing but an effort of conscious thought

[25] Trans. from the French, *L'Homme à la découverte de son ame,* pp. 63-64.

itself to reconstruct a mental universe which, it may imagine, has been torn apart forever.[26]

The ego, the conscious self, is thus like a transparent film at the meeting of two worlds, an inner and an outer world, which still are only one.

The ego finds its double for the outer world in the *persona*. In the ancient Latin theater this was the name given to the mask worn by an actor as he played his role in the drama of life. Molded by social habits, it is even more a projection of the world — and especially of the society in which one lives — upon the self, than it is a projection of the self upon the world. Symmetrically, on the inner fringes of life, the *umbra,* made up of all the instinctive tendencies that the self has checked and repressed continues to follow the ego, which can never be freed from it. It is like the surface of the unconscious, properly so called. The latter, in the layer nearest the light, still manifests a personal character since it is filled with what may be called the preconscious experiences of the individual. But these rise up from a soil where all the experiences of mankind have been deposited. This is what Jung calls the collective unconscious, whose contents are common to all men and where the most highly civilized individual is found on a level with the savage and the primitive. And this collective but human unconscious in its turn emerges from what the universe, seen as it were from the inside, contains of indefinable psychic content for beings which have only become distinct from it by being born from its depth.[27]

Once again, the collective unconscious, as conceived by Jung, is peopled with mysterious archetypes which find their same manifestations in all men. Though Jung readily multiplies the symbolic images capable of expressing them, he refuses to construct a metaphysic out of these archetypes. The descriptions which he gives to them, however, recall the ideas of Plato. As a matter of fact, it is

[26] See in particular *Psychological Types*, or, *The Psychology of Individuation,* trans. H. G. Baynes (New York, 1923),* pp. 207 ff., where he discusses psychology and poetry.

[27] See *The Integration of the Personality,* pp. 13 ff. A synthesis of the Jungian theories on the unconscious will be found in Jolande Jacobi, *The Psychology of C. G. Jung,* trans. K. W. Bash, 5th English ed. (New Haven, 1951).*

rather a question of symbolic patterns which reflect from different angles man's instinctive realization of his place in the world.[28]

One of the first of these to interest Jung was what he called the *anima* in man and the *animus* in woman. By this he meant the supreme aspiration which everyone has for something that will complement his own being, not simply that of another sex in the narrow sense taken by Freud, but of another self which will bring him something which he radically needs, and through which and in which alone he can and must perfect himself. The attraction of the unknown and desired *anima* finds its counterpart in the feeling of dependence upon the *mother,* upon that obscure *mater* which is as it were the matter from which we are made and from which we have been withdrawn, but to which we are still attached by all the fibers of our being.

Behind the *mother* may be seen the profile of another figure upon whom we are even more profoundly, if more distantly dependent. It is that of the *Old Wise Man,* the *father,* from whom we have received everything, but who surpasses, and always will surpass us, and who lives outside all that is in us and all the world besides.

He manifests himself to us through an intermediary who comes close to us. This is the divine messenger *Tot-Hermes,* the *logos,* an initiator who speaks to us in our own tongue even though his words remain mysterious and he speaks only of things which are beyond us.

And the inaccessible Old Man, the "Ancient of Days," is himself in a sense more intimately present to us through his *spirit* than we are to ourselves, but in an elusive way that completely escapes us.[29]

Jung does not deny that this quaternity, as he calls it, took definite shape in his mind as the result of his meditations on the Christian Trinity and the Virgin Mother. But he maintains that its expression springs from a dynamic symbolism that is instinctive in all men. According to him, the same is true of the figure of the devil: the Gospels do no more than define that which the *umbra*

---

[28] *Ibid.,* pp. 53 ff.

[29] On all this, see Jolande Jacobi, *Komplex Archetypus und Symbol in der Psychologie C. G. Jungs* (Zurich, 1957).

becomes when its reality is freed from the luminous and kindly archetypes through which alone man can find peace.

Though these Jungian archetypes could be the subjects of endless discussions, it must be acknowledged that their structure and function is in striking agreement with the hierophanies which Mircea Eliade, following an entirely different route, has separated from the most divergent religious myths—those that are concerned with the heaven, the sun, the breath of the wind and of life, or those which on the other hand are concerned with the earth, or the moon and waters.[30] And just as the archetypes of Jung suggest the hierophanies of Eliade, even if they do not reach the point of being completely identifiable with them, so these mythico-ritualistic patterns brought to light by him find remarkable parallels in the models on which, according to Jung, our dreams are built, and in which the ancestral archetypes are awakened to a new life. Deaths and rebirths, the longings for a *vita nuova* for which one would gladly abandon the dead existences, nostalgias for lost paradises, prospects of unions, of divine espousals where man would be perfected even if he should lose himself in their acceptance — all of these things according to Jung make up the drama and mystery of our nights. Is not this a kind of shadow born in the depths of the soul of every modern man by the ancient rituals of the creation ceaselessly renewed, of the original fall and divine return, of the loves of gods and mortals? Or, rather, does not this mythical dramaturgy bear witness to their indestructible foundations in the soul of the everlasting man?

Only a summary view of these various theories has been given here. Jungian psychology, interesting as it is, and rich in observations and suggestions, is only too obviously in the same state of adolescence that the natural sciences were in the sixteenth century. A lively but somewhat mythological imagination is almost constantly being imposed on what can be considered as scientifically established. But even if one must be prudent in using these analyses of Jung when they lead to hasty conclusions, one cannot ignore the real resurrection which Jung has at least sketched of the human soul. Modern intellectualism, which is responsible for the materialism of our age, should learn a lesson from the exploration of the

---

[30] See C. G. Jung, *The Integration of the Personality,* pp. 52 ff., and Mircea Eliade, *Mythes, rêves et mystères,** pp. 11 ff. in particular.

CANISIUS COLLEGE LIBRARY
BUFFALO, N. Y.

soul made by Jung and his disciples instead of disdaining their false starts and errors. Psychological cures have certainly provided sufficient evidence that these studies are not groundless. The help and clarification which they bring to the history of religion cannot as a consequence be overlooked.

Jung, moreover, does not postulate an artificial, disembodied type of spirituality, any more than Freud. He has stressed the fact that the soul which he would like to reveal to modern man is so closely united to his body that it embraces the material world. He here opens the way to a more profound analysis of the natural symbols for what is spiritual. They should show how the apprehension of the spiritual comes from man's experience of the world, not as a pure spirit which sees it from the outside, but as a living soul which emerges from it. The brilliant but slightly facile studies of G. Bachelard on the poetic conceptions of earth, air, fire, and water at least indicate what a phenomenology of the elements of the world can discover that will serve as supports for, and sensible forms of, the religious experience.[31]

---

[31] Besides his short work *Psychanalise du Feu* (Paris, 1938), one can profitably read, with some reservations, *L'eau et les rêves* (Paris, 1942); *L'air et les songes* (Paris, 1943); *La terre et les rêveries de la volonté* (Paris, 1948); *La terre et les rêveries du repos* (Paris, 1948).

CHAPTER IV

Word and Rite

SINCE man is so deeply rooted in the material world, and since his symbolic representations of spiritual matters have their origin in his composite nature, a study of religion should take these concrete forms of expression as its point of departure. The meaning of these latter should be grasped with the help of a phenomenology which endeavors to embrace their intentionality as it were from within. Only in this way can the integrity of the object under consideration be maintained instead of being distorted in attempts to make it conform to *a priori* suppositions.

Any such study should immediately establish the duality of ritual forms. Sacred words and sacred actions are as a matter of fact always found joined together. But in just as many ways as they are found joined together, so it would seem they have that many different values and meanings. Their constant connection, however, already indicates their original bearing and, also, what is essentially permanent about them beneath the wide variety of forms in which they are found.

If words and rites are distinct and are to a certain extent reciprocally opposed, their constant connection must mean a natural relationship. This is so true that a decisive dominance of one over the other effects a change in the dominant element itself which seems to foretell the downfall of religion and perhaps quite simply of the religious man himself.[1]

[1] See Gerard van der Leeuw, *Religion in Essence and Manifestation,* pp. 339 ff.

53

There actually are religious forms in which the rite has, as it were, absorbed and assimilated the words, and there are on the other hand other forms where the words have practically suppressed the rite. In ancient Rome, for example, there were cults such as those of the Salian priests in which the sacred words had lost all their meaning even for the priests.[2] In a sense they had become nothing more than verbal rites. Conversely, in some extreme forms of Protestantism, the merely spoken word has taken the place of ritual and sacraments. In both cases, little enough is left of religion. In the former, it has degenerated into a senseless superstition, and in the latter it has exhausted itself in a kind of religious intellectualism.

If, as we have already shown, religion is religious to the extent that it is human, it must still be admitted that in the duality inherent in ritual a certain priority must be given to the word. A mere action, one without any real significance, one indeed in which the word does not enter as a determining factor, is by this very fact something subhuman and consequently areligious. On the other hand, it is the word — and therefore humanity itself, which is realized through self-expression — that degenerates whenever it tends to suppress action.

As a matter of fact, action belongs to the original, native essence of the word. And it is only the word faithful to its real nature that can also be truly religious.

The analyses of the Jewish philosopher Martin Buber can help us to understand this.[3] Buber, who has been steeped in the most vital Jewish tradition, that of the Hassidim — a religion that places great emphasis on the word — has shown us the religious tendencies and implications of every word true to itself. What kills or destroys these tendencies is a kind of self-satisfaction found in the over-intellectualized word which, by striving to be nothing more than a word, actually is prevented from truly becoming one.

Fundamentally, the word is only a way to action. It tends toward action. For man it is in a sense the primordial action. It is,

---

[2] See Jean Bayet, *Histoire politique et psychologique de la religion romaine* (Paris, 1957), pp. 50, 86 ff. These curious texts will be found in B. Maurenbrecher, "Carminum Saliarium reliquiae," *Jahrbuch für Philologie,* Supplement XXI (1894), pp. 315 ff.

[3] See Martin Buber, *I and Thou,* trans. R. G. Smith (New York, 1958).*

moreover, the action through which man asserts himself as such. He who speaks, by the very fact of speaking, interposes his own personal existence into the natural course of events.

To this it may of course be objected that the first person of our modern developed grammar was not originally the first. In certain primitive languages such as Hebrew, the first person is not "I" but what we would consider in English or in French to be the third person. But, as Buber has shown, "it" does not represent a person but is a form of the impersonal. This is further indicated by the fact that very small children tend to describe their actions impersonally. Before knowing and expressing himself as "I," a child speaks of himself under the form of "it."

This merely shows that consciousness emerges at a level where it is dependent upon things and seems therefore to confuse itself with them in its first expression. Nevertheless, one who speaks, even if he is not immediately aware of it, does so only because he has a natural tendency to interpose himself in the world. Even if it takes some time for the first person to disengage itself from the impersonal, it would never speak at all unless the tendency was there from the beginning.

If the primitive word is therefore active, it is the first action of *man,* of a being which from its very outset tends to express itself as "I" even if it is not immediately conscious of this fact. As near as it may be in its origins to simple mimicry, the word immediately implies a division between the world and our awareness of the world, even though it is only under the elementary form of imitation.

But, as Buber has again insisted, more must be said. Speech does not simply imply one who speaks and is opposed to the world: it implies another. Someone speaks, but someone must also hear. For speech there must not only be a certain inchoate awareness of oneself, there must also be the certainty, perhaps obscure, but immediate, of another self. Speech is not only personal, it is by nature interpersonal. Dialogue is inherent in the intentionality of all speech.

The various explanations of this fact which can be brought forward do not change it in the least. It has been said that speech postulates another only by the projection of the self upon things. Even if this could be demonstrated, which is far from being the case, it would still be necessary to recognize the harsh fact that I never speak simply to express myself, or, to be more exact, *I* express myself only when I take into account a *thou*. Even if it is said that this *thou* is nothing more than another self, this does not prevent this other self from being as much "other" as it is "self," and being present as such in the intent of every word. If speech is directed to things, it is not because they are looked upon as things but because they are a kind of covering, a sign as well as a screen, of a *thou* sought at the very outset, even if it is as yet no more reflexively distinguished than the I who speaks.

If speech is an inchoative action, it is the action of someone who leaves himself to go to another. It can therefore contain the gift or delivery of oneself to another, or, conversely, the seizure or conquest of another. Actually, in its initial view, it probably includes both. At any rate, under whatever form it may appear, it must be regarded not as a soliloquy but as a kind of dialogue.

It seems necessary to take a further step and not to hesitate to say that the *thou* envisaged by the original word is the *thou* of religion, the divine *Thou*.[4]

What actually is the religious relationship as we have seen it defined, or rather observed, by the phenomenology of religion and depth psychology? It is the basic relation of man to the world in its totality, but in this totality mysteriously apprehended as the unity, or rather the uniqueness, of the sacred, the completely Other. It seems then that the first words of a man are a cry toward God. Speech does not make the gods as Max Müller believed, but speech is rather man's first and profound reaction to the hierophanies.

This is why the myth according to which speech is one of the gods' first gifts to men, and through which they have created man as an essentially religious being, is found almost everywhere.[5] And this is why parents, since they are the first beings to whom it speaks, are veritable gods to a child. They are a kind of first stage in that natural tendency it has from the time it begins to speak,

[4] On the religious character of Buber's analyses, see especially Hans Urs von Balthasar, *Einsame Zwiesprache: Martin Buber und das Christentum* (Cologne, 1958).

[5] The fundamentally religious sense given to the word by all primitives is doubtlessly the element of truth in the fantastic ideas of such traditionalists as Louis de Bonald.

when it begins to acquire the first consciousness of itself, that is, the tendency to address another recognized as the ruler of the cosmos, just at the moment when the self is apprehended as the master of its own actions and its own movements.

From the fact that the word tends toward action, and is an incipient action, this original structure of the word will be found again in, and extended to, action. In other words, a rite is not simply one type of action among many others. It is the typical human action, inasmuch as it is connected with the word as the expression and realization of man in the world, and to the degree that this expression and realization are immediately and fundamentally religious.[6]

A rite therefore is a human action in which man apprehends himself as a religious being, just as in the word which leads to it. The rite will therefore follow the same development as the word. The word is the expression, the realization of man as such; but man comprehends it originally as a gift of God, as God's communication to himself at the same time as it is a communication of himself to God. Likewise a rite is precisely that action in which man feels that he is sharing in the divine activity: what a man does in the rite is a divine action, an action which God performs through and in man, as much as man himself performs it in and through God.

From this it should be clear that if the word becomes obscured, the rite itself will disintegrate. Words that are externally objectified, that develop into a series of techniques, lose their religious meaning. Profane, or rather profaned activity, will correspond to godless speech about the world: the world will no longer be understood as a hierophany but simply as the object of our purely material strivings. Before that, however, the word, having already become self-conscious and self-centered in a naive affirmation of itself, is linked with magical activity, through which man aims at controlling reality by taking the place of the gods and forcing them to reduce their activity within the compass of his own.[7]

[6] See Gerard van der Leeuw, *op. cit.*, pp. 403 ff.

[7] On the present state of research in magic, see the excellent little book of Jérôme-Antoine Rony, *La Magie* (Paris, 1950), and Bronislaw Malinowsky, *Magic, Science, and Religion* (New York, 1955).

From magic should be distinguished the practice of simple superstition, which lacks the former's diabolical character and is a degradation rather than a perversion of true religion. In superstition the word is simply opaque and without meaning. The rite as a consequence has nothing to do any more with either God or man. Or, rather, the rite is there a substitute for God, for a God whom man does not even think of enclosing implicitly in his ritualistic system as the magician does, since the devitalized rite has already imprisoned the superstitious man.

In reaction to all this, the word will tend to become overobjectivized. It will affirm the absolute transcendence of the spirit over the naive reality of a man in search of freedom, over the sophisticated reality of a world in whose objectivity he believes that he marks out for himself a truer autonomy than that of magic, or over the simply hardened reality of a ritual that has fallen into superstition. To become purely divine, the word endeavors to escape completely this sensible world which is the world of man. But it can then well happen that man does nothing more than make for himself a supreme idol, that of the intelligence succeeding to the idols of stone or flesh.[8]

Highly cultured religions are particularly subject to this ultimate temptation. It seems to be fully manifest in certain types of Protestantism. But all modern Catholics can be regarded as being unwitting Protestants in this regard.

Protestantism can only be understood if it is seen as a reaction to a religion that had degenerated, if not into magic, at least into superstition. In the Middle Ages, when few people, even among the priests, understood Latin, the tendency was to make of the liturgy something that took on the character of the incomprehensible, something at which the people assisted but in which they had no part, something that issued from the hands of the priest but like some prodigy that escaped even him. Under the pretext that grace is given, and that the sacraments act, *ex opere operato,* men gave up any attempt to understand them. Words, real words, which make sense and which are spoken with this intent, disappeared from the worship or no longer played an essential role in it. Even in its formulas, worship tended to be no more than a

---

[8] See in this respect Karl Barth, *The Word of God and the Word of Man,* trans. D. Horten (New York, 1957).* Cf. also below, P. 217.

purely ritualistic action. But by the same token, the ritualistic action became dehumanized; and, like it or not, it ceased at the same time to be really religious. This was not necessarily magic since, as we shall see later, unintelligibility is not the essence of magic but rather an intelligibility that is exclusively anthropocentric; but it was certainly tainted with superstition, not in the sense understood by the Romans, of a religion which exceeds its normal activity, but in the analogous sense of a religion which stifles and oppresses the conscience and is therefore degraded.[9]

The Protestant reaction was already lurking among even the best intentioned and most orthodox of the humanist reformers.[10] Simply reversing the general trend of thought, they passed from the correct concept that true religion cannot lose itself in unintelligibility to the much more questionable position that a religion is true to the extent that it is immediately and wholly intelligible. In the end, a religion's truth was placed in its intelligibility, which was itself conceived as being something clear and evident.

This very soon gave rise to an insistence upon the exclusive use of the vernaculars. Next there was the desire, in these languages themselves, to reduce everything to an obvious meaning without any mysteries. And very soon attempts were made to limit everything in worship itself to the communication of this meaning. The consequence of all this was that the rites were themselves painfully reduced to a mere repetition of a verbal pedagogy undertaken for the good of the ignorant or at least the uneducated.[11] This inevitably led to the final suppression of the rites themselves.

The process of this evolution may be seen in the architecture of the times. Altars plainly visible from all sides were substituted for the altars of the Middle Ages which had been completely shut off in a walled chancel. In Lutheran churches the pulpit was brought as close to the altar as possible. On the altar itself, the Bible replaced the sacred vessels, so that the altar came to be regarded as

[9] See below, pp. 75-76.

[10] For the decline in the proper understanding of the Faith among the humanistic reformers who did not subscribe to Protestantism, see H. Jedin, *A History of the Council of Trent,* trans. Dom Ernest Graf, O.S.B., I (St. Louis, 1960),* pp. 355 ff.

[11] See the analysis of the sacramental conceptions of Zwingli, in the excellent article in the *Dictionnaire de théologie catholique* which Père Pollet has dedicated to the doctrine of Zwinglianism.

a kind of secondary, imperfect place for preaching. In Calvinist churches, the pulpit, as a matter of fact, came to dominate the altar and eventually absorb it. In the majority of Reformed churches, the altar soon disappeared. At most it remained as a kind of unrecognizable relic, in the shape of a table, which was used ritually only at intervals, and almost with an uneasy conscience.[12]

It is easy for us Catholics to stigmatize this evolution. It would perhaps, however, be more profitable to ask ourselves if recent developments in many of our own churches are not even more disturbing. What do we actually see taking place under the influence of one aspect of the liturgical movement? Unfortunately, the answer must be: the superimposition of the Protestant evolution upon the medieval one, both stressed to the point of caricature.

On the one hand, a commentator that attracts all the attention to himself has been introduced. In his exposition he aims at being perfectly clear. He makes no allowance for the obscure, for silence, for mystery, for the ineffable; but he absorbs, dilutes, dissolves everything as if he were conducting a kindergarten. His explanations turn his preaching into a matter-of-fact lesson and the rites into a simple illustration of this lesson. They are like a game of charades for the benefit of pupils with small capacity for abstraction.

At the same time a Mass is being duly celebrated in the background without any intrinsic connection with the actual worship of the faithful other than this artificial illustration. To preserve the rubrics, the priest hurries through the required gestures, stammers through words which are supposed to be essential, but which no one could hear even if he wanted, and which are treated as if they no longer aimed at any kind of intelligibility.

The most extreme type of Protestant worship, and usually of the poorest quality, due to the desire to be understood at any cost, is superimposed on medieval worship involved in the fatal logic of its disintegration. One defect exaggerates the other: the ritual service declines under the ever-increasing burden of its verbal trapping; the service of the word competing with the ritual becomes lost in empty phrases. Since it can no longer act as a

[12] On this evolution, see the work of G. W. O. Addleshaw and Frederick Etchells, *The Architectural. Setting of Anglican Worship* (London, 1948), pp. 22 ff.

medium between the rite and the people, it has become a screen shutting the people off from the rite itself.

The plain description of these verbo-ritual behaviors enables us to see how a religion degenerates. It perhaps tells us more than any kind of sociological analysis why it is that Christianity exercises less and less influence upon modern man. If the forms of religion, as they are known today, mean so little to our contemporaries, it is because they are burdened with their own defects. As a consequence, a too facile adaptation of this religion to modern circumstances will only strengthen the barrier instead of bringing men closer to that from which they have become alienated. This happens when they both share the same defects. A ritualistic action without appeal to the mind, words which no longer have contact with reality but actually empty it of its content, resemble only too closely the predicament of modern man. But instead of making religion more accessible to him on this account, they only increase his acquired unawareness of the sacred.

The remedy must be sought elsewhere, in a rediscovery of the original meaning and nature of words and rites so that they are no longer blindly opposed to each other.

This presupposes a restoration of their mysterious density to both words and actions — words which convey nothing more than a reasoning process in which objective reality is practically denied by the mind which substitutes its own activity for it, and actions which no longer make sense since the gestures are so buried in the matter that no mind can penetrate them, cannot be united into an effective ritual.

At the present stage of human evolution we are suffering from the tyranny of the word, or rather of words that have become devitalized by the very stress that has been placed upon them. So that their absorption of the rites may be counteracted, the first thing we need is a phenomenology of a still living rite. This in turn will help us to recover words that will be truly alive in the ritual, that is, words that have been cured of their tendency to reduce everything to themselves.

In the ritual itself actions must be spiritualized by the words. If the meaning of the ritual is not enlightened by an authentic divine word, it degenerates into magic or simple superstition. But the action should not on that account be reduced to a mere clothing of abstract ideas. Otherwise there is no longer any ritual at all but at most a kind of pious charade. Therefore it is the meaning of the ritual symbol which must first be recovered if the words themselves are to become again the words of the divine mystery and not a simple formula which, substituted for reality, can no longer attain it.

CHAPTER V

Phenomenology of Rites:
Sacraments and Sacramentals
and Their Natural Analogues

A rite may be defined as a symbolic action which is religious by its very symbolism. Again it is necessary to pay attention to the meaning of the words. The symbolism which concerns us here is a natural symbolism. It has nothing to do with a meaning added extrinsically to an action which is in itself indifferent to it.[1]

More generally, it may be said that as soon as one considers religious symbolism, and especially ritualistic symbolism, as an action conceived *post factum* to illustrate ideas that were first developed in the abstract, this symbolism will never more be understood. Whenever such artificial symbolism is introduced into a ritual, it means that the latter will soon be dead.[2]

In this respect, the sclerosis leading soon to agony of the sacraments and the ultimate rejection of them in Protestantism is only a product of a real perversion of their meaning which had been prepared by the intellectualism of the Late Middle Ages. The

[1] The symbol always exists prior to the meaning placed upon it. When this meaning is further defined, the symbol becomes a sign. The Christian sacraments are an excellent example of this. On the contrary, any expression of a reality which is conceived without this natural symbolism will be completely artificial and becomes a mere convention.

[2] This is implied since it substitutes for the radical communications of man with God through the interpretation of the cosmic reality, from which man himself emerges, an artificial communication of an abstract nature with no religious connotations.

Protestant Reformation, instead of effecting any reforms in this matter, only brought it to its logical conclusions. Nothing reveals the true nature of rites quite as much as a study of this decline.[3]

What is called the "institution of sacraments," when conceived too narrowly, includes in its definition the seeds of their dissolution. And yet this was not a Protestant invention. Protestantism only brought out all its latent consequences. When the Fathers and the greatest of the scholastics, beginning with St. Thomas, traced the Christian sacraments back to their institution by Christ, they did not understand this at all in the way it was understood by some of those who came after them, and who erroneously used them to support their own teaching.[4] The Fathers did not in the least imagine that the rite of eating or of washing was a profane action, bare of any religious significance before Christ's intervention, but upon which He bestowed a particular meaning by a purely arbitrary decision. According to the classical Christian teaching on the institution of the sacraments, Christ exercised no such arbitrary and unnatural authority over creation. On the contrary, truly traditional theology joins the institution of the sacraments by Christ with the natural symbolism of washing and eating, which of itself has a religious significance. The words of institution simply gave a new meaning to rites already charged with meaning. And the new meaning was not forced upon the natural meaning but rather amplified and enriched it. In no way were the words thought to infuse a wholly accidental, unprepared meaning into actions that were not predestined to receive it.

On the contrary, such an understanding of the institution of the sacraments was a typical product of Nominalism. According to this way of thinking, there are no real essences, and, consequently, if He had so wished, Christ could have as easily given to the Eucharist the meaning of baptism, and to baptism the meaning of the Eucharist. Such a theory, of course, presupposes a radical

[3] For further details, see my volume, *Du Protestantisme à l'Eglise* (Paris, 1955),* pp. 158 ff., as well as the chapter devoted to the sacraments in my study, *The Word, Church and Sacraments in Protestantism and Catholicism,* trans. A. V. Littledale (London, 1961).

[4] See the annotated translation which Père A. Roguet has made of the texts of the *Summa Theologica,* dealing with the sacraments in *Christ Acts Through the Sacraments,* trans. Carisbrooke Dominicans (Collegeville, 1953).

separation of word and rite. From this separation it follows that the efficacy of a rite connected with a word that has no intrinsic connection with it will either tend to attribute to the word a magical efficacy, as if the word itself was a cabalistic formula which charged with mana in a wholly incomprehensible fashion any object however indifferent; or it will tend to degenerate into a mere repetition of the word by means of an arbitrary sign which adds nothing to it except some artificial and useless imagery. An example of the first type of error is the degradation of sacramentalism so typical of medieval piety at its decline. An example of the second may be found in the Protestant reaction which pushed it to its ultimate consequences.[5]

But the same basic supposition is behind the senseless speculations about priests who could, if they wished, change all the loaves of bread in all the bakeries of the world into the body of Christ, and the bloodless sacramentalism of the Protestants. They both hold that in ritual matters it makes no difference what a thing may naturally signify: the meaning of the rites themselves is completely divorced from any natural symbolism. Starting with such a principle, true rites could only take on a magical character, unless they were turned into pedagogical rites, or rather pseudo-rites, doomed beforehand to be stillborn.

In the face of these two equally disastrous consequences of a false intellectualism, which is nothing but a false idealism, a truly Christian sacramental realism demands a rediscovery of the ritual realism common to all unsophisticated forms of natural religion. Rituals are never artificial compositions, the work of theologians who first think in the abstract and then try to the best of their ability to make their creations accessible to a common herd that is little accustomed to their lofty speculations. Quite the contrary, it is everywhere evident that the rites are first and the theological constructions so subordinate to them that they regularly flow from them.

[5] Father Francis Clark, S.J., has accused us of being in general too harsh on Nominalist theology. Nevertheless, he has clearly shown, especially in his discussion of the sacramental theories of Gabriel Biel, the total cleavage between what is revealed and, let us not say what is natural, since the concept itself is tenuous, but what is rational. See especially "The 'Baleful Bequest' of Nominalism," in his *Eucharistic Sacrifice and the Reformation* (London, 1960).

Rites are not actions that are of themselves more or less indifferent and which have been by sheer compulsion impregnated with a meaning for which they were in no way prepared. They are of themselves meaningful actions. A ritual action, far from being a late offspring of a highly intellectualized religion that has to have recourse to gestures to regain contact with the simple-minded, is the most spontaneous and original manifestation of religion. From this ritual action, the later notions about the religion itself are gradually derived. A living rite is not something that has been coldly worked out so that religious ideas which have been put together in the quiet of one's study may have some external manifestation. It is an immediate, primordial creation of religiously-minded men in which they have actively realized their effective connection with the divinity before they explain this connection to themselves.

This is why at all times and in all places rites are considered to be the work of the gods. The men who celebrate these rites would not celebrate them as they do if they thought that they were themselves their authors. And, in fact, the rites soon cease to be observed when men get the idea that they were instituted by other men before them. Rites exist precisely as rites because it is believed that if they can be instituted at all, it is the gods who have instituted them and are the real agents of the rites, working through and beyond the action of the priests.

Far from being an exception to this rule, Christianity is a transcendent realization of it. This is the true meaning of the institution of the sacraments by Christ and of the Catholic belief that the sacraments work *ex opere operato,* that is, that Christ remains their true celebrant. Where this conviction fails or becomes obscured, the sacraments are emptied of their substance, just as in any case where rites come to be regarded as simple human actions, as pious means of teaching the people invented by theologians. In such an hypothesis, the theologians themselves have no need of these rites since they are supposed to have already been in substantial possession of the religion itself and to have later created the rites as a means of transmitting it to the people. Wherever this idea becomes prevalent, the rites themselves cease to be of any consequence because it is felt quite simply that they have ceased to be rites. An edifying tableau has never become a rite for the obvious reason that the spectator does not feel that he is personally involved; neither does he feel that God is there present and active.

This aspect of the matter should be pointed up in more detail since it is so fundamental that if sight of it is once lost, the very possibility of a substantially religious ritual is also lost.

Those in our day, and G. van der Leeuw in particular, who have studied the history and phenomenology of religion, have distinguished two basic types of rites in all religions, analogous to the sacraments and sacramentals of Catholicism.[6]

The former appear as rites in which a properly divine action is present so that the faithful may take part in it. The latter are the ordinary actions of human life which have been, as it were, brought within the sacral sphere. In the former, the sacred action of the gods penetrates the life of men. Wrought at the beginning by the gods, that is, in a mythical time that is nothing more than a sensible image of eternity, it descends by means of the celebration into the here and now of our own existence. Through the latter type of rite, the humble substance of our existence is lifted up to the eternal. They are like blessings which sanctify the life of man and saturate it with divine energy. Contrariwise, through the great "sacraments," it is the divine life itself that becomes our own.

The distinction is well founded. It corresponds to the two separate but complementary reactions which man has to what is sacred. The first focuses upon the *mysterium tremendum* of Otto, the apprehension of the divine as the Sovereign and the completely Other which lifts us out of ourselves and raises us up to a supernatural level in the strictest sense of the word. This is what Friedrich Heiler has called the mystical orientation: one which draws a man out of his own proper world and urges him on to integrate himself with a world which surpasses his natural abilities and which alienates him from his former home, a world where God not only reigns supreme but where He is alone. The second reaction reflects rather the *mysterium* as *fascinans*, the mystery as something attractive and engrossing, that approaches the divine as a beneficent power without peer, that is, God as the Saviour of man.[7]

[6] Gerard van der Leeuw, *Religion in Essence and Manifestation*, pp. 361 ff.

[7] Frederick Heiler, *Prayer: A Study in the History and Psychology of Religion*, trans. and ed. by Samuel McComb, with the assistance of J. E. Park (New York, 1932).

But a distinction does not necessarily imply a separation. The *mysterium tremendum* is also the *mysterium fascinans*. There is, as a consequence, a certain ambiguity in all religious signs; often the same signs, depending upon the stress given them, can become *sacramenta* as well as *sacramentalia*. Moreover, the *sacramentalia* always seem to be more or less dependent upon the *sacramenta*.[8] This is why in Christianity the essentially sacred repast of the Eucharist basically colors the sanctification of every meal by the blessing of the bread, wine, oil, and the fruits of the earth in general. Similarly, all our rites of purification with water, from the *Asperges* before a High Mass to the simplest blessing, are oriented toward baptism, toward the participation in the purifying death and saving resurrection of Christ.

This exchange is due to the fact that the great sacramental acts which deliver the divine acts to us are only possible because of the native symbolism of man's actions in the world in which he finds himself as the central image of God. It can be said that man does not believe that he can share in the life above except by knowing or feeling at the same time that he has an innate relationship with the divine. Here, in the rite, we find again that necessary interrelation already revealed by the word that exists between the expression of our own personality and the apprehension of, or rather the search for, the divine personality.

Nevertheless, the possible, and always at least germinally present, distinction in a rite between God's action laying hold of us and man's action laid hold of by God is the basis for a whole series of different evaluations of the same ritual patterns.[9] Actually, one of the most precious discoveries of the history of religions has been the constancy of certain patterns which make up the primary, and consequently invariable, texture of the rites, but which lend themselves to a great variety of interpretations. If there is an incontestable evolution in religion, it consists in these successive interpretations rather than in any evolution of the rites themselves. Not only is the material of which they are made little subject to modification, but this is equally true of the primary patterns about which this material is organized. What does vary according to the

[8] On this subject, see A. M. Roguet, O.P., in *Theology Library, VI* Chicago, 1958), pp. 36 ff.·
[9] See G. van der Leeuw, *op. cit.,* p. 472.

variations of civilization, is the manner in which they are understood.[10] This in turn does not fail to react upon the ritual. It complicates it and weighs it down with more or less expository repetitions. But these latter are always dependent on the great rites, the primitive *sacramenta*. Or, if these additions acquire an independent status, their parasitical growth simply kills off the ritual as such. This is strikingly evident in the evolution of Greek tragedy, which passed from a kind of liturgy to pure theater.[11] And the same may be found in different aspects of the medieval liturgy. By means of the "mystery plays" and then the "miracle plays," men passed from Christian sacramentalism to the plain didacticism of the Protestant sacraments.[12]

Everywhere, then, may be found the same basic store of sacramental rites. They are modeled after the dynamic representations of the sacred action which are permanently fixed in the religious consciousness, no matter what changes this may have undergone, and their general outline may be seen even in the dreams or poetic creations of men who have apparently freed themselves from the divine. More exactly, it is in the ritual celebration that these representations take their form. The mind only becomes consciously aware of them when it fully realizes what is accomplished in the rites.[13]

What is perhaps the fundamental pattern, that of creation, of an eternal return and a perpetual renewal of all things through a periodic return to the beginning, is clearly manifest in the elementary rituals which form the foundations of the first agrarian civilizations. This is particularly noticeable in the ancient rites of Canaan which, according to the complaints of the prophets, se-

[10] *Ibid.*, pp. 422 ff., where what he says of the many possible interpretations of prayer is equally applicable to rites. See also Mircea Eliade, *Patterns in Comparative Religion*, trans. Rosemary Sheed (New York, 1958),* pp. 23 ff.

[11] On this evolution, see J. Jeanmaire, *Dionysos: Histoire du culte de Bacchus* (Paris, 1951), pp. 268 ff.

[12] See the different works of G. Cohen, particularly his *Anthologie du drame liturgique en France au Moyen-Age* (Paris, 1955).

[13] See Mircea Eliade, *Mythes, rêves et mystères,** pp. 206 ff.

duced Israel settled in the Promised Land.[14] The rite by which a man ties himself to the powers of vegetation is one of the most archaic forms of culture in the primary sense of the word. Cult and culture are as a matter of fact connected, and even indistinct, in their origins as well as in their etymology. The essential activities of the harvest, such as the gathering of the first sheaf of grain, are here of decisive importance. Man recognizes in them the creative power of the divinity by uniting himself with it.

Behind these permanently significant gestures can perhaps be recognized the survival of an even earlier ritual act, that of the simple reaping of the fruits of the earth that would correspond to the very first stage of cultural development.[15] The ear of wheat reaped in silence which, as we are told, gave rise to the most sacred rite of Eleusis, is probably the survival of the most instinctive natural action by means of which man in search of food recognized that he received it from a higher source of fruitfulness.[16] It was for him the first hierophany of God in action.

The theme of the return to paradise,[17] which remedies the damage caused by the fall, flourishes in its turn in the rites of passage, which always deal with a return. This is what lies behind most processions or circumambulations. Here, there is always a question of a rediscovery, an unveiling, and a reconquest of that which had earlier been abandoned. The Freudians have some reasons for seeing in this a correlative of that nostalgia for the maternal womb that fills the dreams of a man worn out with the trials of life.[18]

But there is here a greater concern for an ascent to the paternal heaven than for a return to mother earth. This is what is particu-

[14] See W. C. Graham and H. O. May, *Culture and Conscience* (Chicago, 1936), pp. 16 ff., and especially E. O. James, *Myth and Ritual in the Ancient Near East* (New York, 1958).*

[15] See our remarks above on the work of Father Schmidt, p. 24.

[16] Cf. *Philosophoumena* 5.8. A commentary on this may be found in P. Foucart, *Les mystères d'Éleusis* (Paris, 1914), p. 434. This interprets literally the text of a gesture made under the eyes of the *mystes*. A. Loisy, *Les mystères païens et le mystère chrétien,* 2nd ed. (Paris, 1930), p. 72, note 1, discusses this interpretation in an unconvincing manner.

[17] See Mircea Eliade, *Mythes, rêves, mystères,* * pp. 80 ff.

[18] See what Freud himself wrote on regression in dreams in *The Interpretation of Dreams,* trans. A. A. Brill, rev. ed. (New York, 1937).*

larly noticeable in the ascension rites.[19] God has left the earth, or what amounts to the same, man and the universe with him have fallen from the divine level where they were originally placed to this lower world. Man, therefore, instinctively strives to scale the heights from which he has fallen to recover what he has lost. This is the reason, as Mircea Eliade has shown, why the tree is so important in these rites. One mounts from earth to heaven by being united with its growth, by climbing its branches, and by being borne by them. Circumambulation and ascension are frequently found united in the procession of the felled tree, which on its return is trimmed and replanted, and which is thought to come to life again, as in the mysteries of Attis.

This second kind of rite is closely connected with the preceding. It is perhaps already a more explicit and elaborated copy of it.

In contrast with these are the equally numerous rites associated with hunting and pastoral cultures where everything is centered about the two focal points of a mysterious ellipse, fecundity and death. Life feeds on death; it only survives in perpetual generations. This is the source of the primitive sacrality of the sex act and of murder, almost always found united or closely connected with each other in ritual, which constantly echoes that connection between the libido and the instinct for death revealed by Freud.[20]

In this context, the rituals in which water plays a part seem to be particularly primitive. They are strangely ambivalent: there are the primordial waters, the waters in which life makes its first appearance, fecund waters, and more precisely maternal waters; but there are also the waters of the deluge, the waters in which Leviathan moves about, the waters of the "Death by Water," in which all the living must at last be swallowed up and perish.[21]

Throughout these highly divergent themes and their numerous metamorphoses, there seems to be one rite which remains constant, that of the meal, a repast which unites or reunites one with the creative power, a viaticum for the return to the lost paradise (which is also the land of promise), a nuptial and funeral banquet. We shall have frequent occasion to clarify and illustrate its diff-

---

[19] See M. Eliade, op. cit., pp. 133 ff., and Patterns in Comparative Religion.

[20] See Sigmund Freud, Collected Papers, II, 255 ff.

[21] See M. Eliade, op. cit., pp. 188 ff.

erent meanings, which form, as it were, the backbone of every religion.[22]

If we now pass from these elementary and basically immutable patterns to their mutable interpretations, what do we discover?

A common interpretation of the most primitive rituals at the beginning of the century was to view them as magical practices. This idea is fundamental to all the work of Sir James Frazer in England and to the studies of Hubert and Mauss in France.[23] According to them, a rite would be essentially an act of sympathetic magic. Man takes the initiative by imitating certain natural processes, believing that in this way he can increase their activity and even release those that will be to his own benefit. Thus, ritual orgies should be understood as a means of guaranteeing the fertility of the flocks or even of the earth itself.

Contemporary historians of religion no longer believe that this explains the primitive rites. In fact, a magical mentality is anything but primitive.[24] Since it is closely connected with the first sedentary cultures, it is something decidedly secondary in the development of man's thoughts. It marks a stage of adolescence which man attains when he becomes aware of his own relative autonomy with respect to the cosmic phenomena. Beginning to grow in his own self-confidence and to find his place in the world, he goes on to assert himself against it, that is to say, against the primitive hierophany in which his most elementary apprehensions of reality are bathed. Puffed up by his own relative independence, he strives by means of the rites themselves to make his own will dominate over the will of the deities.

But, at the beginning, man feels that in a ritual action he is himself only when acting within the divine action. Only later, when he begins to reflect on the rites is his attention drawn to his own initiative. Noting its effects and his ability to determine them at his own pleasure, he then comes to interpret the rituals as a means of keeping in check the activity of the gods.

[22] See my chapter on sacrifice.

[23] See along with Frazer's Golden Bough, H. Hubert and M. Mauss, Mélanges d'histoire des religions (Paris, 1909).

[24] See J. A. Rony, La magie, pp. 100 ff.; Raoul Allier, Magie et religion (Paris, 1935); and also the entire discussion of the notion of mana in Eliade, op cit., p. 23.

It may be reasonably asked if the myth, that is, the formulized, or rather typified, image of the divine action underlying the rites is not a primitive reaction against this first debasement of religion. The rites, we must repeat, antedate every detailed explanation of what is done in them. The myth appears as a figurative explanation of the rites insofar as they are divine actions represented in human fashion.[25] As a consequence, it seems quite probable that the myth rises to restate the fact that the rites belong to the gods and not to men, whenever man in the process of discovering himself tends to regard himself as being their principal agent, if not their author. Man's religious instinct then reasserts itself against this magical deformation of religion by expressing the action of the gods in human terms at the very moment when the rites are in danger of being turned into purely human actions.

Perhaps it is possible to be even more precise. It may be asked if it is not through the symbolism of sex that man has conceived the idea that what takes place within himself, the natural functions over which he has a certain control, in some way belong to him more than those with which he is merely associated, such as the harvesting of grain. From this would flow the idea that he there holds, as it were, the key to the forces of nature. At this moment the myth would reintroduce a perception of the divine transcendent action at the price of a first humanization of the gods in the very functions that are most human.[26]

Doubtlessly, viewed in this light, the myth opens the way to mythology, that is, to a deterioration of the idea that one has made for himself of the gods. But it has been first of all a defense against an earlier and more vicious deterioration, that of magic, the attributing of divine powers to man.

In an agrarian ritual as typical as that of Eleusis we thus see the hierogamy superimposed on what was without doubt the most primitive ritual symbol, that of the ear of wheat plucked in silence. The union of the priest and his wife consummated in the

[25] See E. O. James, *Myth and Ritual in the Ancient Near East,* especially the first and last chapters.

[26] This idea has been developed especially by Raoul Allier, in the work previously cited. According to Father Schmidt, magic appears at the time when the invention of hunting equipment furnished man with the hope of subjecting the whole of nature to himself.

hypogaeum came to be regarded as a means of arousing the vege-
tative powers of nature. However, at this point the myth makes its
appearance to explain how the ritual union is not simply the
union of a human couple but of Pluto and Kore-Persephone, that
is to say, the divine source of that fertility of the earth which enables the dying seeds of grain to conquer death despite their own
individual death.[27]

The reinterpretation of the rites in the myth is therefore only a
return in a more advanced culture to the primitive interpretation,
or rather primitive apprehension, of the rites. But this reinterpretation gives rise to a further ritual development. To the bare primary
symbol is added a *dromenon,* a detailed dramatization of the ad-
ventures of Kore. Dragged by Hades beneath the earth, she is
pursued by her mother Demeter until the infernal powers finally
promise that she may return to the light of day. Hence the final
illumination that accompanies the joyful tidings of the divine birth
conceived in darkness. In this way the myth that had been drawn
from the rite returns to the rite. Reinterpreting the archaic ritual
in order to revive its original religious character, it creates a new

[27] In his tenth homily on the martyrs, Asterius of Amaseia describes
this rite in greater detail than is done by others. From Apuleius (*Metamorphoses* 6), it seems likely that it was the union of Kore with Pluto,
as found in the myth, that was imitated. Other authors, however, speak of
a union of Demeter herself, whether it be with Zeus (*Schol. in Georgian*
497c), or with Jasion (Homer, *Odyssey* 5.125-129; Hesiod *Theogony*
969-971). Even at Eleusis it seems that she was believed to have united
herself with the local prince Keleos. (Cf. the scholion on Aristophanes,
Acharnians 55, which seems confirmed by *Orphic Hymn* 41.5-9, and by
an allusion of St. Gregory Nazianzen.) Variations and doublets of this kind
frequently occur in the mythical interpretation of the same rite. They
bear witness to the distinctly secondary character of the myth as compared with the rite. It has been argued that another rite in these mysteries,
the handling of ritual objects, had a sexual significance. But since we
have no certain knowledge as to what these objects were or what was
done with them, it is difficult to draw any conclusions about this. See the
rather inconclusive discussion in Loisy, *Les mystères païens et le mystère
chrétien,* pp. 67 ff.

rite, a later addition to the earlier rite, which it quickens with renewed meaning.[28]

It would be well to emphasize the fact that the new rite was not entirely new. It seems to have been an expressive elaboration of the primitive procession of the mystai toward the sanctuary. It is in this way that the intended symbolism is deliberately introduced into archaic rituals. What were at first only marginal, or even purely utilitarian, rites become interpreted in a legendary fashion. But the interpretation soon tends to accommodate them to itself.[29]

This dramatization of the ancient rites, while seeking to revive them, actually runs the risk of attracting complete attention to itself. The foundations of an intellectualization of religion are thus laid which will ultimately destroy it. But we have not reached this stage as yet. Rather than intellectualization at this stage, we meet the work of the poetic imagination.

Nevertheless this prepares the way for an intellectualization of the rites in the real sense of the word. It makes its appearance when philosophers like Plato try to interpret the mysteries as teaching the immortality of the soul.[30] At this moment the process is set in motion which will gradually substitute a purely literary mystery for the religious mysteries and rituals.[31] The way is thus

[28] Cf. the general evocation of Plutarch (*Stob. Flor.* 4. 107) with the details given in the *Philosophoumena* 5.8, and especially the final formula: "The divine one hath given birth to a holy infant, Brimo Brimos," that is to say: "the Mighty Woman has begotten the Mighty Man." Notice the support given by this text to the version of the myth found in the *Metamorphoses:* Brimo is in effect a proper name of Persephone ("The Formidable").

[29] The liturgist Dom Claude de Vert, a monk of Cluny, was the first to point out the utilitarian origin of many rites, which did not acquire a symbolic meaning until later. See his *Explication simple, littérale et historique des cérémonies de l'Église,* 4 vols. (Paris, 1706-1713). His only mistake was, as a reaction to the fantastic allegorizing of certain medieval scholars, to tend to reduce nearly all ritual symbols to such false symbolisms. See the very curious discussion of this matter in Pierre Le Brun, *Explication de la messe,* I (Paris, 1711; republished as No. 9 in the collection *Lex Orandi*).

[30] See especially *Phaedrus* 250 bc.

[31] See A. J. Festugière, *L'idéal religieux des grecs et l'évangile* (Paris, 1932), pp. 116 ff.

cleared for a philosophical religion whose attempts to explain the mysteries will destroy their usefulness except as expressive, or simply ornamental images. In Hermetism the metamorphosis will be completed. There will no longer be any real mysteries but only mysterious words and images adorning speculations which expressly deny the value of the rites.[32]

This is the same subtly disintegrating process that we see at work in the Christian liturgy during the Middle Ages and at the time of the Protestant Reformation. The use of a dead language and, especially, the interpretation of Christianity in categories of thought that were more and more at variance with those of primitive Christianity created a dangerous spiritual vacuum around its sacramentalism. Temptations to magic were fatally added to simple superstitions. The spontaneous religious reaction found a remedy in the explanations known as the *Expositiones Missae,* which were scriptural in intent but more or less fictional in form.[33] This means that the ancient rites which had become impenetrable to the people were explained as if scenes from the Passion were being carried out in plainly representative actions. The ancient Christian belief that the mystery of the death and resurrection of Christ is present in the Mass was now artificially interpreted as if the walking from the Epistle to the Gospel side represented the return of Christ from Herod to Pilate. The washing of the priest's hands was supposed to correspond with the latter's gesture, and so on.

These fantastic explanations superimposed on the rites could not be satisfied for long with the primitive symbols which quite obviously were not adapted to them. The ancient rites were therefore tricked out with a new ritual. But this was actually no more than a pious dramatization whose spirit was utterly alien to the rites themselves. This explains the representations of the Passion, of the holy women at the tomb, of the empty tomb itself after the Mass of the Presanctified on Good Friday, and the waiting for the return, artificially dramatized, of the Blessed Sacrament on Easter morning.

[32] See A. D. Nock's preface to his edition of the *Corpus Hermeticum,* I (Paris, 1945), p. vi.

[33] See J. A. Jungmann, *The Mass of the Roman Rite: Its Origin and Development,* trans. F. A. Brenner, I (New York, 1951), pp. 115 ff.

The last, or next to last, stage was attained when the Protestants came to interpret the sacramental rites themselves after the pattern of these late pseudo-rites which, while attempting to explain the sacraments, finally supplanted them. In other words, only an imaginative representation could now be seen in all the Church's ritual, with no other content than the pious imaginations or sentimental reminiscences which it could arouse. At this stage, there were no longer sacramental rites in the proper sense of the words. Though apparently still preserved, their ritual was no more than a relic destined soon to be discarded.

The constant reoccurence of these disintegrating processes raises the question as to whether or not they are inevitable. Can they not be effectively resisted so that religion does not degenerate into magic or dissipate itself into a purely intellectual system divorced from life?

Before answering this question, we must first continue our study of the nature of rites by directing our attention to those rites *par excellence* which have come to be called sacrifices.

CHAPTER VI

Sacrificial Rites
and Their Ambivalence

THEOLOGIANS AND HISTORIANS of religion readily admit that sacrifices constitute the most important religious rites. But there is hardly anything on which they hold more divergent opinions than the nature of sacrifice.

Doubtless as soon as men became somewhat civilized, they were struck, if not shocked, by the bloody character of most sacrificial rites. With Virgil, *mactare victimas,* "to slay victims," already means the same as "to offer sacrifice." A modern Protestant theologian has not hesitated to describe Leviticus as a handbook for the perfect butcher.[1] Thus it is not surprising that sacrifice should commonly be taken as being synonymous with a ritual act of slaying, if not of destruction.

For Condren, or at any rate for the one who later edited his *Idea of the Priesthood* (who seems to have been Quesnel), the ideal sacrifice would be the pure and simple annihilation of a creature before God.[2] Without going this far, the whole school of De Lugo, which has for a long time imposed its views about the Mass on the generality of Catholic theologians, takes as axiomatic the idea that the essence of sacrifice lies in the immolation, which is conceived as being one with the ritual slaying of the victim.[3]

---

[1] The saying is from Wilfred Monod.

[2] See Jean Galy, *Le sacrifice dans l'école française de spiritualité* (Paris, 1951).

[3] See Eugène Masure, *Le sacrifice du chef* (Paris, 1932), all of the first chapter.

Modern theologians, following the lead of M. Lepin, P.S.S., reacting to these views of the Baroque Age, have sought to find the essence of sacrifice in the oblation, that is, following the formula devised by M. Masure, a transfer of the ownership of one of the goods which man possesses so that what was his now becomes the property of God. The reason for the mactation, or slaying of the victim, is simply to send it from this world to the next.[4]

In his beautiful and profound study, *The Mystery of Faith,* Père de la Taille maintains that in a state of integral nature the oblation would actually constitute the essence of sacrifice, and that the painful immolation has only come in as a result of sin, which makes it now a necessary condition for an effective oblation.[5] The clues which he has thus given to an interpretation of the cross of Christ through sacrificial formulas and to an appreciation of the role of the Church in offering the Eucharist cannot be denied.

Nevertheless it is doubtful, to say the least, that these refined, highly moralized and spiritualized concepts can give an accurate account of what men have had in mind when offering sacrifice from earliest times.

In favor of a general application of Père de la Taille's thesis to the history of religions it might still be said that it corresponds well enough to the etymology of the word *sacrificium,* that is, *sacrum facere,* "to make sacred." Will not the essence of sacrifice, under whatever forms it may appear, or in whatever way it may be interpreted, actually be in the consecration, in an act, no matter how it is effected or envisaged, that causes an object or being to pass from the realm of the profane to that of the sacred, which will, to repeat, hand over what we possess to God?[6]

Unfortunately, however, this etymological interpretation bears the obvious stamp of an advanced stage of religious development. Originally, *sacrum facere* certainly did not mean "to make sacred"

[4] *Ibid.,* pp. 60 ff. See M. Lepin, *L'idée du sacrifice d'après les théologiens depuis l'origine jusqu'à nos jours* (Paris, 1926).

[5] M. de la Taille, *Mysterium Fid i: De Augustissimo Corporis et Sanguinis Christi Sacrificio et Sacramento* (Paris, 1921). See also his *Mystery of Faith and Human Opinion Contrasted and Defined,* trans. J. B. Schimpf (London, 1930).

[6] This interpretation was taken up again by Jean Bayet in his *Histoire politique et psychologique de la religion romaine* (Paris, 1957), pp. 129-30.

what supposedly was not sacred up to that particular moment, but rather quite simply "to do what is sacred" *in se ac per se*. For the ancient Latins, sacrifice was nothing more than the sacred act. The etymological definition of sacrifice is thus tautological and therefore little suited to throw much light upon our own particular problem.

The reason for this is that the idea of actions which make sacred that which in itself is not sacred could only have arisen in a rather late period, when men in fact had begun to lose their apprehension of what is sacred. For, actually, no matter how one imagines this "making" of the sacred by man, there is nothing that would be less feasible or less likely to be produced by him. Whatever it may or may not be, by definition the "sacred" is that over which man has no control. The sacred is something that surpasses him not only quantitatively but also qualitatively: it is that which belongs essentially to God, which bears His mark, a mark which is both a source of fear and of admiration. The idea that man could himself produce it under one form or another can obviously only come to one who has lost sight of what he is treating.

To put it briefly, we here put our finger on a typical illusion of modern man, so wrapped up in his modernity that he can no longer imagine that things could have been different in the past from what they are today. He therefore assumes that reality was from the first profane and in order to have something sacred it was necessary to take hold of that which was profane and consecrate it. The historical truth, however, is the very opposite to this rather smug opinion. Not only was the sacred never made out of the profane, but, in fact, it is the profane that has come into being through a desecration of the sacred.

In the beginning of man's experiences, the whole of reality is regarded as being sacred.[7] The sacred is precisely man's original apprehension of the world under the aspect of a totality that he seizes at the outset as qualitatively unique. Later, when he arrives at a reflex awareness of himself, of his relative autonomy, he circumscribes a limited area in this reality as his own to the exclu-

---

[7] This does not mean that the origin of religion is to be found in idolatry. From the very beginning a distinction is made between the sacred and what contains it. (Cf. Mircea Eliade, *Patterns in Comparative Religion*, p. 30.) But for the primitive, every object (at least every natural object, where man counts for nothing) can be sacred.

sion of God. At this moment the profane in contrast to the sacred makes its appearance. The more firmly a man establishes himself in the world as in his own home, the more this area of the profane is extended.

Moreover, the farther he extends the boundaries of his own piece of ground, the less interest he takes in the rest. A time finally comes when the profane practically seems to coincide with the real. The sacred has no more than a local survival. The rites then easily appear to man as the making of something sacred. But, actually, as is adequately shown by their common antiquity, they create nothing of the sort, they merely preserve what has been sacred from the beginning.

It is necessary to go still further. Even though it may be true that in the developed rites there are many features that combine to give the impression of a delimitation of a sacred domain, this does not mean that these rites, even at a secondary stage of their development, would have been conceived to produce something sacred. The opposite is true: such rites have been devised to limit the place allotted to the sacred rather than to extend it. The delimitation, or definition, of the sacred with respect to what is profane implied by them does not at all indicate that one intends in this way to include in the sacred something which did not pertain to it, but that one rather intends to exclude the sacred from all the rest.[8]

It is among the primitives on their way to becoming civilized that the rites take on this aspect. But they adopt it quite simply because men become civilized by creating their own proper domain from which God is excluded, who till then pervades everything. When the ancient Romans traced the sacred *pomerium* about their city, it was not so much to enclose within it their tribal gods, who were thought to have been tamed by magical practices, but to keep out foreign gods such as Mars, against whom they felt defenseless.[9]

Here again we see the radical distinction between religion and magic, and the secondary and derivative character of the latter. Magic of its very nature strives to check the divine, to capture and

[8] See the conclusions of Mircea Eliade's *Patterns in Comparative Religion*.

[9] See the observations of Jean Bayet, *op. cit.*, p. 141.

bind it within a ritual system, within a firmly closed sanctuary where it is kept for one's own use. Religion bows down before the presence of the divinity, recognizes it wherever it is manifested, and tends toward it by those means which it believes that God has determined man should use to reach Him. When the so-called consecratory rites are not magical practices used in an attempt to gain control over the divine and reduce it to one's mercy, they are, in fact, a simple acceptance on the part of man of the divine having its own way, a "liturgy," that is, a "service," through which he hands himself over and submits himself to the will on high. In so doing, even if man has some hope of winning over the divine, he acknowledges at the same time its autonomy and final sovereignty.[10] At best, whenever in the beginnings of civilization man is tempted to magic, the rites are more apotropaic than consecratory, if by this is meant something that produces the sacred. They are destined rather to limit strictly the domain of the sacred than to create a domain for it, as if originally there had been none.

If this is the case, if a sacrifice does not in a strict sense create something sacred, if it cannot be made to consist in an offering to God of something which up till then has not been His, if it cannot any more be reduced to an immolation in the sense of a slaying or destruction, in what then does it consist?

The answer that today forces itself upon all the students of the phenomenology of religion is so simple, so obvious, that it is amazing that it has been so lately discovered, and especially that Catholic theologians have had, and still do have, so much trouble in arriving at it, though it should be more patent to them than to any others. What we call by the Latin word "sacrifice" is nothing else than a sacred meal. More specifically, it is every meal that has retained its primitive sacredness, a sacredness that is attached to a meal perhaps more than to any other human action.[11]

Catholic theologians in modern times have taken great pains, but quite uselessly, to prove to Protestants that the Eucharist can

---

[10] See G. van der Leeuw, *Religion in Essence and Manifestation*, pp. 408 ff.

[11] *Ibid.*, pp. 350 ff. Cf. R. K. Yerkes, *Sacrifice in Greek and Roman Religions and Early Judaism* (New York, 1952). The merit of this work lies in its precise and complete description of the rites, as opposed to useless speculations.

also be a sacrifice, *even though* it is obviously a meal. Because of this, liturgists of the Baroque Age were compelled to dissimulate, to diminish as far as possible this aspect of a meal in order to ratify their own concept of a sacrifice, which was that of their adversaries as well — the altar becoming a tomb, communion being set aside, and so forth. This shows on the part of both Protestants and Catholics a strange misunderstanding of ancient Christian tradition and the common customs of mankind. The very opposite is true. In antiquity the Eucharist was seen as the sacrifice of the Christians *because* it was the sacred meal of the Christian community. The texts of the Fathers are so clear and consistent on this point that it can only be denied by a kind of wilful blindness.[12]

When the true nature of sacrifice is once recognized, the so-called oblation regains its original meaning. It is the preparation for the meal through the delivery on the part of the faithful, and the choice on the part of the ministers, of the appropriate provisions for it. As for the immolation, if by that is understood a putting to death, it goes without saying that this is simply the slaughter of the animal victims necessary for a meal at which meat is served. And if, as some have been careful to point out, an immolation understood in this sense is not always present in a sacrifice, there is no need to have recourse to subtleties for an explanation: there simply is no need to slaughter anything in order to eat fruit and vegetables or to drink a cup of wine. As for Condren's theory that the ideal sacrifice would be one of complete destruction and annihilation, which was taken from the concept of a holocaust, that of a victim consumed by fire, it must be admitted that it starts from a complete misconception. The exposing of victims to fire for some purpose other than cooking them for a meal seems to have been originally done (as the Bible explicitly states) for the purpose of separating from the victims the delightful aroma which pleases and satisfies the gods, who are presumably more subtle than humans.[13] Moreover, as has been frequently observed, fire is a particularly impressive theophany. But whether one concentrates on the fire or simply on the smoke produced by it, the idea of destruction is not prominent here, and even, it may be said, has no place whatever.

[12] See my study on the "logical sacrifice" of St. Justin, in *Spiritualité du Nouveau Testament et des Pères*, p. 272.

[13] Cf. *Genesis*, 8:21. Cf. Yerkes, *op. cit.*, p. 129.

These elementary observations may seem to be prosaic. As a matter of fact, they do not altogether invalidate the speculations of contemporary theologians on the oblation and immolation and their relative place and importance in sacrifice. However, they should at least alert them to something about which they are at times too little concerned: sacrifice is not originally a subtle notion; it is a fact, a fact whose material reality should be taken into account before hasty attempts are made to give it spiritual explanations that run the risk of soon exhausting themselves in useless argumentation when they lack this concrete point of departure.

We should hasten to add that the determination of a sacrifice according to its true essence, that is, a sacred meal and nothing more, is only an apparent reduction to a more prosaic reality. Such an impression only betrays the incurable idealism of our own sophistication. A sacred meal, by itself and without the need of anything else, actually constitutes the richest hierophany there is. It is in the sacred meal that man sees the sacredness of life, of his own life, and as a result apprehends himself as being dependent upon one who is almighty and all good, or, to express it more accurately, upon the singular and superabundant fruitfulness of the divinity. To recognize the sacredness of a meal as being the highest form of human activity is to recognize man's total dependence, both for his creation and his continued existence, upon a God who is at the same time apprehended as the one who possesses the fullness of life.

This is the reason for the many meanings of sacrifice which follow the multiplicity of forms under which it is found. It is from these different forms that we must start if we are to appreciate the various meanings of sacrifice. We can do this no better than by studying the different types of sacrifice known to the Israelites as described for us in the Bible. The history of comparative religion has proved that the Israelites did not invent any essential form of sacrifice and that there was none which they refused to take from the peoples who surrounded them. All this rich and varied material was bound to lend itself, not to a kind of artificial spiritualization imposed from without, but to a higher awareness of what sacrificial practices could mean in a profound and pure religion.

When we say that a sacrifice is a sacred meal, we must understand this in the sense of its being a meal which is fundamentally a meal of the gods but with which man is associated, whether it be because he has paid for, or prepared it, or even, as frequently happens, because he takes part in it in some way or other. There can even be cases among primitives where man himself eats all the food that makes up the substance of the sacrifice. But the meal is not the less sacred for this since the food taken is recognized for what it is, that is, something belonging to God and connected with God's own life communicated to man. This was certainly the case with with the sacrifice of the Pasch,[14] which according to some was the only sacrifice the Israelites had before they settled in Canaan, and it is also the case with the Eucharistic sacrifice of the Christians.

Nevertheless, alongside the Pasch, the Jews recognized sacrifices in which a part of the victim, after its slaying, was burned on the altar, while another part was eaten by the faithful. This is true of the *zebhach* (sacrifices of peace, of praise, and so forth). In the sacrifices "for sin," the *chatta'th* or *'asham*, the priests, but not the faithful, ate a part of the sacrificed animal, the remainder of it being consumed by fire.[15] Finally there was the *'olah,* or holocaust, as it is translated in the Septuagint, where the entire victim was burned on the altar and neither priests nor faithful partook of any of it.[16]

But in addition to these bloody sacrifices there were the *minchah,* a sacrifice of grain, which also could be either burned entirely on the altar or eaten in part by the faithful, and the *nesek,* a libation of wine upon the altar, always accompanying another rite, and never appearing by itself, which emphasizes the fact that a sacrifice is a complete meal, but nothing more than a meal.[17]

Other bloody rites were assimilated to the sacrifices, although they originally seem to have been merely apotropaic in intent. This was the case with the red heifer and the scapegoat, where the slaughtered animals were not burned upon the altar, but the former simply "in view of the priest," and the latter "outside the camp."[18]

Throughout all these rites we perceive, or suspect, an extensive development of secondary themes. We have already indicated the

---

[14] See G. van der Leeuw, *op. cit.,* and also Robertson Smith, *Religion of the Semites,* 3rd ed. (London, 1927), who was the first to clarify the fundamental identity between the primitive sacred repast and sacrifice.

[15] Cf. Yerkes, *op. cit.,* pp. 171 ff.

[16] See Yerkes, *op. cit.,* pp. 115 ff.

[17] *Ibid.,* pp. 161 ff.

[18] *Numbers* 19:1-10, and *Leviticus* 26.

importance of fire as a hierophany, and, we might say, for Israel in particular, as a theophany.[19] We should also note again the importance of blood as another hierophany. It is identified with the principle of life and therefore with that which is quasi-divine in man, and which in sacrifice somehow returns to its source.[20]

More complex, and much more difficult to determine is the connection of sacrifice, or at least of some sacrifices, with what is pure and impure, and as a consequence, especially in Israel, with sin. However, since there is a danger of distorting the issue, care should be taken not to exaggerate this connection. The Middle Ages again are primarily responsible for this abuse, though it was only the theology of the Reformation and of the Counter-Reformation that brought it to full flowering.[21] This consisted in identifying sacrifice with a propitiation for sin. But as a matter of fact, neither Scripture nor the manifold varieties of natural religion make any essential connection between sin and sacrifice. As we have just seen, the ancient Jews knew only two categories of sacrifices related to sin, the *chatta'th* and the *'asham*. To these could be added the liturgy of the *yom kippurim*.[22] But it would be completely wrong to believe that these represent the highest forms of sacrifice. The very opposite is true. As is indicated by the fact that the priests alone, and not the faithful, took part in these sacrifices, we have here purificatory rites that had only become a necessary condition for the celebration of the ordinary sacrifices as the result

[19] See C. M. Edsman, *Ignis divinus* (Lund, Sweden, 1949).

[20] See Yerkes, *op. cit.*, pp. 42 ff.

[21] The struggle against Pelagianism in the time of St. Augustine already tended to reduce all religion to the alternatives of sin and grace. During the late Middle Ages, which enjoyed an Augustinian renaissance, this tendency became more pronounced. But the Augustinianism of this period was in many respects simply a reduction of the teachings of the great Doctor of the Church to their most negative aspects. Luther made a theological principle out of this opposition. But, as Aulen has shown, the opposition which Luther placed between sin and grace had a much deeper meaning than it did in Pietism. It is in this last context that the Anselmian theory of satisfaction was taken as the only real interpretation of sacrifice. See G. Aulen, *Christus victor; An Historical Study of the Three Main Types of the Idea of the Atonement*, trans. A. G. Hebert (New York, 1931).

[22] See Yerkes, *op. cit.*, pp. 125 ff.

of some accident making it temporarily impossible for those for whom they were offered to offer them themselves. The Epistle to the Hebrews, correctly understood, although it only refers to the ritual of the great annual expiation, shows clearly that the essence of a sacrificial act is not this expiation for, or purification from, sins. This factor is only the necessary prelude to going into the sanctuary, which the priest enters not as the substitute for, but as the leader of, all the people.[23]

Again, it is worth pointing out how the sacrifices for sins in Israel and, more in general, the rites of expiation through blood poured upon the altar and even upon the assistants themselves were originally understood. It is quite obvious that we are here touching upon aspects of the sacred which are not peculiar to the tradition of Israel. Rather, we find there the most primitive reactions of a religious consciousness, but expressed in Israel with a remarkable clarity.

In other words, these rites are intimately connected with the notion of what is pure and what is impure. And this explains those prohibitions, so strange to us, which ceaselessly threatened the pious Israelite.[24] It goes without saying that this opposition between what is pure and what is impure does not correspond to our modern concept of morality. But it is necessary to stress the fact that this opposition cannot with any greater accuracy be reduced to a purely physical, or even quasi-physical, reality as some historians of religion, misled by the material aspects of the rites, have maintained. To the religion of the primitives the "purely physical" is something just as foreign as the "purely spiritual." The basic idea behind a sin of ritualistic nature, which the rites themselves must remove, is that of the sacred character of certain great realities, and those especially which impinge upon human life.[25]

Above all, when blood has been shed, whether it is a question of homicide or sexual activity, even that which is the most positive such as in childbirth, one becomes impure. And when one is impure, one cannot offer sacrifice.[26] Why is this? Can it be that sex,

[23] See my *Spiritualité du Nouveau Testament et des Pères*, p. 185.
[24] See Yerkes, *op. cit.*, pp. 33 ff.
[25] See G. van der Leeuw, *Religion in Essence and Manifestation*, pp. 343 ff. and M. Eliade, *Patterns in Comparative Religion*, pp. 14 ff.
[26] See Yerkes, *op. cit.*, pp. 154 ff.

or more fundamentally, that life itself should seem to be essentially impure? Nothing is further from the truth. This cannot be better illustrated than by recalling the fact that contact with the scrolls of the Torah, the sacred object *par excellence* of Jewish worship, made one equally impure.[27] In other words, what caused the impurity was not contact with something that was impure but rather with something so holy that the man who had the temerity to approach it was presumed to be guilty of sin. Similarly, in the Old Testament, the sight of the Lord was regarded as being fatal to the viewer, though He is, or rather *because* He is, life *par excellence*.[28]

The sacral, ritual root of the idea of sin is the feeling which man has of God's radical transcendence whenever he is moved to have recourse to Him. It is practically the counterpart of that holy familiarity to which man is called in sacrifice, and it is that which keeps this familiarity from becoming sacrilegious. The expiatory ritual ceaselessly reminds man that he is of himself basically unworthy of that contact with the divine which is effected in sacrifice. But, as in the vision of Isaias, God Himself purifies man so that he can endure the heavenly vision and still live.[29] This purification is accomplished through the instrumentality of blood, since it is by means of blood, as in the maternal waters of creation, that God transmits life. Blood returned to God at this time, by being poured upon the altar or upon the mysterious "propitiatory," and by being sprinkled upon man, restores the latter to his original nature as a creature of God, ready to meet Him since he has been begotten by Him.

But behind all this, a sacrifice remains essentially a meeting with God in a sacred meal. To repeat, it is originally a meal in which man recognizes that in every meal he meets God. He meets Him there because it is God who provides him with food, who is present there with him, and who is at once his fellow sharer in the meal and his provisioner.[30] Emphasis on the fact that in a sacrifice man in his turn nourishes God seems to be a later development.

---

[27] The rabbis, in their discussion of whether or not such a relatively late book as the *Canticle of Canticles* is inspired, declared that it "soils the hands," thus indicating that it was.

[28] Cf. the vision of Manoah in *Judges* 13, or *Exodus* 33:20.

[29] *Isaias* 6:6.

[30] G. van der Leeuw, *op. cit.*, pp. 350 ff.

This element is apparently predominant, if not exclusively so, in the holocaust. But this predominance may be taken in two senses. The holocaust can express a man's conviction that he holds God at his mercy in some magical way since he feeds Him, or it can express a lofty religious concept in which man recognizes that all he has, or can enjoy, belongs ultimately to God alone.

If we go back beyond these evolved and contrasted concepts of sacrifice, we shall undoubtedly find that at the beginning there was the idea of an exchange between God and man, of an alliance that naturally took the form of a business transaction: *do ut des*.[31] But as G. van der Leeuw has rightly observed, we should not be misled by interpreting such expressions according to our own way of thinking, which is not at all that of primitive man. When we think of business transactions, we understand by them material operations with no spiritual overtones. But nothing is further from the primitive mentality than such a line of thought. For the primitive, business implies some form of fellowship. Possessions are exchanged only by those who trust each other. When an agreement is reached, an alliance is at the same time made which includes all those sacral and spiritual factors which can be presumed to be connected with friendship. To interpret the archaic sacrificial formulas of the type *do ut des* as if they were purely profitable, selfish transactions is to miss the point completely. What is actually meant is that by means of a gift and an exchange, one takes one's place in the beneficent but also sacred circle of creation. Where God himself lives and communicates His life in such a way, we live divinely by sharing in His own dynamism.

So essential is this to the living concept of sacrifice as a meal of communion and alliance that certain historians of religion have even come to the paradoxical conclusion that it is not because one believes in the gods that one offers sacrifices to them but it is because one offers sacrifice that one believes in the gods. According to this opinion, the dynamism of the exchange in which one is placed by sacrifice would be prior to belief in the gods. A good many archaic texts, especially some of the Vedas, seem to favor this interpretation, improbable as it is in itself.[32] When such im-

---

[31] *Ibid;* see also van der Leeuw's study "Die *do-ut-des* Formel in der Opfertheorie," *Archiv für Religionswissenschaft,* XX (1920-21), pp. 241 ff.

[32] See H. von Glasenapp, *Die Religionen Indiens* (Stuttgart, 1943).

plications are drawn from them, it means that they have been taken too literally. Nevertheless, they contain an element of truth: man does not recognize God in the abstract before entering into a living relationship with Him through an exchange of goods that are both material and spiritual. Rather, it is through this exchange that man comes to realize the sacredness and profundity of his own existence.

Thus it is in a study of sacrifice that we can discover the whole range of profoundly different interpretations that men have given to a ritual that has changed surprisingly little in its substance or in its imaginative representations.[33] We have already considered certain aspects of the development of this ritual, and we have paid particular attention to the impasse into which it sinks when some of man's natural tendencies are given free rein. But now a consideration of sacrifice, and especially of what sacrifice has become in the Old and New Testaments, should enable us to see more positive developments.

The primitive view of sacrifice, and this is something more permanent than a temporary phase preceding the later developments, is the meeting *par excellence* of God and man. It is an act that is inseparably social and individual. Each man feels that he is personally engaged in what is basically a common celebration. It is at the same time a full realization of God's interest in mankind. All this comes from the fact that a common meal makes men appreciate their relation with the cosmos which provides the natural resources for their life. Eating in common is the human act *par excellence,* where society is built up as from within, while each man perfects himself by integrating himself with the universe. It is moreover the first and supreme act in which man apprehends himself in his living relationship with God. Man undoubtedly comes to the meal to secure this relationship, and, in a way, to secure everything, since he there receives nourishment for his life. But he also goes there to give, to give himself. In other words, he realizes, not in thought, but in a decisive act, that his life is not his own, that it depends upon God alone. And thus, at last, in sacrifice the life of man comes, or comes again, to participate in the life of God.

[33] See Yerkes, *op. cit.,* pp. 161 ff. and 190 ff.

Later, when man becomes civilized, he discovers his control over nature and, at the same time, his relative ability to regulate his own life. He tends to assert his own personality. His own self-consciousness is gradually separated from, and opposed to, his earlier, basically religious consciousness of reality. When this happens, the gods do not disappear but appear to him as sources of power which he strives to capture and control, if he can, for his own advantage or that of the group. It is then that man, by means of ritual, seeks to make himself the master of the gods, to tame them just as he tames nature for his own ends at this stage of his development.

This is what the prophets of Israel saw in the cults of Canaan.[34] This is what they condemned in the cults of the alliance of the *Baalim*. These were the gods whom the Canaanites hailed as the lords of the earth but whom they at the same time tacitly enslaved with their cults. It is in this context, as we shall see later, that the notion of a temple, a fixed sanctuary which men claim to be the home of the deity but which is really his prison, acquires all its importance. By regaling the god with sacrificial offerings which preserve his vitality, men exploit him for their own needs. This is why Nathan rose up and opposed David's plan to build a temple to the sovereign and free Lord who had manifested Himself to Israel: "God does not dwell in a house made by the hand of man."[35] In other words, man cannot boast that he put God at his mercy. Later, when the temple actually had been built, Jeremias announced its destruction and the collapse of the false hopes of an indestructible alliance which Israel had placed in it.[36]

Nevertheless, it is still true that the Canaanite rituals in their material aspects were almost entirely taken over by Israel. But the prophets, following the plan that was certainly begun by Moses, were able to give a radically new meaning to them.[37] In the alliance with Israel that was consummated through this ritual, the prophets tell the people that they cannot deceive themselves by claiming that they have entered into a bilateral contract according to which

[34] See Adolphe Lods, *Israel from its Beginning to the Middle of the Eighth Century*, trans. S. H. Hooke (London, 1932).

[35] *II Samuel* 7.

[36] *Jeremias* 7.

[37] See my study, *The Meaning of Sacred Scriptures*, trans. by M. P. Ryan (Notre Dame, 1958),* pp. 32 ff.

God would be chained to them through sacrifices in such a way that they could shamelessly exploit Him. Even in the alliance He remains the true and sole master. The sacrifices offered according to the Mosaic law have value only because they have been sovereignly prescribed by God. Their efficacy is that of an act of faith and obedience to the God who spoke on Sinai. To the extent that Israel, thus submissive and believing, ceaselessly affirms and reaffirms its will to be faithful to the Torah, God will also be faithful to His promise to make His Name, that is, the virtue of His presence, dwell in Israel.[38] But this presence remains mysterious, unattainable, even in its manifestation. It is the presence in the luminous cloud, the impenetrable cloud of the heavenly storm on Sinai, the inaccessible light where man cannot seek to dwell without condemning himself to death.[39]

If man should grow so bold, as will be the case, to imagine that he has thus laid hold of God, that he can make use of Him at his own good pleasure, the blessing of the alliance will be turned into a curse. The prophets will announce the destruction of the sanctuary which the impious piety of the people has already profaned. Ezechiel will see the invisible presence depart and leave Israel to a cult that has been deprived of its object, before this presence turns against the people to destroy the holy city with its sanctuary. Thus the way will be prepared for Christianity.[40]

In Christianity, not only will the sacrifice offered by man appear as an act of faith and obedience to the free and sovereign Word of the God of the alliance, but it is this God who becomes in the most explicit fashion the offerer, the priest, and the victim.

Some passages in the Old Testament already hint at such a transformation. This is the case in the account of the sacrifice which Abraham offered of his son Isaac.[41] God intervenes, providing Himself with a victim to replace the lad. The Christian Paschal liturgy stresses this account as a forecast of that which was finally fulfilled: God refused the sacrifice of the first-born and only son which man had been willing to accord Him. For in reality it was God Himself who was to offer on the Cross His only Son as the

---

[38] As a comparison, see the discourse and prayer of Solomon at the dedication of the Temple, *I Kings* 8:14 ff.

[39] Wm. J. Phythian-Adams, *The Presence and the People* (Oxford, 1942).

[40] *Ezechiel* 9:14.

first-born of many brethren whom He would associate with Himself in the Eucharistic celebration.[42]

All of this will receive its full meaning when we consider it again in the light of the wholly new concept of the divine Word which will begin to vivify the Jewish ritual before it becomes, in its final development, the soul of the Christian ritual.

Before returning thus to a study of the word and its role in the celebration, we must, following the lead of Gerard van der Leeuw, mention a fifth stage of development, or in this case, of decline, in sacrificial rites.[43] After our consideration of natural religion, magic, Judaism, and Christianity, it should be profitable to consider the religious romanticism that is characteristic of a decaying Christianity. We find at the end of the evolution that which a number of historians of religion have sought to find at its beginning: a religion and a sacrifice without God. Every period of decline in worship caused by the rationalization of religion, described in the preceding chapter, has been marked by this meaningless reaction. But never has this reaction been so clear and manifest as in modern times.

When man loses the faith that animated his rituals and especially his sacrifices, he comes to regret this loss. If he does not miss the substance of the religion, he at least misses the emotion and the feeling of exaltation that were associated with it. He then seeks, either by reviving the past or by instituting new techniques with a psychological basis inspired by the ancient rites, to recover something of that psychological atmosphere which surrounded them, without however giving credence to the original beliefs that had been connected with them.

There are individuals who experience a keen aesthetic pleasure in dead religions, and in their imagination, at least, they strive to revive their lost pomp. We thus understand the enthusiasm which some atheists have for the liturgy and plain chant, the ambiguous ecstasies of Des Esseintes, the more substantial dreams that Walter

[41] *Genesis* 22.

[42] See the prayer which follows the third lesson of the Paschal vigil in the old liturgy. Cf. the beautiful and exact study of G. de Broglie, S.J., "La Messe, oblation collective de la communauté chrétienne," *Gregorianum*, XXX (1949), 534 ff.

[43] G. van der Leeuw, *op. cit.,* pp. 350 ff.

Pater could project upon his Marius the Epicurean, without however committing himself to them.

Or there may even be the attempt, such as we find in the strange positivistic religion of Auguste Comte,[44] or in the pageantry of Nazism or Communism, to restore to the masses who seem to have lost their religious convictions the emotional drive that accompanied them. Examples of such an attempt may be found in the displays staged by Hitler in the Sportspalast, in the tomb of Lenin, and in the astonishing Russian military cemetery at Treptov in the suburbs of Berlin, with its funerary chapel, its perpetual lamp, its book of the dead, its altar, and its colossal statues in an attitude of prayer. But all these efforts of an ersatz religion that has no basis in faith, whether they be crude or refined, whether perverse or pathetic, are only a dim confession of defeat. The hidden recesses of the soul of modern man are there laid bare to the penetrating gaze of psychoanalysis without his even knowing it.

---

[44] See Charles de Rouvre, *Auguste Comte et le Catholicisme* (Paris, 1928), pp. 101 ff.

CHAPTER VII

The Different Religious Uses
of the Word:
From Myth to Creative Word

THE VARIATIONS which we have traced in the meaning of the same sacrificial rites bring us to a consideration of the usage or, rather, the different usages, of words in worship. Actually, it is by means of words that a man determines the meaning he puts into his rites as this meaning develops and becomes progressively clear.

It is fairly obvious that words are used in religion in a great many strikingly different ways.[1] At the outset it is difficult to determine which of these is the most fundamental. Nevertheless, modern research in the history of comparative religion has established the central, if not fundamental, character of one of them, which may be compared to a nucleus about which the clouded meanings of primitive religions have gradually condensed. Starting from this as from a source of numerous reflections and radiations, all the other forms of sacred speech attain their meaning. This nucleus is myth.[2]

This term adequately designates the reality which has slowly forced itself upon historians of religion. The meaning which they have attached to the word is actually that of the Greek *mythos* as this was originally understood. But it is necessary to insist at once

[1] See Gerard van der Leeuw, *Religion in Essence and Manifestation*, pp. 403 ff.

[2] *Ibid.*, pp. 413 ff.; see also E. O. James, *Myth and Ritual in the Ancient Near East* and Mircea Eliade, *Mythes, rêves et mystères* and *Patterns in Comparative Religion*, pp. 410 ff.

upon the fact that this meaning is not at all that which the word generally has today. When we speak of myths, our first thought is of Homeric mythology, which is made up of highly evolved though somewhat degraded forms of myths, so much so that they were destined soon to become nothing more than a literary fiction. In other words, a myth, as we conceive it, is synonymous with a fable. In this banal usage of the word, myth has come to be the unsubstantial counterpart of positive reality. It is a game, a fiction of the imagination, which we oppose to the high seriousness of scientific truth. But in the beginning a myth was nothing of the sort, nor do the modern historians of religion have this later meaning in mind when they use the term.

As understood by them, a myth is not a seductive, though false, fancy of the mind opposed to the bare but substantial truth. It is the primitive, spontaneous expression of reality as man intuitively perceives it, and is only opposed to that view of reality which he attains at the end of a logically deductive train of thought. It is above all the total expression of this reality as opposed to its fragmentary expression. As such, it is the basically religious expression of reality in contrast to every profane expression of it. It is a projection of man's first experience in its original unity which, as we have noted, was spontaneously, essentially religious.

Though modern historians of religion soon sensed the importance of such an understanding of the myth, they were not able to see at once all of its many implications. Two general lines of interpretation were laid out in turn. The first was defined by Andrew Lang in his work, *Myth, Ritual and Religion,* which appeared in 1899. According to him, a myth is man's first expression of the phenomena which he experiences, an imaginative explanation that precedes a rational one. A myth is thus "etiological": it points out the cause, or causes, of the world as understood by primitive man. This view is quite close to that of Lévy-Bruhl who regards the primitive mentality as being prelogical.

Lang's theory was demolished by Hocart in a study which he contributed to *The Labyrinth,* a collection of essays edited by Hooke in 1935. According to Hocart the motivation behind the myth is not at all etiological. The myth is anything but a first attempt at an explanation of the universe, or kind of infantile cosmology. It has always been linked with ritual and should not be conceived as an attempt to explain human events, and more in general, the origin of the universe. It is merely a description of ritual, but a poetic and imaginative one. Stated more precisely, a myth is the spontaneous expression of what ritual means to primitive man.

More recently, E. O. James has taken up the whole question again in his *Myth and Religion in the Ancient Near East* and has shown that both of these interpretations are unsatisfactory, though Hocart came nearer to the heart of the problem than Lang.[3] Hocart oversimplifies and, as a consequence, confounds the issue by rejecting all etiology in the myth. But he is right in affirming the natural and enduring connection between myth and ritual. A myth is always derived from a ritual. But for the primitive, ritual is absolutely central to man's life and that of the world. It is a kind of résumé or focal point for all human life and for life in general. A myth, therefore, in expressing the meaning of a ritual for one who performs it, actually explains the whole world to him. But this explanation has not only been built about the rite, it remains centered upon it.

Lang's explanation of the myth was inadequate in that he had not as yet been able to distinguish the myth as such. He still confused it with those secondary degradations commonly attached to the meaning of the term according to which a myth is a simple stammering explanation of reality. Three stages may be noted in this decline from the original meaning of myth.[4] The first of these is the myth of epic poetry such as is found in the *Iliad*. Here we begin to find "mythology" in the pejorative sense of the word. The gods of Olympus have simply become a half-imaginative, half-rational explanation of the forces of nature. But correlatively, it is quite obvious that the gods and their worship are no longer taken in all seriousness. They tend simply to provide material for tales that man arranges as he pleases and which, as a consequence, no longer deceive him.

A further step in the evolution of the myth is the saga, the heroic tale of a fabulous past. The mythological gods are still present, but they visibly recoil before the apparition of the heroes, who are more or less openly demi-gods, that is, men who claim to be endowed with quasi-divine virtues. Moving from the *Iliad* to the

[3] London, 1959.
[4] See Gerard van der Leeuw, *op. cit.*, 414 ff.

Odyssey, we can see the change in progress. In the latter, the theme is no longer the rivalry of the gods actively engaged in the conflicts of men, but the deeds of Ulysses, where the divine activity is pushed into the background and becomes hardly more than an embellishment.

A third stage is reached with fables, the fairy-tales of folklore. Here, though there is no complete rejection of a belief in hitherto sacred persons, their only real interest is the pleasure they afford in the telling of a story. Since the greatest liberties are taken with the narrative, the characters are no longer really respected. They are no more than puppets in a kind of daydream, elaborated at will, but with a more than half-awareness of the fact that it is only a pleasant dream.

Nothing is more alien to all this than a myth that has retained its original vitality. It has already been cast, it is true, into the form of a story; but it is a symbolic story, a story of the gods which does not happen in time, at least in our time, but in a transcendent time, which is only a human image of eternity.[5] It is, in fact, eternity as man can apprehend it, that is, as the living source of his own history and that of the whole universe insofar as man's time meets this eternity, or, rather, insofar as eternity meets him in his ritual. The full meaning of life and of its stage, the world, is illuminated by this special fact. The sacred action develops its meaning there as being the focus of every action, where the world is invaded by that which is beyond all reality, judged by human standards.

We see, for example, the mysteries of Eleusis, springing from a worship of nature and finding their place in the alternating rhythm of spring's rebirth and winter's death. The kernel of these mysteries is a symbolic rite: the ear of wheat plucked in silence. In this rite, man meets the forces of nature as the source of life and death. He deliberately associates himself with them in the inaugural act of the harvest. At the other end of its evolution, the mystery will find expression in the liturgical drama of Kore-Persephone, her abduction by Hades, her desperate pursuit by Demeter, and her final but transitory return to the light of day. All this elaborate drama was germinally within the elementary ritual act. But the myth is the intermediary between the two, not so much the explanation as the

---

[5] Mircea Eliade, *op. cit.,* pp. 394 ff.

poetic expression of the ritual act. And the drama in its turn is only the materialization of the myth in a new rite.

To repeat what has already been said, it seems that the myth develops at the very moment when magic tends to pervade religion. But it appears as an instinctive religious reaction to magic.

Primitive man comes to a rite as to a reality which completely surpasses him. He surrenders to it, abandoning himself to it with mingled emotions of fear of, and attraction for, what is sacred. But with the progress of civilization man becomes more self-conscious. He tends to use even the ritual as a means of imposing his own will upon the gods.

Once again it may be asked if this stage is not reached when a ritual in which man and his own actions have become central is superimposed upon a primitive ritualistic action which obviously surpassed man though he took part in it, as was the case in directly agrarian rites. To the rite of the ear of wheat plucked in silence at Eleusis was added the hierogamy, the renewed union of the priest and priestess. In the sexual act of which he is the author, but in which the natural powers of fertility are also engaged, man believes that he holds the key, as it were, to a beneficial release of these same powers.

At this very moment, the mythical projection of the union of Kore and Hades under Demeter's motherly auspices, herself subject to the higher Fates, will re-establish a divine meaning to the rites and the sovereignty of the gods over the ritual. What is done by man, even when his actions seem to be essential, will be regarded as being nothing but a sacred representation of a divine story. The union of the hierophant and his wife is in reality, according to the myth, merely the epiphany of the union of Kore and Hades. And all this remains subject to the deity of the Earth Mother, who is herself under the sovereignty of the celestial powers while being blessed by them.

We thus find in the myths the ordered layers of the primitive hierophanies: the heavenly gods, the mother goddess, the divine pair to which the human pair is assimilated while remaining subject to them. For the heavenly gods, transcendent indeed, but whose transcendence had gradually alienated them from men, was first substituted the closer image of the sovereign Earth Mother, then still without a partner. Later a divine pair was introduced in the mystery of life further humanized. In return, the myth restored in reverse order the higher reality of the divine couple behind the priestly pair, the Earth Mother behind the divine couple, dangerously humanized, and finally the supremacy of Zeus and the heavenly Fates.

The myth therefore reaffirmed the divinity, the transcendence of the ritual action at the moment when this seemed on the point of becoming completely humanized and coming under the complete control of man.

The liturgical drama does nothing more than make the divine story, which is to remain the soul of the rite, evolved as it may be, concrete and perfectly explicit.

If this sheds light on the central place of the myth in the evolution of religion, it shows also that the myth cannot be considered as the primary form of the sacred word. Prayer rather than myth must have been this primary form.

Taken indeed in its basic form as a supplication for the help of Another, who is completely Other and All Holy, prayer seems to be the most elementary form of the sacred word. In its developed forms, prayer will express what man has in mind when he draws near to God in his rites. But prayer soon fluctuates between a personal appeal to another and a conjuration, that is, words used as a charm in a magical formula to constrain the other. Nonetheless, we must must not be too hasty in drawing conclusions from the imprecatory form of certain prayers to a necessarily magical content. When a man wishes to change the divine will for his own advantage, even though he ardently longs for this, as long as he entreats this will in fear and fascination of what is sacred, he at least implicitly recognizes the divine sovereignty, even if his attitude is much like that of a spoiled child with its importunate pleadings. And to this extent, crude as his religion may be, it is still authentically religious.[7]

Prayer is perfected to the extent that it ceases to seek to impose man's will upon the will of God and tends to be conformed to the latter and to adhere to it, whether this will is known or not. Prayer

---

[6] Debatable as is Friedrich Heiler's theory on the essential opposition between what he calls prophetic and mystical prayer, because of its wealth of material, his *Prayer* remains irreplaceable. F. Heiler, *Das Gebet, Eine Religionsgeschichtliche und Religiospsychologische Untersuchung*, Munich, 1923. See also G. van der Leeuw, *op. cit.*, pp. 422 ff.

[7] *Ibid.*

which seeks to know this will, to surrender itself to it, has been defined by Heiler as the typically prophetic prayer.[8] Mystical prayer,
on the contrary, would be that which tends to lose itself in God,
foregoing any demands, renouncing all activity, and seeking simply
to merge itself in Him. But such a losing of self would in fact be
merely the counterpart of a veritable divinization of man by fusion
with the divine. Heiler here has failed to take into account another
side of reality, which was to be brought forward by the Anglican
Bishop Kirk. The same ambiguity may be found as well in what
Heiler has called prophetic prayer. An ardent petition, "Thy will
be done!" can, as a matter of fact, involve a questionable collabo-
ration with this will: God may be sought and entreated merely as
a potential means of salvation, for nothing more than man's own
good.[9]

Actually the opposition between prophetic prayer, dominated
by a vision of a personal and free God, and mystical prayer,
dominated by that of a "Supreme Good" in which one desires to
be immersed and swallowed up, is quite artificial. A truly mystical
prayer is one in which the vision, even though obscure, of the
transcendent personality of God and of its intrinsic value, sweeps
away the vision of all the individual goods that man could ask of
God. In this way, growth in mystical prayer, in a search for union
and conformity with God, is mixed in with growth in prophetic
prayer, in a love of the personal God which becomes the intrinsic
end of prayer.[10] Conversely, it must be repeated, the so-called prophetic prayer is liable to decline into a religious utilitarianism
which desacralizes religion no less than an ambiguous mysticism,
where man's search for divinization is nothing more than the
apotheosis of his will for power.

One could be tempted to believe that the prayer of praise
escapes these perpetual ambivalences of the other forms of prayer
and of religion in general. Is not the disinterestedness of this
prayer, which asks nothing of God, neither His gifts nor even Himself, but which adopts an attitude of joyful adoration of His great-

[8] See Heiler, *op. cit.,* pp. 227 ff.

[9] See K. E. Kirk, *The Vision of God,* 2nd ed. (London, 1932), pp.
428 ff. and 466 ff.

[10] *Ibid.;* see also my *Spiritualité du Nouveau Testament et des Pères,*
p. 485.

ness, the purest form of homage that His holiness can receive? Indeed, this can be the case, but it can also be the contrary. There can be no doubt that a religion that is tending toward magic can be accompanied by an increase of praise.[11] A number of cult hymns composed in such an atmosphere seem at first sight to be pure litanies of titles, attributes, transcendent qualities of the divinity. But their purity is no less strongly suspect, for it may be that such an accumulation of divine names and epithets only covers a conviction of being able to excite the divine power that is being invoked in order to profit by it.

We here touch upon the special ambivalence of "consecratory" prayers, that is, those prayers which are most closely united with the rites in that they express and determine their contents.[12] It is chiefly here that real magical conjurations may be found: the evocation, or "calling up," of the divine power which one desires to elicit through the efficacy of the words and to infuse into the sacred action. But the same formulas which can be the vehicles of such an intent, can also become the expression of an earnest supplication whose exasperated fervor implies the profound conviction that all depends absolutely on the sovereign will of God alone, who is invoked with so much ardor precisely on that account.[13]

More generally, those prayers which accompany the rites and which are thought to assure their effective content by defining the meaning which is put on them take on the shape of a particularly actualized form of praise. These prayers are in effect the setting forth and glorification of the divine fact recognized in the experience of the ritual as that which constitutes its religious substance.[14] It is probable that every form of praise of a less ritualistic character is only an extension of this initial proclamation which not only accompanies the rite but is really one with it. Such an evolution may be traced in the Hebrew sacrifice of praise. Originally it was a sacrifice that was accompanied by a psalm glorifying the divine epiphany proclaimed in the rite itself; but, at a second stage, it became a sacrifice whose doxological character was specified by the psalm, which was now referred to a previous providential

[11] See G. van der Leeuw, *op. cit.*, pp. 430 ff.
[12] *Ibid.*, pp. 422 ff.
[13] *Ibid.*, pp. 408 ff.
[14] *Ibid.*, pp. 430 ff.

manifestation, itself non-ritual in character. At a still later stage, the sacrifice of praise became the praise itself, now completely separated from any ritual activity and regarded as a higher substitute for it.[15]

In the course of such an evolution as this, we detect what could be called a progressive spiritualization of the rites through the development of the word. But it is necessary to emphasize the fact that this progress is again ambiguous. Actually, it runs the risk of being only an intellectualization of the rite in which the latter, instead of being spiritualized in the proper sense of the word, simply vanishes into an abstraction. In such a case, as we have already observed, the word finally attains a relative omnipotence, but at the cost of a fatal devitalization. The reality of the word, like that of religion in general, has been taken over by a pure idea, whose purity is only synonymous with lack of reality.

Whatever be the case, the hymn which accompanies the carrying out of the ritual and which expresses the contents of the ritual in a praise which constitutes its explicit consecration, appears to have been the matrix for the myth. It is there that the myth seems to have taken form. Texts such as those of the Homeric hymns, even if they are not of very great antiquity, can make us realize how the meditations of the priests on the rites under their care could have for the first time poetically expressed all their meaning.[16]

We should also note that it is there that we see the birth of "theology" (Θεολογία), as this was understood by the ancient Greeks even up to the time of the Fathers of the fourth century. To them, theology was not so much a rational reflection upon divinely revealed truths as the contemplation and lyrical expression of the *mirabilia Dei,* the "wondrous things wrought by God."[17]

[15] *Ibid.,* pp. 433 ff. See also my *Spiritualité du Nouveau Testament et des Pères,* p. 43, note 75.

[16] It may well be that the Hymn of Demeter has preserved for us the best of Eleusinian piety, when it had not yet evaporated into philosophical speculation.

[17] Fine examples of these may be found in the French translation of the hymns by Mario Meunier in *Hymnes philosophiques* (Paris, 1935). A very interesting Christianization of this type of hymn may be found in the writings of Synesius of Cyrene (see the edition and commentary by N. Terzaghi, *Synesii Cyrenesis Hymni* [Rome, 1949]).

It was essentially a religious, and even a cult activity. It did not express the sacred verities in order to subject them to speculative analysis, but to exalt the faith in its very definition. Thus it quite naturally constituted a glorification of God. However developed the thought might be in the hymn of praise, its development was all imbedded within a doxology. This is precisely what we still see in the great Christian Eucharistic anaphoras or in other texts of the same sort such as the *Te Deum*. The confession of faith is there inseparable from the praise. It remains an act of adoration.

What is intellectual in this form of particularly concentrated praise is so lyrical in its inspiration that the most fully developed hymns tend through their very development to become ineffable. Enigmatic formulas as a consequence tend to be uttered in a kind of ecstasy either of pure rejoicing, such as in the *alleluia* and the melodic prolongations of the last syllable (the *jubilus*), or of prostrate adoration, such as in the Jewish *Kedusha* or the Christian *Sanctus*. Better still, the result of this lapsing into the ineffable will be the pure and simple ecstatic silence which the ancients already regarded as the ultimate form of praise when it strives to lift itself up to its object but cannot do so without fainting away: *Tibi silentium laus* — "To you, silence is praise." [18]

A discussion of the connection between the prayer of praise and the performance of the rites must take into account another even more important factor. This is the way in which one passes insensibly from prayer to another use of the sacred word which is, as it were, the very opposite of prayer, the sacred oracle. Actually, only this passage from prayer to oracle can give an account of the truly religious meaning of consecratory prayer. We are, so to speak, at the antipode of man's effort to arouse by means of his own words a content in the rites which he might master when it appears that the praise of the god of the rites, on the lips of the priest, has ceased to be the words of a man addressed to God, but has now become the very words of God addressed to men. [19]

It would be well here to note the importance of a genuine intellectual revolution that has taken place in the course of the last generation. Originating in the history of comparative religion, this

[18] See R. Otto, *The Idea of the Holy*, pp. 79 ff.
[19] See G. van der Leeuw, *op. cit.*, 435 ff.

change soon had a profound impact on Biblical exegesis and caused a complete reversal of some hitherto accepted views.[20]

Protestant Biblical exegesis, which was still handicapped by the unquestioned acceptance of Hegelian dialectics, had accepted as an axiom an essential opposition between prophet and priest, that is to say, between the man of the word, individually inspired by God as he was thought to be, and the man of the rite and religious institutions.[21] But the great Norwegian exegete Sigmund Mowinckel called attention to the fact that the prophets of Israel belonged at first to associations connected with particular sanctuaries and that it is impossible to discover, even among the greatest and most original prophets, any change of surroundings as radical as has been postulated.[22] It was in the Temple that Isaias had his inaugural vision that germinally contained all his later prophecies.[23] Both Jeremias and Ezechiel were priests.[24] It is a complete misunderstanding to regard the former's sharp criticism of the worship at Jerusalem in his day as a criticism of the worship as such. And Ezechiel, though he unreservedly adopts the position of his predecessor, concentrates so much on a resoration of the ideal cult that some modern scholars, with a show of plausibility, have gone so far as to attribute to him the origin of all the Israelitic priestly legislation.[25]

After Mowinckel, the school of S. H. Hooke was able to throw light on the fact that priestly inspiration was found generally, but was particularly noticeable among the Hebrews. The origin of the idea of a divine word appears in the priestly oracles pronounced at the time of the ritual celebrations. More definitely, the word "Torah," before coming to mean a systematized collection of laws,

[20] See O. Eissfeldt, "The Prophetic Literature," in *The Old Testament and Modern Study,* ed. H. H. Rowley (Oxford, 1956), pp. 115 ff.

[21] The very remarkable work of Adolphe Lods, *The Prophets and the Rise of Judaism,* trans. by S. H. Hooke (London, 1937), is strongly biased in this regard.

[22] See his *Psalmenstudien III: Die Kultprophetie und prophetische Psalmen* (Kristiania, 1923).

[23] *Isaias* 6.

[24] *Jeremias* 1:1, and *Ezechiel* 1:3.

[25] This was the thesis of Wellhausen's school.

was a mandate from God issued at the time of the sacrifices of the alliance.[26]

Later, the Scandinavian school, with Alfred Haldar and Ivan Engnell, was to draw out the consequences of this new point of view so enthusiastically that with some reason it can be accused of substituting a scarcely less exclusive pan-ritualism for the blind anti-ritualism of the older Protestant exegesis.[27]

What is at least certain is that the divine word, the ἱερὸς λόγος, in all living religions and particularly in those of the Mediterranean basin, is not only incorporated into the ritual but is essentially one with it. At first the words are not so much an explanation of the rite as its fully conscious expression. They are at the same time that which, because of their intelligibility, guarantees the rite its fully human reality and that which, in the rite, imposes a divine form upon humanity. They are a formal recognition of the divinity, which cannot be real without such a surrender as that which the sacred demands of us, aptly described by Joachim Wach as the last constitutive, and not least important, element of the religious fact.[28]

The ways in which the divine word in the cult-experience is formulated are infinitely varied.[29] We see the divine word and the rite born together when the latter is distinguished from any natural phenomena, as a sign in which the theophany is apprehended in a special manner.[30] Thus the flight of sacred birds will be interpreted as indicating the divine approval or disapproval of some projected form of human activity. Then will come the examination of the entrails of victims offered in sacrifice. The casting of lots, whatever form it takes, is never anything but a particularly significant rite. The murmuring of the oaks in the sacred wood of Dodona about the sanctuary of Zeus marks a further step in making the heavenly voice more precise, but also more material. In

---

[26] See the two volumes of collected essays, edited by S. H. Hooke, *Myth and Ritual* (London, 1933), and *The Labyrinth* (London, 1935).

[27] See particularly A. Haldar, *Associations of Cult Prophets among the Ancient Semites* (Uppsala, 1945), and I. Engnell, *The Call of Isaiah* (Uppsala, 1949).

[28] See above, pp. 30-31.

[29] See G. van der Leeuw, *op. cit.*, pp. 380 ff.

[30] See R. Otto's reflections on divination, in *The Idea of the Holy*, pp. 147 ff.

the Hellenic world the Delphic oracle was thought to reveal truths to men through the priestess of Apollo, the Pythia, sitting upon a tripod and chewing bay leaves that put her into a kind of trance. This is a typical example of a "prophet" in the original meaning of the word, that is to say, someone who "speaks for another," the other in this case being God.

Just as in the case of sacrificial rites, so we find all these different forms of the divine word or their equivalents in Israel. Of what use was the *ephod,* or even the *urim* and the *thummin,* if they were not means of divination analogous to the Hellenic lots? [31] The origin of a good number of sacrificial psalms appears indeed to have been in a Torah interpreting the way in which the sacrifices were performed. [32] The very strange phenomenon which the rabbis called the *bath-qôl* [33] appears to be closely connected with prophetic inspiration in the strict sense of the word. This was the heavenly voice that was heard on Mount Sinai, or in the sanctuary "between the cherubim," according to the vision of Isaias and the Mosaic accounts. Prophetic inspiration in its turn seems to have been for a long time steeped in the collective excitation of the "enthusing" rituals celebrated by the bands of prophets. [34]

Among the prophets who appear to us to be the most evolved, such as, for example, Amos, we still find the vision properly so-called and the dream along with the inspiration that is only an interpretation of an unusual fact regarded as something sacred, and therefore as a sign. And this inspiration, even when it seems to rise up spontaneously in a mind free from all this ritualistic conditioning, is still concerned with the religion of the people, and more precisely with their ritualistic observances. [35]

It is therefore not in the materiality of these manifestations of the word that Israel is really distinguished from other nations, not any more than it was by the materiality of its rites. The fact of a

[31] See Adolphe Lods, *Israel,* pp. 301 ff.

[32] See Mowinckel, *op. cit.*

[33] See "Bat Kol," *Jewish Encyclopedia,* II (1925), pp. 588 ff; *Exodus* 19:6 ff., 25:22, and *Isaias* 6:8.

[34] See also A. R. Johnson, *The Cultic Prophet in Ancient Israel* (Cardiff, 1944).

[35] See the remarks of Haldar, *op. cit.,* on this prophet who has been made into the anti-priest *par excellence.* He deals especially with *Amos* 1:1 and 7:14.

divine word in itself, is not enough to set Israel apart. Whatever may be the defects of the Scandinavian school of exegesis, it has at least utterly destroyed the hypothesis that a kind of pre-Protestantism could be found in the Old Testament, so that the word would be already set off against the rite.

But once the terrain has been cleared of wrong oppositions, it is possible to see more exactly what constitutes the real originality of Old Testament propheticism and Christianity. It is due not to the form but to the content of that word which re-echoed in Israel before it became embodied there, in the most literal sense, in Him who was to be called the Word made flesh.

A comparison of that which the word impressed of itself upon the religion of the Hebrews alone and that received by neighboring religions will show the original character of the former.

In the Hellenic world the Delphic oracle enjoyed a unique position as an example of the sacred word.[36] Nowhere else among the Greeks was there to be found such a constant tradition of relatively coherent oracles. But an examination of this tradition will show that the divine word was humanized only by becoming absorbed in the minutiae of human activities which, in the end, had nothing religious about them. If one seeks to find a constant in this tradition, as the best Greek philosophers attempted to do, and to this extent something that transcended the individual oracles, this can only be achieved by a process of abstraction, which is only another, though more subtle, means of humanizing them. As a consequence, the oracle, the alleged voice of Apollo, either lost itself in "politics," the building of a city in which man gradually became his own master, or it raised itself above the temporal vicissitudes of this world only to become an interior ideal like the "know thyself" of Socrates, or the ideal of a harmonious order, the beauty of the cosmos, which is only a higher projection of a perfect but finite humanity as expounded by Plato in his *Republic* and *Laws*. In both instances, the figure of God speaking to man is taken over by that of man creating a world for himself in which he perfects himself.

Better than Nietzsche, who somewhat exaggerates the opposition between Dionysiac and Apollonian inspiration, Dodds has shown that the Delphic oracles, in which the god only reveals

---

[36] See Marie Delcourt's work, *L'oracle de Delphes* (Paris, 1955).

himself by reducing himself to an abstraction manifests but one aspect of Greek religion, even if it is the most prominent one.[37] A sense of the divine irrational was constantly struggling with the too perfect rationalization of what has been called "the Greek miracle." [38] The fascination that the "mysteries" had for Plato, and more in general his insatiable curiosity for the Semitic East, and for Egypt in particular, betrays the attraction of the opposite pole. This certainly has some connection with the tension which Plato took pains to preserve between the myth ($\mu\hat{\upsilon}\vartheta os$) and the now rationalized word ($\lambda \acute{o} \gamma os$).

In late Hellenism, in Hermetism and Neo-Platonism, these tendencies were reversed. The return of the ever-threatening tide, as may be seen in the *Bacchae* of Euripides[39] and the whole of the Orphic and Pythagorean traditions, eventually caused the waters of the Orontes and even of the Ganges to sweep over the small clear stream of the Illysus and empty themselves in the Tiber.[40]

In the guise of "mysteries" the ancient religions of the East acquired a pseudo-Hellenic character. Their contribution to the Hellenistic world and to developed Roman paganism was what later became known as "a sense of mystery." It was not that the gods of these cults were more supernatural than Delphic Apollo, but rather that their *hieros logos*,[41] even when tricked out in the

[37] See Charles Andler, *Nietzsche, sa vie, sa pensée*, II (Paris, 1958), pp. 19 ff., on "La naissance de la tragédie."

[38] E. R. Dodds, *The Greeks and the Irrational* (Berkeley, 1951).

[39] Particularly characteristic are verses 72-77:
>"Happy is he to whom it has been vouchsafed
>To know the divine rites,
>To lead a holy life,
>Consecrating his soul
>On the heights of the Bacchic frenzy
>In sacred purifications."

[40] See the brilliant studies of J. Jérôme Carcopino, from his *Basilique de la Porte Majeure*, 7th ed. (Paris, 1944), to *De Pythagore aux apôtres* (Paris, 1956), despite the fact that a considerable part of his work is based on pure conjecture.

[41] On the revival of the *hieros logos* in the Hellenistic world, influenced by the Oriental religions, see A. J. Festugière, *La révélation d'Hermès trismégiste*, I (Paris, 1944), pp. 1-67 and 309 ff. On the specificity of the Jewish, later Christian, Word, see especially the article by G. Kittel, "$\lambda \acute{o} \gamma os$" in *Theologisches Wörterbuch zum N. T.*, IV, pp. 69 ff.

philosophy of the time, preserved a good many elements of un-tamed primitiveness that the civilizations of Athens and Rome had gone too far in repressing — the mystery of life and death, the mystery of a creative, and perhaps saving, *eros*. In short, the sacred there rips apart the flattering figure of narcissistic beauty with which man had become enchanted. And at the same time something entirely different from a simple lack of elegance is redis-covered in the evils that beset man and the world. The *hybris* of sin is no longer judged according to merely human standards of perfection.

To this extent, the invasion of Hellenism by these mysteries was certainly able to prepare the way for Christianity, but their chief contribution was to stir up sluggish aspirations rather than to furnish any real satisfaction for them. In the religion of the He-brews and later of the Jews, all this irrationality which the Greeks had tended to remove, had also undergone a progressive purga-tion. But instead of dissolving through it, it had deployed in all its sovereign liberty.

The divine word affirmed in Israel — and which took on a completely new aspect with the preaching of the Gospel — is actually no less different from the *hieroi logoi* with which Hellen-ism, by contact with primitive revelations, sought to revitalize it-self in its decline than it is from the devitalized Greek and Roman oracles. These oracles claimed to give divine answers to human questions asked of them, but the answers were themselves all too plainly human. This was not the case with the Eastern oracles. There nonetheless, man still sought God and asked for an answer from on high to his questions. Here, on the contrary, whether in what we are told about Moses or of the patriarchs before him, be-ginning with Abraham, or in what we learn from the lives of the great prophets themselves, it is God who questions man, challeng-ing his ways. The Word intervenes, tearing apart the web of human affairs to take them back again into His mighty hand. Those who hear the Word which they have not requested and those whom it has chosen as its instruments are troubled and even terrified by it. To a greater or lesser extent all hear that which was heard by Saul of Tarsus: "It is hard for thee to kick against the goad." Still they murmur: "This word is a hard saying, who can listen to it?"[42]

[42] *Acts* 26:14, and *John* 6:61.

The divine Word has retaken the initiative in the dialogue with man, and this initiative is not disputed.

And if ever a word has been act, a personal act in the highest degree, it is this Word of God that speaks to proclaim Himself as King. From generation to generation His Word has proved itself creative of an incomparable history. This history may rightly be called sacred, for it is the history of the sacred seizing this human history again as if from within, which till then had only been the history of the gradual profanation of the universe by man.[43]

Therefore it is as a presence, not only all-invading but also all-dominating, that a divine personality without parallel is revealed to us. As becomes progressively more clear as this revelation becomes more explicit, this personality has nothing in common with mythological personifications, mere glorified images of men, with their vices as well as their virtues. But its purity, instead of being that of a progressive abstraction in which the sacred only dissolves into moral and intellectual concepts, as in Greek thought, is that of a sovereign grandeur and condescendence, which is never so formidable as when it is most freely communicated.

Moses' experience at the burning bush may be given as typical of all the various revelations made to Israel and of that unity behind the revelations, unbroken throughout all the highly individualized prophets who were to be its instruments.[44] It is the living unity of a Name that is disclosed in proportion to the realization of a design. The God who speaks to Israel, speaks to man only in order to mold a people, a man according to His heart, and it is in and for this work that He himself is gradually to be known.

At once, then, the ancient hierophanies, still alive though badly distorted in the mystery religions, are reanimated and transformed. The preternatural meaning of love and death is revealed with unheard-of clarity in the espousals of Yahweh with "the virgin without spot or wrinkle" whom He has resolved to draw miraculously from the corrupt mass of humanity. The virgin will come forth indeed but through a succession of mysterious trials through which

[43] See the first chapter of my volume, *The Meaning of Sacred Scripture.*
[44] *Exodus* 3.

the Lord Himself will be revealed in the unique faithful Servant, suffering and dying for the redemption of the unfaithful.[45]

Similarly, in a praise of God no less new than the Word that arouses it in Israel, a praise which will have its final bloom in the *berakah* of Judaism and its definitive fruit in the Christian Eucharist,[46] the heavenly or earthly powers through which men obtained their first apprehension of the sacred, regain (or acquire for the first time) a remarkable transparency. When all the cults were more or less entangled in an idolatry of the symbols expressing the fundamental sacred word, Israel initiated the first monotheism that was more than a paralyzed reminiscence of the primitive apprehension of the divine as transcending all its particular manifestations. And this was not effected through a process of devitalizing abstraction, nor can this experience be confused with the different forms of tribal henotheism that characterized the "gods of the alliance" among the other Semitic peoples. In this recognition of God revealed to Israel as the sole God, the individual revelations and the manifold and partial words did not disappear. They had only to confess their radical insufficiency and their dangerous ambiguity.

The prophetic reaction to idolatry cannot be formulated in the simplified terms that modern rationalists have erroneously suggested.[47] When the prophets declare that "the gods of the nations" are "false gods," or that the idols "are nothing," they do not mean to say that there was nothing but an illusion behind the non-Jewish cults.[48] They wish to affirm the unique transcendence, the

---

[45] This theme of the betrothal of Yahweh to His people is the entire theme of Osee, which was taken up again by Ezechiel. That of the salutary sufferings of the Servant was developed in the Songs of the Servant which form the nucleus of the *Second Isaias.*

[46] On the *Jewish berakah* and the Christian Eucharist, see *The Meaning of Sacred Scripture,* pp. 224 ff. The essential texts may be found in the *Tractate Berakoth,* trans. A. Lukyn Williams (London, 1921), and *Seder R. Aman Gaon,* Hebrew text with English trans. and notes by David Hedegard (Lund, 1951).

[47] See the unconvincing foreword by Henri Berr to Adolphe Lods, *The Prophets and the Rise of Judaism,* trans. S. H. Hooke, (New York, 1937), pp. xi ff.

[48] See for instance *Jeremias* 10:1-16, and its parallels in the *Second Isaias.*

absolute omnipotence of the God who has revealed Himself to Israel. But according to the tradition of the Jewish rabbis and that of the Fathers of the Church, this affirmation of the prophets did not prevent their recognizing some truth in the oracles of the pagans and in the worship they offered to their numerous gods. These were indeed revelations of an authentic, but limited and fallen, spirituality insofar as they were incorporated in a worship stained by superstition and magic. In this view, the gods of the pagan oracles appear as the powers which impregnate the world with sacredness as they sustain it. These powers, all emanating from the one Creator God, because they are, as it were, His angels, that is, His messengers, are an original refraction of His own power and sanctity. But since they have themselves fallen, at least some of them, they have embroiled man in their fall by abusing him. Just as they were themselves cast down from their original state after their foolish attempt to free themselves from God, or even to make themselves equal with Him, so they have tricked men, making them revolt in their turn, but promising them that which they themselves had been unable to attain. While promising man complete possession of this world over which they had thought they could establish their rule in defiance of the Lord, they have chained man to themselves through his uncontrolled desires.[49]

Man, in his turn, adoring the rebellious servants instead of the sovereign God, yielded to their corrupting influences only by being himself corrupted. The false worship which man renders to the false gods is consequently not so much a worship as an attempt to satisfy the appetites which those powers who have both enslaved and enervated him by their revolt have aroused in him. This gives rise to the magic which accompanies idolatry and superstition.[50]

Nevertheless, neither the ancient Jews nor the primitive Christians were completely pessimistic about the pagan cults and oracles. The worship of the fallen angels that had been substituted for the worship of God remained interwoven with authentic revelations which the good angels continued to transmit. Consequently, if the present world appears as a closed field where "Michael and his

[49] See my study "The Two Economies of Divine Government: Satan and Christ," trans. Charles Miltner, C.S.C. in *Theology Library*, II, ed. A.M. Henry, O. P. (Chicago, 1955), 465-497.

[50] See E. Langton, *Essentials of Demonology* (London, 1949).

angels" are lined up against the great enemy, "the ancient Ser-
pent"[51] and the angels that he has debauched, even in the most
vicious cults there remain traces, and even more than traces, of
man's primitive familiarity with the heavenly spirits that should
have led him to the true God. The "oracle of lies" cannot refrain
from bearing witness at certain times to the victories of the angels.
Thus it should not be surprising that the Jews and the early Christians were ready to recognize even in the Sibylline oracles echoes of
the unique Word.[52]

Where this word, however, has regained all its purity, and come
to a gradually evolved fullness, it can well be imagined how radical
the change will be. It will not destroy the materials of the ancient
myths, for this would be to destroy all possibility of a human apprehension of the sacred. Rather it will lay hold of them for its
own purposes, and remodel them to express the divine design. Instead of limiting itself to restating once again, even though with a
clarity never before known, the divine origin of the world in general and of human life in particular, it will trace out sacred history.
It will proclaim that God, from whom human history had withdrawn, has reappeared in that same history to take again in hand
His spoiled work.

The ritual action will therefore no longer be a simple memorial
of the creative act underlying the whole of history, but soon denied and disavowed by the course it had taken. It will now be
referred to the personal, saving, redemptive intervention of the
God who has spoken to announce His intention to regain His
rule over the world, and who by this announcement has already
turned it toward His coming. The pure and immediate resurgence
of the divine word in Israel is indeed inseparable from the saving
event, that is, from the redemptive coming of the creator God. He
has come straight to the bosom of a world which had progressively
moved away from Him and taken to itself the place it had denied
Him. The ritual figurations of the sacred originally evoked the
creative virtue hidden under the whole of life, and they evoked it
precisely under the present shape exhibited to us by the cosmic

---

[51] *Apocalypse* 12:7, 9.

[52] Both the Jews and Christians interpolated the texts. See Lanchester's
introduction to them in R. H. Charles, *The Apocrypha and Pseudophi-
grapha of the Old Testament*, II (Oxford, 1913), pp. 368 ff.

powers, in its rhythm of eternal births and deaths, in the relentless pursuit of a union, a reunion which inevitably vanishes again. These ritual patterns, unchanged and unchangeable as they are in their materiality, together with the expressions taken up from the myth will now undergo a radical transformation. This re-fashioning will proceed directly from the word itself which casts a new light upon the ancient myths in order to express as last through their own symbols both the eternal truth and the newness of salvation.[53]

The ancient seasonal rituals will thus become commemorations of the first historical deliverance wrought by the sovereign God, who has in some way descended into the history of His people. The sacrifices of alliance, through which man had attempted to ally himself as best he could with the cosmic powers in order to lay hold of their superhuman energies for his own advantage, will now be imposed and consecrated by God through His word which gives them a new meaning. In carrying out these sacrifices, man does nothing more now than attest his faith in the word which offers him the alliance as a free and royal grace, which he had hitherto not anticipated, nor for which he could even have hoped. For these sacrifices have themselves become for him the very seal with which God has marked His determination to espouse in the loyalty of His own love the people whom this love has recreated.

We can thus begin to see how true it is that with the invasion of the divine word, of the God who Himself speaks, into sacred history, the sacred is effectively preparing to invade the whole life of man. This does not happen in the illusory way of a "consecration of the profane as such" which would still leave it unchanged. Instead, it is an historical, clearly dated, and completely individualized insertion of the divine word in the affairs of men, but which for all that, is not a mere miracle in which the divine word would strike the earth like a meteor. It is a slow germination, which is gradually to regain control of human history, beginning with a particular area of providential events in which the decisive coming event is prepared and outlined in advance.

These events, whose continuity gradually traces the outline of sacred history, do not represent an invasion of the world by a strange God, but a reconquest of creation by its Creator. Their

---

[53] See Adolphe Lods, *op. cit.*, pp. 281 ff.

first effect is to give sense to this creation, to restore its primitive meaning. But the restoration of this sense, of this primordial revelation included in creation itself, occurs simultaneously with the effective retaking of it by the divine hands, from which sin, the fallen powers, and man after them, had wished to withdraw it. It is therefore necessary that both revelation and the reconquest of man, reaching him through the world in which he lives, should seize him through the witnesses to, or at least the vestiges of, the sacred which were left in this world. This is why the traditional signs of the sacred, either *sacramenta* or *sacrificia,* were retaken by the word, but in such a way as to signify henceforth the divine redemptive act and the coming of a Saviour.

The seasonal feast of the cosmic rebirth now becomes the Pasch in which Israel, in her deliverance from Egypt, commemorates the new creation of a new humanity from sinful humanity. What had been sacrifices of alliance with the Baalim of vegetation become the sign of the alliance concluded through faith in the sovereign word, by the revelation made on Mt. Sinai. The sacrifices are now endowed with their full meaning and receive all their virtue from the fact that God has begun to reveal Himself to those whom He has freely chosen, has begun to communicate with them, and has already descended among them to espouse them through the liberating activity of His strong hand and extended arm.

At the end of the experience, of the long trial during which the sacred history of the Old Testament brought together the will of the Almighty and the rebellious wills of His children, the meaning and the effective import of this history was to be revealed in a new type of prayer that is inseparable from a completely new concept and realization of sacrifice.

This prayer, and the sacrifice inseparably linked to it, is the Jewish *berakah* which was the predecessor of the Christian Eucharist.[55]

As Audet has rightly insisted, the *berakah* is something more than a simple "thanksgiving," if we understand this word in its re-

[54] *Exodus* 12. See the *Haggadah* of the Passover meal, as it is still used in the Jewish ritual.

[55] See J. P. Audet, "Esquisse historique du genre littéraire de la 'Bénédiction' juive et de l'Eucharistie chrétienne," *Revue Biblique,* LXV (1958), pp. 371 ff.

stricted sense of thanks given for a particular gift. It is a confession (ἐξομολόγησις) in the Biblical sense of the word, a
laudatory heralding of the *mirabilia Dei* which, instead of turning
us back upon ourselves and upon the mere satisfaction of our own
interests, should open and dilate us in the enthusiastic acceptance
of God's design.

But it would be no less erroneous to exclude from it every
human concern, as Audet tends to do. The *berakah* is not simply
a "purely disinterested" contemplation of the wonders of the
divinity, unconcerned, or at least not directly concerned, with
man's lot. It is rather the contemplation of God *as revealed in His
Word,* with all the intervention that this implies in human history
— the intervention of a presence that does not act with respect to
mankind in general but with respect to a chosen people. In speaking to this people God acts upon it with the intent of drawing it
out of the corrupt mass of sinful humanity.[56]

Undoubtedly the first effect of the word thus reintroduced into
the heart of the history of the world, and particularly that of man,
is to enable man to rediscover the first meaning, the divine meaning of all creation in its entirety. And this is the intent of the priestly account of the creation in Genesis, which shows us this same
word that has spoken through the prophets at the beginning, and
being itself the beginning of all things, whether of the world or of
man.[57] But this rediscovery cannot be separated from the new discovery of God intervening on behalf of Israel, freeing it from the
slavery of Egypt and false gods, warning it about the adulterous
cults of Canaan, delivering it by His omnipotence, but also purifying it by mysterious trials in which He seems to abandon it. The
berakah is the acknowledgement of all this: it is a complete act of
faith which accepts the word as revealed in sacred history and
which by this very fact alone restores to creation a meaning which
had been lost through the Fall.[58]

[56] See in Hedegard, *op. cit.*, pp. 147 ff., the great *berakah* for the conclusion of the meal.

[57] *Genesis* 1.

[58] The great *berakah* mentioned above unites the thanksgiving for food
with thanksgiving for the *Torah.* In the same way, the "berakah" of the
Didache in a single blessing mentions both food and a knowledge of God.

And just as the faith which is commanded by the word is expressed and prolonged through obedience, so the *berakah* is an acknowledgement in an even more profound, more living sense. It is the contemplation of the divine design and, through it, of the word of Him who reveals Himself by delivering Himself through His activity to those it touches. This faith will, moreover, consent to this design and deliver itself to its exigencies and its promises; hence it will be the conformation of the people to their God whom they have come to know. The Jewish *berakah* therefore encloses all the existence of the believer in a universal acknowledgement of the active presence of God who created all things through His word.[59] No matter what he did, the pious Israelite was taught by the rabbis to begin all his actions, even those which seemed to be the most secular, with the formula: "Be blessed, Lord our God, King of eternity. . . ." This was immediately followed by an express memorial of the divine word as seen as the source of that which was to be immediately used. Thus, for example, when lamps were lit, a Jew would say: "You who have created the stars to watch over the day and night." It is in this sense that St. Paul would later be able to say that "Every creature of God is good, and nothing is to be rejected that is accepted with thanksgiving. For it is sanctified by the word of God and prayer." [60]

But the heart of all these blessings, and that without which they would lose their reality, is the twofold and inseparable blessing "for knowledge and food," as it is expressed in one of the greatest and most important formulas of the *berakoth,* which (through the *Didache*) passed from Jewish into Christian usage.[61]

The knowledge here in question is the "knowledge of God" which the prophets had made the ultimate goal of all their preaching. It is that knowledge which consists of union and conformity with the revealed God, in a believing and loving submission to His word, to His revealed Name and His design as accomplished in this word to which faith surrenders us.[62]

[59] *Tractate Berakoth* (ed. Lukyn Williams), pp. 70 ff.
[60] *I Timothy* 4:4-5.
[61] *Didache* 9.
[62] See my *Spiritualité du Nouveau Testament et des Pères,* pp. 34 ff.

The objects of food thus connected with knowledge are first of all the fruits of the promised land. They are, as it were, the perfect signs of God's alliance with his people, of His promises that have been realized solely through the virtue of His word that had formulated them. But above all this food is the ritual nourishment of the festal banquet in which the community of believers realizes its unity in the celebration of the *mirabilia Dei,* the wonders of God, of which this unity is the final aim.

It is here that the *berakah* again meets the sacrifice. Just as a celebration of the Paschal meal with a modified meaning seems to have originally been the only sacrifice of the Hebrews, so it is a sacred meal, permeated with the Paschal atmosphere and infusing the whole life of the Messianic community with it, which in Judaism contemporary with Christian origins, assimilates all the contents of the gradually transfigured Jewish sacrificial rites.

At this moment we can see how, after the different types of sacrifices employed by the Semites had been progressively reinterpreted by virtue of the divine word, this new meaning was to free itself from their materiality. We should be careful to note, however, that this did not mean a pure and simple spiritualization of the sacrifice of praise into a praise described as sacrificial, that is, into "the sacrifice of lips," as it is called by Osee.[63]

This would mean giving an interpretation far too literal in its false spirituality to his famous saying: "It is *hesed* (piety towards God accompanied by compassion for men) that I desire, and not sacrifice." [64] This is better understood as a renewed sanctification of every festal meal of the community, outlining and foretelling the Messianic banquet announced by the prophets.

Beginning with the short *berakah* pronounced by the "Master of Justice," the Teacher of the Word, over the bread which he breaks for the community of his disciples, these meals were brought to a final close with the great *berakah* sung over the last cup before the group disbanded. It is there that the redemptive action of the Creator God, who had chosen, prepared, established and consecrated His people for Himself throughout sacred history by making Himself known through His word, was formally recognized in all its fullness. It is there especially that this people, arriving at its

---

[63] *Osee* 14:2.
[64] *Osee* 6:6.

final stage, becoming fully aware of the last and imminent realization of the divine design, surrendered itself to it.

This is why it was held, as attested by Josephus for the Essenes and manifested at Qumran, that the sharing in a repast of this type, even for the Jewish priests themselves, was more than equal to all the sacrifices.[65] It is, as it were, the final preparation for the renewal of the alliance that had been announced by Jeremias,[66] for the founding of an alliance not only new but eternal, and which Ezechiel [67] in his turn had described as the removal of the old heart of stone, rebellious to the divine word, and the replacing of it in the breast of man with a true heart of flesh [68] on which the divine word, according to the saying of his predecessor, would be engraved.

At this point it is perfectly natural that the most primitive form of prayer should reappear at the summit of the most evolved prayer of praise, that is to say, an earnest supplication. Actually we see such a prayer, though greatly changed, rising up as an integrating element in the fully developed *berakah*. The request is no longer opposed to contemplative praise, to the simple and joyful acceptance of the divine will. Rather, drawing support from the first and merely incipient realization of the divine will in the past as a pledge of what is to come, the *berakah* comes to an end with the ardent entreaty that it should reach its full and complete accomplishment. In other words, man having now been made cognizant of the divine design, and through this knowledge beginning to reflect on his own countenance something of the divine Visage, touched and marked as he already is in his entire being by the sacred Name, finally asks from God nothing except that "Thy will be done on earth as it is in heaven. . . ." [69]

At this stage all is ready for the passage from Judaism to Christianity. This passage is simply the consequence of what the Word

[65] Jewish Antiquities 18:1-5. See G. Vermes' commentary on this text in *Discovery in the Judean Desert* (New York, 1956), pp. 54 ff., and what this same author has to say about the analogous text from the *Manual of Discipline*, p. 213.

[66] *Jeremias* 31:31-34.

[67] *Ezechiel* 37:26.

[68] *Ezechiel* 36:26.

[69] See in Hedegard, *op. cit.*, the *Tefillah* of the Eighteen Benedictions, pp. 83 ff.

announced to Israel, the re-creative action that had been fore-shadowed, the Presence that had already been given but under a veil, would itself complete. In the person and life of Jesus of Nazareth we have the Word made flesh, an action of man which is consequently God's own action, a living Presence, which hence-forth is His, no longer veiled but manifest, incarnate in humanity.

This is fully realized by the acceptance of the Cross, in the circumstances in which Jesus accepts it, and with the meaning He gives to it in His discourse after the Last Supper which is the full development of all His preaching, just as the Cross is the full realization of all His earthly life.[70]

When He rises up at the Supper, he first takes in His hands the bread and breaks it; He then takes the cup of benediction, and He gives them to His disciples as the efficacious signs of His broken body and His shed blood — efficacious since they are given by the divine Word made flesh to the extent that it took upon itself all the infirmity of our flesh. The eucharist which He pronounces thus consummates all that to which all the Jewish *berakoth* were tending, and particularly the *berakah* of the ritual repast in the communities expecting the Messianic alliance.[71]

The recognition of the divine Name communicated to man, of the divine design for man, is here made perfect since it is that of a man who is God made man. In the Word made flesh, man's answer to the Word of God at last adheres perfectly to the Word itself. At one stroke, just as sacred and profane history meet in their com-mon consummation at the Cross on which Jesus hung, in the Great *Berakah* for the Cross, in all the eucharists which will now draw their efficacy from the living memory of the Cross, the perfect sacrifice is accomplished, perfecting the praise, the confession of the divine Name in the definitive fiat given to His design.

Henceforth, as a consequence, the sacred rite which only re-peats the action of Christ at the Last Supper on the evening before He was crucified, a ritual action in which all human life is taken up in the redemptive action at its height, is no longer, like the rites of the Old Testament, merely a human action drawing its efficacy from a divine command, but is now an action whose unique

[70] *John* 13:31-17:26.
[71] See the final appendix to *The Meaning of Sacred Scripture*.

efficacy comes from the fact that it is the Act of God accomplished at the height of human history.

We have thus come to the point where a comparative study of Christian sacramentalism and the pagan mysteries — in which some have tried to see the former's shadow and outline — may help us to catch and understand more perfectly the significance of Christian sacramentalism.

CHAPTER VIII

Pagan Mysteries
and Christian Sacraments

I F WE WISH to understand Christianity within the general background of history and comparative religion and religious psychology, we must, after having seen it evolve out of ancient Judaism, place it in the context of the "mystery religions" of pagan antiquity. When Christianity broke its ties with Judaism, it was surrounded by a number of other Eastern, and, particularly, Semitic religions, that were expanding toward the West. And ever since then, both pagans and Christians have been impressed by the resemblances that may be observed between the religion of Christ and these other religions.

In modern times, the study of these analogies has led some scholars such as Richard Reitzenstein and Wilhelm Bousset [1] to ask if what Christianity added to Judaism should not at least in large part be explained by the influence the pagan mysteries had upon the Christian mystery from the time of its first formulation and its first ritual developments. More specifically, is not the concept and reality of a Christian sacrament, bringing salvation through participation in the death and resurrection of a Saviour God, a particularly successful instance of those mystery religions which were in competition with one another but which all had more or less the same general theme?

[1] I noted their essential works on page 34.

Dom Casel and his school, as is known, believed that it was necessary to answer this question in the affirmative.[2] At first sight there seem to be striking points of convergence between these pagan myths and the doctrinal preaching of the *kerygma,* the Gospel of Christ, between the rites which surrounded these same myths and the Christian sacraments, and even in the vocabulary used by both pagans and Christians, not only in the use of the key word "mystery" itself but also in that of such words as "initiation," illumination," "rebirth," and so forth.

The validity of these analogies cannot be determined until a thorough study of each individual resemblance has been made. Then, and only then, should the question of possible dependence be posed. Moreover, as we have already emphasized, even the most perfectly verified analogies will not suffice to determine this. There will have to be a careful scrutiny of the historical channels through which they may have happened to come. It cannot be repeated too often that depth psychology has lent support to the findings of ethnologists indicating that everywhere certain mythic patterns are to be found that have arisen independently of any possible historical influence.

If during the past century the study of the mystery religions has produced a vast number of works, it is unfortunately necessary to admit that their most common trait is an almost total ignorance of these elementary rules of methodology. When one begins by describing the mystery religions and Christianity without distinguishing their essential characteristics, and by transferring ideas and expressions from one to the other, it should be quite obvious that it will become impossible after that to determine their mutual differences and influences.

In recent decades, however, a saner type of criticism has been coming to the fore and a number of definite conclusions can now be formulated,[3] although there are still a good many scholars who continue to splash about, confusing the issue rather than contri-

---

[2] *The Mystery of Christian Worship,* trans. T. T. Hale (Westminster, Md., 1962).*

[3] Remarkable in this sense is the fine essay by Hugo Rahner, "Griechische Mythen in christlicher Deutung," given at an 'Eranos' session, and later published in the volume mentioned in the following note. See also the excellent study by Bruce Metzger, mentioned on page 36.

buting anything to its clarification.⁴ The results of these investigations have been both a confirmation and a denial of the original unity of the mystery religions. They have confirmed it by proving that these religions had a common origin in the agrarian rites of the ancient Mediterranean civilizations. They have at the same time denied it by demonstrating the late and artificial character of the common mystery which was formerly regarded as being the principle of this unity, and by pointing out the utter ambiguity of the word "mystery" as used in pagan religions and in primitive Christianity.

With respect to the common origin of the mysteries, there is no longer any doubt that the rites of Eleusis, just as those of the worship of the Syrian Adonis, or of Attis in Asia Minor, or of Isis and Osiris in Egypt, and of many other deities which sooner or later came to resemble them, such as the Thracian Dionysus or the Iranian Mithra, were originally agrarian rites that consecrated the processes of vegetation.⁵ In the early stages of civilization man believed that he was able, by means of these rites, to stir up the forces of nature for his own material advantage, long before he saw in them a means of attaining a happy immortality.

Frazer was the first to make these nature rites an object of special study, but his hasty, superficial, and at times *a priori* assimilations must now be corrected with the help of the more recent works of E. O. James.⁶ Nevertheless, one of the solid contributions made by Frazer in his famous *Golden Bough* was his discovery of the importance in all these cults of an archaic mythic figure. This figure, which was to give rise to the priest, king, and inspired wise man of later civilizations, may be compared with the archetype of the "Tot-Hermes" described by Jung, although the former is richer in content and more clearly defined. Sigmund Mowinckel has demonstrated the importance of this figure in the

⁴ This is unfortunately the case with most of the other contributors in the 'Eranos' sessions who have dealt with these questions. Most of their studies touching on this problem will be found in *Papers from the Eranos Yearbooks, II: The Mysteries* (New York, 1955).*

⁵ See particularly E. O. James, *The Cult of the Mother-Goddess: An Archaeological and Documentary Study* (London, 1959).

⁶ Especially his great work, already cited several times, *Myths and Ritual in the Ancient Near East.*

early development of Jewish Messianism.[7] But at the same time, no one has shown better than he the variations to which this figure, eminently sacral, was subjected, and in whom the people through an obscure identification with the gods themselves were believed to find their unity and their vital principle. And no one indeed has more clearly demonstrated than Mowinckel the change that this archetype was to undergo in Judaism, at the sources of Christianity itself.

We shall have to return to this matter later. For the present we should note that these different religions, before they could constitute the mysteries of the Hellenistic Age, had to pass more or less rapidly through three or four stages of evolution. These have been particularly well defined by Angus in his *Mystery Religions and Christianity*.[8] As we shall see, the fourth stage was completely unknown to the mysteries of Eleusis. But it was under the influence of these mysteries and even at times through the direct interference of the priests of Eleusis that the other mystery religions were to experience the same kind of evolution as that of the Attic mysteries. We shall therefore begin to trace their history beginning with these latter.[9]

In the first stage there were no mysteries at all, at Eleusis no more than elsewhere. There was merely the seasonal worship, open to all, well known to all, observed by the natives of this small farming community.

The mystery as such only made its appearance at the time of the Dorian invasions. The newcomers were thoroughly intrigued by the practices which the supplanted populations preserved as the last remnants of their autonomy, even though these latter had begun to lose their understanding of the original rites. The old native families, the Kerykes and the Eumolpides, who jealously guarded the tradition of their ancestral rites, had to permit the Dorians to be initiated into them. But they represented the rites as being a priceless secret and their own exclusive property, and they clung to them all the more tenaciously as a kind of rare compensation for their loss of political prestige.

[7] Sigmund Mowinckel, *He That Cometh* (Oxford, 1956).

[8] S. Angus, *The Mystery Religions and Christianity* (London, 1925), pp. 44.

[9] See particularly P. Foucart, *Les mystères d'Éleusis* (Paris, 1914), and Victor Magnien, *Les mystères d'Éleusis* (Paris, 1929).

A third stage in the evolution of the rites was reached when their reputation was extended far beyond the environs of Athens, their original theater. From all over the Greek-speaking world people came to be initiated into the mysteries. They were curious and attracted by the antiquity of the rites, but their devotion was probably more superstitious than mystical in character. The Kerykes and the Eumolpides made no objections but continued to initiate these strangers indiscriminately, demanding nothing more of them than a knowledge of Greek.

At this stage the mysteries became completely mysterious. No one, the hierophant apparently no more than the initiates, any longer had the least idea about their primitive meaning. But for the sensitive and imaginative Greeks, the rites served as a providential compensation for the increased rationalism of philosophy. All, even the philosophers themselves, were charmed by the strange and pompous ritual which each one could interpret to suit himself. A glance at the dialogues of Plato should furnish sufficient evidence of this.[10]

But all of these beautiful speculations were the work of litterateurs. There are no indications that the worthy Kerykes or Eumolpides took the least part in them, though these pious imaginations must have contributed considerably to making the local industry—which could possibly be compared with the Passion Play at Oberammergau, if not with the festival at Cannes — more attractive.

We must, however, insist on the fact that these various speculations about the mysteries, which modern scholars are inclined to regard as being at the heart of the mysteries, never had any part in them, at least at Eleusis. The mysteries, as such, had nothing to do with them. The mysteries were rites, and nothing more than rites, carefully preserved by the priestly families as a kind of monopoly. Everyone could speculate about them at leisure. The Eleusinian priesthood, once again, did not take any interest or part in these speculations, except perhaps insofar as they contributed to the fame of their profitable enterprise.

The secret of the mysteries was so scrupulously kept that we are not too well informed as to just what they were, except for a few rites, though even here the details are lacking. Some skeptics have even maintained with a slight show of probability that the secret

[10] See, for example, *Phaedo* 69c or *Phaedrus* 250b-c.

would not have been so well kept by great numbers of Greeks and free-speaking metics if it had contained anything of really intrinsic interest. At any rate, the least that can be said is that which has come from Aristotle, who knew well what they were: it was not so much a question of learning something there as of simply experiencing the rites: οὐ μαθεῖν ἀλλὰ παθεῖν.[11]

Certain it is that those who like Plato gave the most wonderful spiritual interpretations to the myths were not disturbed in the least by anyone. But, on the other hand, Alcibiades, though he was highly popular with, and extremely useful to, the Athenians, was exiled as a profaner of the mysteries for having parodied the rites during a night-time spree with some of his friends.[12] One cannot imagine anything that would more plainly indicate the fact that the mysteries, that is, the secret things, were simply rites, and nothing more than rites, a fact that was constantly neglected by historians of religion in the nineteenth century.

Moreover, still within the confines of ancient Greece, we find other examples of ancient rites passing through a similar evolution. This is particularly true with respect to the "mysteries" of the Cabiri on the island of Samothrace, which received this title because of their resemblance to those at Eleusis.[13] But the obscurity and even the incongruity of the myth about the three Cabiri does not seem to have had anywhere near the same interest for the ancients as the Eleusinian myth dealing with Demeter and Kore, though it has been the object of a considerable amount of speculation in modern times. It must be confessed that the Boeotians were obviously less able to exploit their local resources than were the Athenians. Thus, except for some transient seamen, the Cabiri do not seem to have secured many adherents.

But it was different with the so-called mysteries of Dionysus.[14] In his *Bacchae,* Euripides has described, and certainly idealized, the kind of general madness that this barbarous cult imported

[11] The formula has been handed on to us by Synesius of Cyrene. See Synesius Dio 7 (*Patrologia Graeca* 66:1136).

[12] He was brought to trial after the mutilation of the statues of Hermes during the night of June 6, 415 B.C.

[13] See C. Kerényi's study in *Eranos Buch* (1944).

[14] See H. Jeanmaire, *Dionysos: Histoire du culte de Bacchus* (Paris 1951).

from Thrace (despite fierce opposition) brought to the lively Greeks. It is important to note, however, that no one at this period describes the orgies of the bacchants as mysteries.[15] The objection to them, the same that would later be raised against them at Rome, was rather their notoriety and complete lack of restraint. These meetings of frenzied madness ended up with the maenads indulging in omophagy, that is, in the tearing asunder and devouring a goat that was slaughtered, rather than sacrificed, at the height of the Bacchic revels. Care must be taken not to confuse, as has too often been done in the past, this hysterical ritual, which soon disappeared, with either the Orphic speculations which had their origins in it or, still less, with the late mysteries of Sebazius, which gave them a new life. These latter mysteries, however, which were of a more or less Neo-Pythagorean character, included nothing of the ancient Dionysic orgies, and were even marked with a dualistic asceticism that was poles apart from them.[16]

From the beginning of the Hellenistic Age, however, the philosophically minded were struck by the general resemblances between the Eleusinian mysteries and others that were of a decidedly exotic nature. But this did not take place without these latter cults being more or less remodeled after the former, before something of what the indigenous cults had evoked in the Hellenistic mind was transferred to them also.

The first, and certainly the most striking instance, is that of the mysteries of Isis and Osiris. The religion of the ancient Egyptians is a remarkable example of Semitic nature-worship, centering at first about the person of the king, the more or less magical principle of vitality for the earth itself as well as for his people.[17] Osiris, the mythical ancestor of the Pharaohs, dying and being reborn through the charms of his sister-spouse Isis, had been from earliest times the object of a cult whose liturgy was the center of the royal function in Egypt. Yet, apart from the progressive democratization of the rites of embalming, there was not the least suspicion of a

[15] One can realize this by examining the texts collected by N. Turchi, *Fontes historiae mysteriorum* (Rome, 1930), pp. 3 ff.

[16] Franz Cumont, *The Oriental Religions in Roman Paganism,* authorized translation (Chicago, 1911),* pp. 64 ff.

[17] See Mowinckel, *He That Cometh,* pp. 28 ff.

mystery into which one could be initiated. These rites were first
reserved for the Pharaohs, but when they became more common,
they gradually extended the relative identification of the Pharaohs
with Osiris to all the dead.

The assimilation of this cult to the Greek mysteries was effected
in a completely artificial manner, and for motives, it must be confessed, that were purely political. It was brought about by the
Ptolemies who were anxious to weld together in language and culture the indigenous Copts with the Greek colonists. In setting up
the mysteries of Serapis at Alexandria, they strove to introduce the
myths and some of the practices of the ancient Egyptian cults into
a setting that would be familiar to the Greeks. For this, the
Eumolpid Timotheus was brought to Egypt, and with the help of
the poet Demetrius of Phalerus, who composed the Greek formulas for the new rites, he succeeded in effecting the desired religious
syncretism by casting the old beliefs into a mold that to a certain
extent resembled the rites at Eleusis.[18]

This is perhaps the only case in history where we can see a religion having its origins according to the postulates of the philosophers of the eighteenth century, that is, in the cleverness of
priests who constructed a ritual and dogmas to satisfy the wishes
of politicians.

In spite of this fact, this highly artificial religion was destined
to enjoy a remarkable success. Local Serapeia were set up in all
the Mediterranean colonies founded by the merchants and sailors
of Alexandria. And thus the Egyptian mysteries were the first to
reach a fourth stage of development, one never attained by the
Eleusinian mysteries, but soon shared wtih the other mysteries.
The first stage was simply that of the original primitive religion,
the second, its somewhat incongruous survival in the midst of a
more advanced civilization, the third, the acceptance of foreigners,
and the fourth, and last, a kind of missionary preaching of the
mysteries throughout the whole Greek-speaking world.

In those troubled times marked by a great deal of intellectual
curiosity and anxiety, the artificial but glittering ritual, exotic
enough to arouse interest and Hellenized enough to be readily
adopted, attracted great numbers of adherents and sympathizers.
A clergy that could be described as being congenitally inclined to

[18] Cf. Plutarch, *De Iside et Osiride* 28.

make-believe had little difficulty in satisfying the aspirations of these neophytes. They simply gave them in a popularized form something of the speculations that the Greeks had themselves made about their own mysteries. We can see the procedure at work, though not free from a considerable amount of charlatanism, in the *Metamorphoses* of Apuleius, the sole direct witness, even though fictionalized, that we have of the piety of an initiate and of what he got out of the mysteries.[19] This was nothing more than a hope of a happy immortality derived from the ritual consecration to the god or goddess, but without any moral or mystical concerns. As has been well expressed by Glover, Isis did not seem to be very squeamish about her worshippers.[20]

At about this same time a second, and more genuine, Oriental cult crossed over to the West where it was in its turn dressed out as a mystery like that of Eleusis, again with the assistance of the Eumolpid Timotheus. This was the cult of the Great Mother of Asia Minor, Cybele, who was an equivalent of the Greek Demeter. And with her was also introduced her consort Attis.[21]

Two stages should be distinguished in the transfer and later transformation of this cult. When the Great Mother of Pessinus was installed at Rome in 205 B.C., this was done on the advice of the Sibylline oracles as a means of diverting the disaster that was constantly threatening the city in the person of Hannibal. But as soon as Scipio had received the black stone sent by King Attalus and the procession of Roman matrons had solemnly enthroned it with its priests on the Palatine, attempts were made to check the cult's further spread. The Romans were horrified by the ecstatic cult of the goddess which included the mutilation of the Galli, her servants. As a consequence, the worship of Cybele was strictly limited to its allotted precinct until the beginning of the Empire. Claudius, however, authorized public feasts on the twenty-fourth and the twenty-fifth of March. The ceremonies began with a procession of the dendrophori carrying the felled pine dedicated to Attis that recalled his death through emasculation. After a show of

[19] See the whole of Book 11.

[20] Cited by A. E. J. Rawlinson in his excellent note on "Christianity and the Mystery Religions," in *The New Testament Doctrine of the Christ* (London, 1929), p. 79.

[21] See Cumont, *op. cit.,* pp. 46 ff., and also the two works of E. O. James already cited.

grief, during which the Galli, the priests of Attis, mutilated themselves, there was a day of rejoicing on the twenty-fifth, when his return to life was announced. Joy followed the tears and the shedding of blood. It all ended with the joyous procession of the silver statue of Cybele through the city, amidst a shower of blossoms, on its way to bathe in the Almo.

Details with respect to the initiation undergone by the men, and more especially by the women, who wished to be associated with the worship of the goddess and her dubious companion are rather scanty. But the resemblance which an extant ritual formula bears to that of Eleusis seems to betray the hand of the indefatigable Timotheus, the promoter of decidely universal mysteries, though always by the mere adaptation of any kind of foreign material to the rites familiar to him.[22]

Closely connected in its origins with this cult of Cybele was the worship of the Syrian goddess and her consort Adonis. The latter had a more developed role than that of his counterpart Attis, but it was still the expression of the natural powers evidenced in winter's death and spring's return to life.[23] The cult was introduced to Rome by Heliogabalus, once again through the worship of a stone, the black meteor of Emesa, which probably had phallic connotations. The savagery of the primitive rites connected with this cult was bound to offend the *gravitas Romana* even more than the worship

[22] Clement of Alexandria cites in his *Protrepticus* the two formulas for the mysteries of Eleusis: "I have fasted, I have drunk the cup, I have received from the box, having done, I put it into the basket, and out of the basket into the chest"; and for the mysteries of Attis: "I have eaten out of the drum, I have drunk out of the cymbal, I have carried the cernos, I have slipped into the bedroom." (*Protrepticus* 2.21, 15). Firmicus Maternus gives a slightly different version of the latter: "I have nourished myself from the drum, I have drunk from the cymbal, I have become an initiate of Attis" (*De err. prof.* rel. 18.1). Arnobius (*Adv. nationes,* 5.5) tells us expressly that Timothy had written on the Phrygian mysteries, and Pettazzoni (*I misteri: Saggio si una storia storico-religiosa* [Bologna, 1924], pp. 119), followed by other authors such as Th. Zielinski (*La Sibylle* [Paris, 1924], pp. 83), thinks that he must have made them over on the Eleusinian model.

[23] See again Cumont, *op. cit.,* pp. 103 ff., and the two volumes by James already cited for the mysteries of Attis. Lucian's treatise furnishes us with adequate information on the Syrian goddess.

of Attis, for they included sacred prostitution and human sacrifice. The astrological speculations then so much in favor, however, secured the late favor granted to the worship of Adonis. But it was difficult to see a real mystery in this cult even when it was transferred to the West. The nearest thing to it was the purely literary mystery of the *Oracula Chaldaica,* which in the third century interpreted the Syrian myth in terms of Greek philosophy, though with an Eastern cast, much like the somewhat earlier Hermetic books of Egypt.[24]

But the most directly astrological of all the mysteries, and certainly the most original, was that of Mithra.[25] This sun-god, the conqueror of the powers of darkness, was of Iranian origin. His cult, which apparently only consisted in purifying lustrations and a common banquet, was introduced into the Roman empire together with that of the Great Mother. His sanctuaries were usually to be found in the buildings connected with the temples of Cybele.

The cult's militant dualism, no less than its progressively graded initiations, can explain its popularity in military circles. *Mithraea* are to be found on the sites of many camps of the third century of our era, especially along the *limes Romanus,* the Roman frontier. A result of this worship of Mithra was that a kind of solar monotheism, decidedly syncretistic in character, almost became the religion of the empire under Constantius Chlorus, and it doubtlessly prepared the way for the adoption of Christianity by his son Constantine.

The statue of Mithra sacrificing the primitive bull to give life to the world, found in Mithraea, has at times created the impression that the rite of the *taurobolium* was part of his worship. Actually, as Cumont has shown, this was not the case. The rite, which had its origins in Anatolia, was immediately connected with the worship of the Great Mother.[26] The Christian poet Prudentius, who could have himself been present at such a ceremony, describes it in the following terms: The one to be initiated leaped down into

[24] See W. Kroll, *De oraculis Chaldaïcis* (Breslau, 1894), as well as J. Bidez, F. Cumont, *Les Mages hellénisés* (Paris, 1938), pp. 158 ff.

[25] F. Cumont dedicated an excellent study to it: *Les mystères de Mithra,* 3rd ed. (Paris, 1913). See also his *Oriental Religions,* pp. 150 ff., and G. Dumezil, *Mithra-Varuna* (Paris, 1940).

[26] See Cumont, *op. cit.,* pp. 205 ff.

a trench and through a grate was bathed in the blood of a bull that was sacrificed over him.[27] A famous inscription of one who claimed that he had been reborn for eternity through the *taurobolium* and *criobolium (taurobolio criobolioque in aeternum renatus)* has caused some to believe that the Pauline notion of baptism as a mystical burial in the blood of Christ producing a rebirth to His resurrected life could have been drawn from this rite.[28] But the relationship should be understood in the opposite sense. At the time of St. Paul the *taurobolium* was completely unknown outside a few places in Anatolia, whereas at the time of this inscription the mystery religions were running their final course in an atmosphere that was already impregnated, and even saturated, with Christian concepts.

Moreover, it is important to note that much earlier another Phrygian cult, that of Sebazius, locally connected with the worship of Cybele and Attis, shows how these cults were subjected to Jewish influences. From the beginning of the Hellenistic Age the adepts of Sebazius formally identified him with the Lord Sabaoth of the Bible. This is all the more interesting since the Phrygian Sebazius is a counterpart to the Greek Dionysus.[29] This can explain the hopeless confusion in late Orphism of themes derived from the ancient religion of Thrace, ideas derived from a revived Pythagoreanism, and Oriental influences in which were certainly entwined Hebrew and perhaps even Christian threads of thought.

With the Neo-Orphic and Neo-Pythagorean thiases of the second and third centuries we encounter an entirely new stage in the evolution of the mystery religions, and one which actually outgrows them.[30] But historians of the last century were too prone to project the characteristics of this phase on the earlier ones. Here must be considered not only the *Oracula Chaldaica* already mentioned but also the Egyptian Hermetic books[31] with which they have so much in common, and also Neo-Platonic theurgy, which

---

[27] *Ibid.*, p. 63. See Prudentius, *Peristephanon* 10.1011 ff.

[28] *Corpus Inscriptionum Latinarum* 5.610. Found at Rome, the inscription can be dated from A.D. 376.

[29] See Cumont, *op. cit.*, pp. 48 ff.

[30] See the works of Carcopino cited at pp. 74, note 40.

[31] Père Festugière has published four volumes dealing with these with a wealth of material and reflection that is almost discouraging; *La révélation d' Hermès trismégiste* (Paris, 1944-54).

was to find there some of its sources. But what is too readily glossed over is that these late mysteries, according to the felicitous phrase of Père Festugière, are chiefly, and even exclusively, literary mysteries.

This should be understood in the sense that there was no longer any question of real religions but only of religious philosophies. They had no special rites: their adherents could give their own interpretations to any rites that they might adopt. We even see here rising up, particularly in the Hermetic books, a formal condemnation of all rites and of any hopes that one could have in them, except as symbols which themselves became useless as soon as one had learned their secret meaning.[32] As a consequence, the only thing that these sects had in common with real religions, with which they have been too long confused, was that kind of connection which exists between modern theosophy or any other form of occultism and the great religions which they claim to surpass by deciphering their symbols.

We are here confronted with the final development of that which had already been outlined by Plato when he drew his inspiration from the mysteries, as in the *Phaedo*. Their rites and formulas are used only as a kind of language, in a purely mental way. And this language, it must be remembered, had by this time become so trite that it no longer implied something that was necessarily religious. It served as a cloak for any kind of difficult knowledge, whether this was some rhetorical question in Quintilian, or, in Philo, abstruse theories of Stoic physics and the allegorical interpretation of Biblical texts. Even St. Paul in one of the rare, and perhaps only certain instance, in which he makes use of the language of the mysteries says: "I have been initiated (μεμύημαι) on how to be filled and to be hungry, to have abundance and to suffer want."[33]

As a consequence, neither the Hermetic books — or rather the different religious treatises that they include in the midst of much magical and astrological rubbish, like the *Poimandres* or the *Asclepius* — nor the Chaldean oracles should be considered as a source of a theology of the mysteries. There never was such a theology. These writings, in themselves, are only different forms of

---

[32] See the remark of Nock, following Festugière, cited above, p. 76.

[33] *Phillippians* 4:12.

a syncretistic gnosis in which the mysteries are never a major source of inspiration, and often nothing more than a mere medium of expression or means of ornamentation.

The Neo-Orphic or Neo-Pythagorean thiases (the two are hard to distinguish) such as that which must have convened in the basilica near the Porta Maggiore were more theosophical than religious in character, even if the meetings themselves, including the banquet which could have occasioned them, were cloaked in a kind of half ritual. It is only much later that an attempt was made to reanimate these gnoses with concrete religious forms. But this took place only with a late and degenerate Neo-Platonism at the center of the general movement fostered by Julian to restore a dying paganism, and particularly within the theurgy of Iamblichus.[34] But this artificial attempt proved to be quite fruitless. It is, or at least should be, obvious that these late forms which strove to wrestle with Christianity by meeting it on its own ground cannot contribute anything to the explanation of the origins of Christianity.

In addition, it must be stated that it would be equally illusory to seek an antecedent to the Gospels, or even to the faith of the early Church, in either Hermetism or Neo-Platonism. Not only did these schools rise up after the foundation and early organization of Christianity, but they owe much to the influence of first the Jewish, and later the Christian, community at Alexandria, from Philo to Ammonius Saccas. As a consequence, the seed of anything essential in Christianity certainly cannot be found in them. If we look for the sources of whatever resemblances there may be between Hermetism or Neo-Platonism and Christianity, they should be attributed to their common Jewish background, whenever directly Christian influences must be ruled out.[35]

Before passing on to the Christian mystery, it will be useful to assess here, even provisionally, the data which we have thus far collected.

The history of the mystery religions which we have traced throws light on the way religion develops within the total evolu-

[34] See J. Bidez, *La vie de l'empereur Julien* (Paris, 1930). On Iamblichus, see Cumont, *Lux perpetua* (Paris, 1949), pp. 372 ff.

[35] See on this question my *Spiritualité du Nouveau Testament et des Pères,* pp. 318 ff.

tion of a civilization. This is highly instructive and furnishes us with some very practical lessons. From this history it appears that when civilizations make progress mainly along intellectual lines, as was the case with the Greco-Roman civilization, a reaction sets in that is marked by a decline of religion. To state this more precisely, a loss of contact with the living sources of a religious experience seems to go along with this advance in intellectualization.[36] The primitive reaction to the great realities of life and death that are at the source of a religious apprehension of human existence is gradually weakened. Religion does not immediately disappear, but it undergoes a change. The problem of salvation, that is to say, of an end of life to be obtained by an adherence to a transcendent revelation at the heart of human experience, is transformed into a search for an idea: a simple explanation of the world tends to take the place of salvation through religion. The problem of God, if it survives, is no longer that of a vital encounter but the rational solution of a metaphysical puzzle.[37]

In such circumstances, the evolution of the mystery religions betrays that a kind of collective unrest and sentiment of frustration is the inevitable consequence of such a process. Instead of rendering the old religions of no concern, the failure to understand them, unchanged as they are by the ambiguous progress of knowledge in other areas, makes them all the more fascinating. Antiquarianism soon proves to be insufficient. What had been lost will now be sought in highly exotic rites. Nevertheless, it is believed that it can only be found there by artificially imposing upon outmoded or barbarous rituals an interpretation which in reality bears the stamp of a highly cultured mind returning to that which its very culture has made inaccessible. In contrast with what was originally sought in the rites, all that is now asked of them is a quest for a happy immortality, and then a purification which will only be defined in philosophical terms and concepts. In this quest, which those who are engaged in it pursue with an anxiety unknown

[36] See the text of Jung quoted on pp. 47-48.

[37] This devitalizing transposition, which has been a danger at all times, has been remarkably analyzed by the Anglican archbishop, William Temple, in a work written in 1939, which his present successor, Arthur Michael Ramsey, cites and comments upon in *From Gore to Temple* (London, 1960), pp. 160-61.

to their immediate or remote ancestors, there is something more than they can themselves define. Something of that has gone into formulas such as that which the hierophant whispered at an initiation, which may have been that of Attis, though it is not certain: "Take courage, mystai, for the God being saved, you also will be saved from your toils." [38]

We are probably not mistaken in saying that this familiarity with the divine has a new ring to it. It is no longer the naive spontaneity of the primitive, quite naturally absorbed in the epiphanies of the sacred with which his whole life is crossed. And it is no longer the essentially speculative quest of a religious philosopher for whom a higher understanding of life can take the place of this telling experience. It is a *pati divina,* an experiencing of divine things, where again, according to the Aristotelian formula, one longs for experience ($\pi\alpha\vartheta\epsilon\tilde{\iota}\nu$) rather than information ($\mu\alpha\vartheta\epsilon\tilde{\iota}\nu$), but with the keen and painful awareness of those who believed that they had solved the riddle of the universe but are disappointed with their own solution.

A formula such as we have cited is, however, weighed down with further disappointments, which are betrayed by the multiplication of these increasingly involved initiations which are heaped up as if their very number could make up for their inadequacy. Can gods who are so close to man as to be able to have compassion on his miseries really save him if they themselves need to be saved? It can be seen, therefore, how the circle of knowledge substituted for reality, from which one sought to escape, is soon closed again in the pursuit of a salvation based more and more upon gnosis alone, that is to say not in the rites themselves, which do not keep their promises, but in a new interpretation once again substituted for the rites, even though it is the rites themselves which one wishes to explain now.

It is this movement, this religious aspiration, which is the source of Plotinus's flight toward God, so new in Greek philosophy. [39] But what, according to him, is the purification, the conversion which brings us back to God, or more accurately to the One, except a renewed intellectual process substituted for that conquest,

---

[38] Cited by Firmicus Maternus, *De err. prof. rel.* 22.
[39] E. Bréhier must himself recognize it. See *La philosophie de Plotin* (Paris, 1928), p. 102.

or reconquest, of reality that the ever more demanding spirituality of the age had tried to regain?

It is precisely here that we see how the mysteries prepare the way for Christianity. This preparation is not in any way a fore-shadowing of the Christian solution. We can only see it by projecting upon them the outline of what in fact was not to come until later. The preparation is in the new consciousness of a problem to be solved which can no longer be satisfied with the old solutions, and which cannot be eluded again by an intelligence escaping from reality.

With the Socratic interpretation of the Delphic oracle, "Know thyself," the human subject as a thinking subject and as an agent endowed with a moral conscience, both reflexive and critical, must find a place for itself in any religion which it may accept as its own. The pity is that man, in thus conquering himself, seems to have left the divine hands, and the presence of these hands evades him even in the traces they have left in the world which man is trying to reanimate. What man needs is to meet a transcendence which will be more than a mere abstraction. Yet, this transcendence must now meet him in his newborn consciousness, that of a mortal and sinful being. It is in this way that Christianity will come to him.

The Christian mystery, when we find its first expression in St. Paul, appears in complete opposition to the other mysteries contemporary to it. This opposition has not always been clearly seen.[40] As we have insisted before, the other mysteries have nothing mysterious but their rites. The meaning which could be ascribed to these rites was certainly not at all mysterious. Anyone who so desired could argue about it since it never really belonged to the rites but was imposed upon them. Or, when the terminology of the mysteries comes to be applied to that meaning itself, we are no longer within the compass of these religions but have entered into Gnostic occultism which took nothing from them except their language and images.

On the contrary, the Christian mystery, when it makes its first appearance, is not at all a secret rite. Nor is it an idea unveiled for

---

[40] It is to D. Deden, "Le 'mystère' paulinien," a study which appeared in the *Ephemerides Theologicae Lovanienses,* XIII (1936), that the credit for having been the first to establish it with full clarity must be given.

an elite, but a design of God inaccessible to any creature as long
as God Himself has not revealed it to the world and its powers. It
is a fact, an historical event, in which human history reaches its
summit. It is a unique fact in which God Himself takes that history
back into His hands while He Himself descends into it.

There is in the beginning no connection between the Christian
mystery and a ritual initiation whose beneficiaries keep it to themselves. Nor is it any philosophico-religious esoterism. Its first mention, in St. Paul's First Epistle to the Corinthians, has reference to
the preaching of the Gospel, seen as the announcement which
must be made to the world of that which God has kept hidden for
all mankind. The wisest of men and the angels themselves have not
had access to it. It is the eternal will of God which is discovered in
this mystery, when God comes to judge, the time has come for
the entrance of His Son into the world, bringing to every man
His definitive Word by realizing it in Himself.[41]

It is not in relation to any ritual, not even to the ritual of the
temple or the synagogue, that the Christian mystery is to be defined. But this mystery is what will introduce a fully new meaning
into these rites themselves, which it will keep while transforming
them. It has, however, known some providential preparations, and
even some that were inspired. They are to be found in the apoca-
lyptic trends of Judaism, that is to say, in that phase of Judaism
already prepared for a purely supernatural intervention. The
apocalypse in turn had come from wisdom, but from a wisdom
that had been transformed in Israel by the coming to it of the
divine Spirit, of the breath of the living word of God.

To understand this transcendent newness, we must look into its
antecedents.

Wisdom is a typical phenomenon of the whole Mediterranean
civilization at the time of its highest development. It is like a nebula
from which were to come the Greek philosophies as well as the
last developments of the divine Word in Israel.[42] For wisdom is
actually the most characteristic product of every civilization. It is
an art of living based on experience, and, above all, a tradition of
experience criticized by rational reflection. It is in this that wisdom

---

[41] *I Corinthians* 1:17-2:16.

[42] The best study is still that of H. Duesberg, *Les Scribes inspirés*, 2 vols.
(Paris, 1938-39).

is opposed to the intuitive spontaneity of primitive man. Wisdom is a work of the leaders who first organized the human city. It will be fixed by the "king's men" as these leaders have been called — these ancestors of our officials who will extend and secure the royal authority in the first great sedentary monarchies which were to succeed the tribal authorities.

Assyria and Egypt will be the principal sites where wisdom will be put down in writing, at the end of an evolution which started with the first leaders who laid the foundations for the Mediterranean civilizations by outlining, through the expansion and stabilization of their own authority, the passage from a nomadic to a sedentary mode of life. This explains why wisdom, with the royalty which it upholds, will not in the beginning be looked upon favorably by the prophets of Israel. For this people, for whom Yahweh is King by His word, to seek wisdom will seem to be an abandonment of this word, just as to seek for a king is to deny God.[43]

Isaias will say: "I will destroy the wisdom of the wise, and the prudence of the prudent I will reject."[44] However, just as Samuel, under divine inspiration, had finally consecrated a king by making of him the anointed of Yahweh, so wisdom along with kingship will be naturalized in Israel. But it will be with the essential reservation that "the fear of the Lord (Yahweh) is the beginning of wisdom."[45]

This does not mean that wisdom had not been religious from the first. Far from it. But the religion with which it had been saturated from its birth had been that ambiguous religion whose teachers and priests were the first kings — who tended also to become its gods. It was a religion tending to magic, in which man imagines he can dominate the world by using the rites to chain the divine powers for his own designs. The vision of the Messias-King will be opposed to this kind of kingship in Israel. For he is only the anointed of the Lord, and his own will tends to disappear before God's will, and his reign before God's reign. In the same way, for that earthly wisdom, either skeptical or superstitious, will be substituted the wisdom of which the divine teachings will be the soul. But wisdom will not on that account cease to be nurtured by ex-

[43] *I Samuel* 8.
[44] *Isaias* 29:14 (which will be cited in *I Corinthians* 1:19).
[45] *Proverbs* 1:7.

perience and rational tradition. But the basis for its judgments will no longer be human intelligence tending towards its own autonomy but the intelligence of inspired wise men, who clarify the experiences of the ancients, as well as their own reasonings, by the light of the Torah of Yahweh.

Thus the wisdom of Israel will be ever more and more saturated with the divine Word to the point that Ecclesiasticus will be able to identify them. After describing wisdom he will say: "All these things are the book of the alliance of the God most high, the law that Moses has given as their inheritance to the assemblies of Jacob." [46]

Did he not say of wisdom itself shortly before this, "I am come out of the mouth of the Most High"? [47]

It is true that the deacon Stephen in accordance with rabbinic tradition will say on the other hand that Moses had been instructed in all the wisdom of the Egyptians. For the divine Word is as well able to seize upon the civilized man enjoying the riches of Egypt, as upon the primitive man in his poverty. [48]

In this way we understand how wisdom, for a pious king, will come to appear as a gift of God, as his gift *par excellence* which has to be obtained through prayer. It is thus that Solomon will appear in Israel as the perfect wise man in spite of his fault, which is a permanent reminder to a just Israelite of the dangers of wisdom as well as of kingship. [49]

In effect, the Davidic kingship will come to its end by succumbing to the temptation of idolatry. But wisdom, far from disappearing, will only relinquish what it had kept until then of the earth. Just as God will be revealed in the trial of exile as the only king, not only of Israel but of the world, and of the powers which rule the world through successive kings, so it will be seen that He is also the only Sage. Wisdom, then, as we see in the eighth chapter of Proverbs, will be the divine design, the supernatural design, in virtue of which God had created the world and which He will fulfill in spite of anything in human or cosmic history. It is in this way that wisdom, paradoxical as is this term of its evolution, will come to flow into the apocalypse, the revelation.

[46] *Ecclesiasticus* 24:32.
[47] 24:3.
[48] *Acts* 7:22.
[49] *I Kings* 3:4-15, 4:9-14.

We come across the actual transition from one to the other in the book of Daniel.[50] Daniel is presented to us as a wise Jew, the ideal wise man even more than Solomon. He is however only a pious youth, fearlessly faithful to Yahweh, transplanted to the court of the all-powerful king of Babylon. But it is he alone who will be able to solve the riddles against which the proud wisdom of this latter comes to stumble. Daniel will take great care to point out that he does this only through an inspiration of the Most High. It is He alone, indeed, who holds in His hand the *kairoi,* that is the key to the decisive events of history, not only because He alone knew them beforehand but because it is He who determines them as King of Ages. And He *reveals* their mystery to whom He wills (this is precisely the meaning of the word apocalypse), not through any wisdom which His elect would possess as their own, but by His sole grace.

We are here at the exact source of the mystery of St. Paul as it is to appear in the First Epistle to the Corinthians. The whole literary context of this mystery is the same as in the second chapter of Daniel. The mystery there likewise appears as the secret of divine wisdom, queen of human and cosmic history, which God alone reveals when He wishes, to whom He wishes, thus confounding the wisdom of the wise and the intelligence of the intelligent.

But this mystery, for the first time, discovers its full dimensions. It is not a fragmentary or transitory aspect of it that is to be revealed. The hour has come for the revelation of its center and its all.

But we speak the wisdom of God, mysterious, hidden, which God foreordained before the world unto our glory, a wisdom which none of the rulers of this world has known; for had they known it, they would never have crucified the Lord of glory. But, as it is written, "Eye has not seen nor ear heard, nor has it entered into the heart of man, what things God has prepared for those who love him." But to us God has revealed them through His Spirit. For the Spirit searches all things, even the deep things of God.[51]

[50] *Daniel* 2.
[51] *I Corinthians* 2:7-10.

That σοφία ἐν μυστηρίῳ — wisdom in mystery — is Christ. It is the event of Christ given to the world, as the revealer and accomplisher of God's designs. As Paul described it a few lines above,

> For the word of the cross is foolishness to those who perish, but to those who are saved, that is, to us, it is the power of God. For it is written, "I will destroy the wisdom of the wise, and the prudence of the prudent I will reject." Where is the "wise man"? Where is the scribe? Where is the disputant of this world? Has not God turned to foolishness the "wisdom" of this world? For since, in God's wisdom, the world did not come to know God by "wisdom," it pleased God, by the foolishness of our preaching, to save those who believe. For the Jews ask for signs, and the Greeks look for "wisdom"; but we, for our part, preach a crucified Christ — to the Jews indeed a stumbling-block and to the Gentiles foolishness, but to those who are called, both Jews and Greeks, Christ, the power of God and the wisdom of God.[52]

The mystery, the great secret of wisdom, in which the depths of God are revealed, is therefore Christ. It is not only what He has said, but what He has done, and above all His Cross, His Cross seen in the full perspective of His resurrection, together with the communication of the Spirit and the building of the Church, His body, in which men are reconciled among themselves at the same time as they are with the Father. It is what the captivity epistles will develop and deepen.

In the Epistle to the Colossians, Paul identifies with the fulfillment of the word of God "the mystery which has been hidden for ages and generations, but now is clearly shown to His saints. To them God willed to make known how rich in glory is this mystery among the Gentiles — Christ in you, your hope of glory!" [53]

This is obviously what the Apostle meant to describe earlier in the same Epistle when he said: "It has pleased God the Father that in Him (Christ) all His fullness should dwell, and that through Him he should reconcile to Himself all things, whether on the earth or in the heavens, making peace through the blood of His Cross." [54]

[52] *I Corinthians* 1:18-24.
[53] *Colossians* 1:26-7.
[54] 1:19-20.

And, again, this is what he will later expand when he says that "all the treasures of wisdom and of knowledge are hidden in Him," [55] before finally saying:

When you were dead by reason of your sins and the uncircumcision of your flesh, He brought you to life along with Him, forgiving you all your sins, cancelling the decree against us, which was hostile to us. Indeed, He has taken it completely away, nailing it to the Cross. Disarming the Principalities and Powers, He displayed them openly, leading them away in triumph by force of it. [56]

These texts leave no doubt about either the significance of the Christian mystery or the intellectual world in which it is to be found. It does not proceed from the mystery religions but springs from what is most original in Judaism. It is not one of the ancient rituals where we can see the birth of the great myths which are behind all the natural religions, nor again is it an explanation of these rituals along the line of Greek philosophical speculation, if only as a reaction to it.

It is an event unique in human history, when the word, itself without an analogue, opened a way through the sacred history of Israel and broke once and for all the network of the universe closed upon itself. What is this event if not the taking again of the creature into the hands of the creator? This is why the great event of Christ and His Cross is presented to us as the entrance of the divine king into His kingship, who reduces to nothing all the usurped kingships. Such is the meaning of His victory over the powers who crucified Him, and who, as St. Paul tells us, would not have done so if they had known that they were thus consummating their own eviction. These powers are not simply the earthly powers of the kings and the priests, of the Roman empire represented by Pilate and the Aaronic priesthood by Annas and Caiphas. Behind these visible possessors of authority, ἐξουσία, are the invisible powers of the demonic kingdom to whom the world was enslaved after the fall of the angels and of man himself after them. For a hierarchized economy in a cosmos ruled by spirits who should have been the first servants of God is substituted a new economy in which man is made free from the bondage

[55] 2:3.
[56] 2:13-15.

of sin and the natural world. The divine power of Christ now acts immediately in man and for man, thus associating him with the divine kingship reconquered on the fallen cosmos.[57]

This explains how St. Paul sees the cross as a liberation not only from sin and idolatry but also from the Mosaic law.[58] For the law, according to an opinion of the Rabbis which has some foundation in the Bible itself, had been revealed "by the ministry of the angels," as St. Paul says in his Epistle to the Galatians; and the same may also be found in Stephen's speech as recorded in the Acts of the Apostles, and in the Epistle to the Hebrews.[59] In contrast to the ambiguous words of the oracles, the word of the Old Testament thus appears as the word of the faithful angels in which an authentic echo of the divine word can be heard. But this divine word has made itself heard to us in Christ. In the cross of Christ it is not simply the angel of the Lord that has intervened in His name to save His people, but the Lord Himself has come down to them to lift them up unto Himself. From this comes the whole significance for us of the glorification, through the Cross, of the Word made flesh, as found in St. John,[60] and of the ascension of the one who was crucified and rose again now entering the heavenly places to meet the Father, as we see in the Epistle of the Hebrews where He is represented as our precursor.[61] The only-begotten Son, through His effective condescension, through His redemptive incarnation in the flesh of sin, will thus make us all sons in Him through the Spirit, that is to say, sons of the heavenly Father.[62]

When these "depths of God,"[63] as St. Paul says, have been revealed, we see how the mystery of His will, that is, His design for us and the world, was to discover for us, and to give us to, God Himself.[64] It is not only with His work that God associates us in the fulfillment and the plenitude of the mystery. It is with His own interior life, with Himself. We are therefore His adopted sons and,

---

[57] See in "The Two Economies of Divine Government: Satan and Christ," cited on p. 113, pp. 471 ff.

[58] *Ibid.*

[59] *Acts* 7:38 and 53; *Galatians* 3:19; *Hebrews* 2:2.

[60] *John* 3:13-16; 8:28; 12:32-3.

[61] *Hebrews* 6:20.

[62] *Romans* 8:14-17; *Galatians* 4:4-7; *I John* 3:1.

[63] *I Corinthians* 2:10.

[64] *Ephesians* 1:9.

as St. John will say, "Behold what manner of charity the Father has bestowed upon us, that we should be called, and should be the sons of God." [65]

The Christian mystery is neither an ancient rite, nor the interpretation of an ancient rite: it is only the revelation of a divine design. In that revelation our history is recapitulated short of sin and consummated in the very life of God.

Nevertheless, the Christian mystery will find in its turn a ritual expression. It will take up again and recast the ancient material of the natural rites that Judaism had already purified and transfigured. It will do this by bringing to fulfillment their "historization." It means that their primitive, cosmic meaning will have been absorbed into the final meaning of sacred history.

Christ expressed the divine meaning of His cross at the Last Supper by changing bread and wine into His body and blood. Through the shedding of His blood, He has substituted His death for the sacrifices of the Old Testament. And as St. Paul says, every time we celebrate this renewed Eucharist as a memorial of Him, "We proclaim the death of the Lord, until he comes." [66]

Therefore, among the first Fathers of the Church will be found some apparently contradictory statements concerning the sacrifice of the Christians. [67] Some of them will say, especially in their apologies addressed to the pagans: "We have no sacrifices," meaning by this that we have no bloody sacrifices, the only ones known either to the pagans or to Leviticus. And they will take up again, like St. Paul, the philosophical formulas used in the Hermetic and Gnostic writings for the "logical sacrifice," meaning by this the offering of oneself to the divine will in a life according to reason. Thus they will seem to identify the evolution of Jewish and Christian wisdom with that of the pagans in Greek rationalism. And this will accompany their description of Christianity as the true philosophy.

We have here, however, only one side of a picture, the other being no less important. What the Fathers borrowed from pagan philosophers in their criticism of sacrifices and of ritualistic religion, is only a negative side — the incapacity of any ritual to

[65] *I John* 3:1.

[66] *I Corinthians* 9:26.

[67] See my *Spiritualité du Nouveau Testament et des Pères*, pp. 272 ff.

sanctify a man as long as his thinking personality, his moral conscience, and finally his whole life, is not embraced by his religion. But to this first view of Christianity we must always add the other, which is the one the Fathers describe not for the Greeks but for the Jews. The same Fathers who portray Christianity as a true philosophy because it has no other ritual than rational worship describe it also as the "pure offering" which was to be offered everywhere according to the well-known prophecy of Malachias.[68] The full meaning of this new affirmation can be understood only when we see it explained, as, for example, in St. Justin's *Dialogue with Trypho*.[69] The apologist takes his start with the explanation of the contemporary rabbis, who held that this pure offering, to be offered everywhere, was constituted by the *berakoth*, that is to say, by the blessings or eucharists which the pious Jews in the diaspora pronounced everywhere, exercising in this way their function of "a holy nation, an elect race, a kingly priesthood." But following the teaching found in the Epistle of St. Peter,[70] St. Justin now applies to the Christians and their Eucharist the formula taken from Exodus to express the fact that the whole people of God is to be a priestly people. The Christians, he says, taken from the pagan nations themselves, were the only ones to realize the prophecy to the letter. Their sacrifice is that sacrifice of pure lips mentioned by the prophet Isaias, that is to say, the sacrifice in which is fulfilled the design of God to impose His name upon man and upon the whole world. But the Christian Eucharist is such only because it contains in a mysterious way the oblation of Himself that Christ has made to His Father in the Last Supper and brought to consummation on the Cross.[71]

The description of Christianity as the true philosophy and at the same time the fulfillment of the true Israel opens the way to later assimilations. These will occur when the formulas and images borrowed from pagan mysteries are applied to the Christian sacraments.[72]

[68] *Malachias* 1:10-12.

[69] *Dialogue* 117 (P.G., t., 6, col. 746 BC).

[70] *I Peter*, 2:9; citing *Exodus*, 19:5-6.

[71] Cf. Irenaeus, *Adv. Haereses* 5.2, 2nd ed. (Harvey), II, 319-21.

[72] See Hugo Rahner, *op. cit.*,* pp. 37 ff. and my study "Mysterion," first appeared in the *Supplement de la Vie Spirituelle*, XXIII (1952) and republished in English, in *Mystery and Mysticism* (London, 1956).

With Clement and Origen, following a line first traced by Philo the Jew, the terms used in the mysteries will be transferred not to the Christian ritual but to the Gospel teaching. More in particular, Clement of Alexandria will use the language of the mysteries to interpret Scripture as referring entirely to Christ. He will gain support for this from the use which St. Paul himself made of the word "mystery" in order to indicate that Jesus and His Cross are what gives the divine word its full meaning. Thus, at Alexandria, the mystery into which we must be initiated to find there the saving illumination, will be a reading of Sacred Scripture in the light of Christian tradition, which discovers Christ for us there as the "Spirit" to whom the "Letter" leads.

It is only later, when the Christian faith has been so fully expressed that it can no longer be influenced by paganism, that we shall see parallels being drawn between the adhesion to Christ in baptism and the initiations of the pagan mysteries. But this will only be in the fourth century, when paganism, under the influence of Julian the Apostate, will tend to model itself on Christianity and not the opposite. Then, for the first time, baptism will be described as a kind of ritual mystery. We find one of the first examples of this in St. Basil's treatise *On the Holy Spirit*.[73] A little later, St. Cyril of Jerusalem will be the first to describe his instructions to the Christian neophytes as being "mystagogical" catecheses.[74]

Much later, the *Mystagogia* of St. Maximus,[75] directly inspired by Pseudo-Dyonysius, will be an explanation of the Eucharistic liturgy itself.[76]

Then also a wide use will be made within the Church of a whole body of material that had now become innocuous: secondary symbols, like white vestments, lamps, incense, and so forth, which had been sparingly used before because they were so common in the pagan mysteries.[77] But this is no more than a mantle

---

[73] *De Spiritu Sancto* 27.66 (*Patrologia Graeca* 32:188).

[74] *Patrologia Graeca* 30:332 ff.

[75] *Patrologia Graeca* 92:657 ff.

[76] See my study of him in *Spiritualité du Nouveau Testament et des Pères*, pp. 473 ff.

[77] The restrictive decisions of the Council of Elvira are the last we know in this respect.

for the Christian faith and has nothing to do with the creative elaboration of the Catholic ritual itself.

Nor should we forget that the Greek Fathers who showed themselves to be the most liberal in the acceptance of this material were at the same time those who were most severe toward Hellenistic paganism. No one has been more critical of the ritual and myths of paganism and their Gnostic interpretations than Clement of Alexandria, despite the fact that no one has been more liberal than he in making use of their images.[78] If the Fathers admitted that the Christian mystery could take to itself something of the literary imagery of the pagan mysteries, it is because they saw in Christianity the fulfillment of the obscure desires and latent aspirations which the very popularity of the mysteries betrayed, but which neither natural religion nor philosophical criticism had been able to satisfy. Yet no one more than these men, who have been so lightly accused of Hellenizing Christianity, has ever been so conscious of the fact that the non-Christian mysteries could never have procured or determined the fulfillment of these desires and aspirations.

[78] His *Protrepticus* passes without stopping from evocation to criticism.

CHAPTER IX

Sacred Space

W HAT WE HAVE discussed thus far has kept us at the center of the liturgical function. But if we should stop here, our study would remain somewhat abstract. The liturgy of the Church, like that of every other ritual, is a concrete action that is unfolded in a definite place and at a given time. We must see it as it is actually carried out to interpret it as a truly living reality and be able to distinguish clearly what it shares with other rituals as well as what marks it as distinct from them.

Accordingly, we must now undertake a discussion of the sacred place, the Christian church, and see more intimately what goes on within it. But we should begin by asking ourselves the precise meaning of the consecration of a particular space, first in the natural religions and then in Judaism. It is necessary to point out the different ways in which man's religious consciousness becomes aware of the special consecration of a definite space. We may here distinguish three of them which are more or less successive.

In the beginning, it is not space as such that appears to be sacred, for the simple reason that as yet there is no notion of space. The sacredness of a given place, therefore, first comes from the special presence of the sacred recognized in it. Here we encounter the influence of the different fundamental hierophanies already described.[1]

---

[1] On sacred space in general, see G. van der Leeuw, *Religion in Essence and Manifestations,* pp. 393 ff., and Mircea Eliade, *Patterns in Comparative Religion,* pp. 369 ff.

The mountain is a sacred place *par excellence,* quite simply because it is the closest place on earth to heaven.[2] The fact that man cannot live there, the solitude and silence which surrounds it, and the absence, at least relative, of animal and even vegetable life, heightens this character. The frequent presence of clouds, and especially of lightning, seems particularly theophanic. The importance of Horeb-Sinai for the religious consciousness of Israel is typical of this.

In more advanced civilizations, this motif continues to survive, especially in the domes, and still more in the steeples, of our churches, or quite simply in the rising thrust of their arches, or even of a whole style such as that of English Perpendicular Gothic. Earlier than this, it was the same more or less clearly conscious inspiration which had moved the architects of the Babylonian ziggurats (the prototypes of the Tower of Babel), the pyramids of Egypt, the temples of Angkor, and the remarkable Mayan buildings in pre-Columbian America.

Just as there is a profound relationship between the sacredness of the tree and that of the mountain, the forest enjoys a role like that of the latter in specifying a sacred place.[3] But here chthonic themes are doubtlessly already joined with heavenly ones: life emerges from the earth, even if it is true that it is directed toward the light of the sun. This is what lies behind the often disturbing ambiguities of the forest. It is regarded as the meeting place of similarly, if not equally, sacred forces, and even as their battle-field. It is into the forests that the more or less mythical St. Georges, the messengers of light, are called to meet and conquer the dark dragons formed from the fires hidden within the bowels of the earth.

The theme also survives in the sacred wood, which was first itself the sanctuary and for a long time continued to enclose the temples made by the hands of men. The survival, and even the

[2] On the sacred mountain in general, see Mircea Eliade, *op. cit.,* pp. 100 ff., 375 ff. On Sinai-Horeb, see Paul Marie de la Croix, O.C.D., "Hauts-lieux élianiques," in *Élie le Prophète,* I (Paris, 1956), 23 ff.

[3] On the symbolism of the tree, see Mircea Eliade, *op. cit.,* pp. 271 ff. On the linking of the sacred tree and ascensional themes see, M. Eliade, *Mythes, rêves, et mystères,* pp. 80 ff., 133 ff. The ambiguity of the forest symbolism has been well brought out by Marcel Brion, in the chapter devoted to this subject in his book, *L'art fantastique* (Paris,. 1961).

possible resurgence of primitive themes, may be seen admirably
suggested in the *Oedipus at Colonus* of the highly cultured Sopho-
cles.[4] With good reason a survival of this theme of the sacred wood
has been found in the countless pillars and semi-darkness of
Gothic churches. Further removed in its outward shape, but more
closely connected with the prelogical or metalogical mentality, is
the *achera,* the sacred stake of the Canaanite sanctuaries, which
symbolically represented the ancestral forest in the midst of urban
life.[5] The oaks of Mambre, under which Abraham experienced
what is perhaps the most telling theophany reported in Genesis,[6]
like those of Dodona, betray the persistence of this sylvan sacredness even in the most evolved religions.

With the chthonic hierophanies is immediately associated the
grotto.[7] Here again its survivals are legion. We need but recall the
Cave of the Nativity, the sanctuary of St. Michael on Mount Gar-
gan, and the Grotto of Lourdes. With the grotto is easily connected
the spring, just as the sacrality of earth is connected with that of
water. This is still attested by the pre-Christian sanctuary of
Chartres, with the connection it has maintained between the "well
of the holy and sacred places" and the chapel dedicated to the
virgo paritura (the virgin that shall bear a child) "of the under-
world." Modern psychologists have rightly insisted upon the relationship of this sacredness of grotto and spring with a longing for
the Maternal Womb, for Mother Earth and the maternal waters.

Sanctuaries built with a cupola are a refined development of
this sacredness of primitive caves. Their cosmic meaning is often
indicated by the paintings that cover them. Byzantine symbolism
naturally introduced there the figure of Christ Pantocrator as Lord
of the powers. The way in which old ideas tainted with magic can
rise up again may be seen in the dome representing the vault of
heaven which Chosroes ordered built to shelter his own throne,
next to the true Cross which he placed in its center after taking
it from the Christians.

But with these examples we pass, almost without noticing it,
from the first concept of a sacred place, which is defined by par-

[4] Particularly at the beginning and at the end.
[5] See Adolphe Lods, *Israel,* pp. 87 ff.
[6] *Genesis* 18.
[7] See M. Eliade, *op. cit.,* pp. 244 ff.

ticularly numinous natural objects found there, to a second concept of it. Here it is actually the place itself which becomes sacred, either because of its shape, or its orientation in space, or simply its location, prescinding from anything found or not found in it. We thus obviously touch here upon secondary motives for the sacred, since they presuppose a knowledge of the distinction between space and that which it encloses.

We know that the decisive factor in the choice of Fleury-sur-Loire as the sacred place of the Druids, long before it became the tomb, real or imaginary, of St. Benedict, was its location at the center of Gaul,[8] just as its site in the great forest at the height of the bend in the Loire retains its connection with the most primitive themes. Similarly, at Delphi, the location of the omphalus as the center of the universe soon enjoyed a role no less important than that of the fissure from which could have risen telluric fumes intoxicating the Pythia.[9] These navels of the "mother land," or even of "Mother Earth," are everywhere of great importance, either the stone of the *mundus* at Rome,[10] or Jerusalem, still considered in the Middle Ages as the center of the world,[11] or the altar of heaven on which the emperors sacrificed once a year at Pekin, located not only at the center of their empire but also of the cosmos.[12]

But the center is not the only significant site: there are others, determined by astronomical considerations. This was the case with the sanctuary of the Cathari at Montségur, determined, as is said, by the spot in a circle of mountains struck by the rising sun at the time of the equinox. A later development was the deliberate creation of such sites as Carnac and Stonehenge by the arrangement of upright stones which indicated, by the shadows cast on a determined day, the place for sacrifice.[13]

[8] Caesar, *De bello gallico* 6.13.

[9] See Marie Delcourt, *L'oracle de Delphes,* pp. 146 ff. Also Eliade, *op. cit.,* pp. 231 ff. Cf. Pausanias, *Description of Greece* 10.16.2.

[10] See Eliade, *ibid.;* cf. Varro, cited by Macrobius, *Saturnalia* 1.16.18.

[11] On the entire significance of this theme of the center, see Eliade, *op. cit.,* pp. 380 ff.

[12] See Marcel Granet, *La pensée chinoise* (Paris, 1934), p. 93.

[13] See Louis Hautecoeur, *Mystique et architecture: Symbolisme du cercle et de la coupole* (Paris, 1954), pp. 155-156.

We may thus pass on from the site of a sanctuary to its orientation. In all the solar cults, like those of the Iranians, this will obviously be of primary importance. And we should note here how it is maintained, or rather given a new meaning, with the orientation of Christian churches, altars, and even tombs, but we will have to return to this later at some length.[14]

We advance further in our understanding of sacred space when, after noting its site and orientation, we consider the shape of the sacred place. In this way, every place can become sacred, provided it has a shape that can be taken as a cosmic image. This explains the importance of circular, octagonal, and even spherical shapes, such as have been carefully studied by Louis Hautecoeur.[15] The motif is undoubtedly already present in the Canaanite gilgal, that is, a circular alignment of upright stones.[16] It soon gained dominance over the purely chthonic motif in sanctuaries with cupolas inspired by caves and grottoes. Man there received the impression that he was being given a kind of summary of the world, where all its sacredness was found concentrated through some mysterious sympathy. Something of this persisted in the decoration of medieval cathedrals in the West, and still more in Byzantine churches, where the symbolic figures prove the desire to consecrate a miniature universe. The theme was explicitly developed in the *Mystagogia* of St. Maximus and the *Church History* (understood in the sense of a description of the church) attributed to St. Germanus of Constantinople.[17]

Just as important as the shape of a sacred site or building can be its measurements. Since it is impossible to determine these exactly for the Great Pyramid because of the erosion of the sands, the cosmic meaning of its dimensions will doubtless remain an object of endless dispute.[18] But there can be no doubt that all kinds of golden numbers played a great part in the construction of Greek temples and many other sanctuaries. And the meaning of these numbers was doubtlessly mystical and magical long before it became aesthetic. What men sought was a building in tune with the

[14] See below, pp. 169 ff.
[15] See note 13.
[16] See Adolphe Lods, *Israel*, pp. 42 and 94.
[17] *Patrologia Graeca*, 91:657 ff.; 98:384 ff.
[18] See C. W. Ceram, *Gods, Graves, and Scholars*, trans. E. B. Garside (New York, 1953),* pp. 148-149.

rhythms of the universe, and which was as a consequence a kind of resonator of the sacred.[19]

The determination of a sacred place, however, may be due to something completely different from these scientific, or pseudo-scientific, factors, namely, to some happening or event that is taken as a divine manifestation.[20] This is the case with all the sites that have been favored by an apparition, whether it be the temple of Castor and Pollux in the Roman forum or the shrines that have been built in modern times to the Virgin at Lourdes and Fatima. The localization of sacred objects, certain meteorites in particular, like the Black Stone of Pessinus, may be associated with such apparitions, though this brings us back to the first category of sacred sites. But it is not so when emphasis is placed on the humanization of the sacred as happens in the case of the tombs of saintly individuals, and more generally in the case of buildings erected to their memory, such as the Christian *martyria* and the Moslem marabouts. As we shall see, every specifically Jewish or Christian consecration of space springs ultimately from the accomplishment of the saving event or events.

In addition to these two ways of conceiving sacred space there is a third, which attributes the sacredness of a site to the act of consecration by a human agent. Here also must be mentioned the sacredness of the hearth, whether this belongs to the family or to the city, as in the case of the temple of Vesta. The making of fire is a typical human activity, as everyone knows, even though fire itself is regarded as one of the most striking hierophanies. From this it follows that man soon finds in the building and maintaining of a hearth a means of localizing the sacred that is dependent on his own will and which can even share in his own mobility.[21]

Nevertheless, the production of a sacred place at one's own pleasure is more readily attached to other rites. Romulus, who fixed the site of Rome, the sacred *pomerium,* by tracing a circular furrow with his plow, provides us with a particularly interesting example. But the question may be asked: Was not the rite which we regard as consecrating a sacred place originally desecratory?

[19] See P. M. Schuhl, *Platon et l'art de son temps,* 2nd ed. (Paris, 1952).

[20] See G. van der Leeuw, *Religion in Essence and Manifestation,* pp. 52 ff.

[21] See M. Eliade, *op. cit.,* pp. 372 ff.

In other words, when a man traced a boundary, did he intend to establish within it the sacred which had not been there before, or, on the contrary, did he intend to exclude it more or less completely from the area which he was reserving to himself?

We are here confronted with a question which we have already posed: Was there originally any consecratory rites properly speaking? Or rather were not these rites originally apotropaic, and only later considered to be consecratory? Actually, as long as man believes anything to be really sacred, it seems contradictory that he could think of producing it. The most he would attempt to do would be to try to rid himself of the fear he felt of it. When it seems to us that he is consecrating something that was not sacred, it is more likely that he is actually trying to preserve from a sacredness that worries him something that he would like to make his own. Only later, at a time when he has exchanged these longings for freedom for a bold practice of magic does man, by means of his rites, want to shut up the sacred in an enclosure where he will have it at his disposal.

As a matter of fact, to return to Romulus, it seems that the reason for the *pomerium* was at least as much the wish to keep out of the city the gods that were not wanted there as to keep in those with whom an alliance was desired. The Field of Mars will get its name from the deliberate installation of the god of war *extra muros,* outside the walls of the city. And we find a parallel to this at Athens in the Areopagus.

On closer examination, this ambiguity is found in all sacred and magical circles which, under certain conditions, must be traced in the ritual consecration of a definite space.[22] The circles with which magicians surround themselves for their operations, and which are still found in the pentagram of the Dr. Faust study, are intended to place the operator outside the influence of possible counterattacks from the forces he is attempting to constrain. This sense of magical protection seems to be behind the famous *rotae* of the old St. Peter's on the Vatican. These were two circles on the pavement which defined the respective places of pope and emperor. Later these circles were taken as a symbol of the universe and of the

[22] Jung has studied the significance of the circle with respect to the Tibetan *mandala* in a particularly interesting fashion. See *The Integration of Personality*, pp. 127 ff.

Church, over which the prince and the pontiff, like angels of the Church and of the people, extend their power, as is still the case with the carpet embroidered with an eagle thrown under the feet of a Byzantine bishop when he pontificates. The circle marked with the signs of the zodiac under the feet of the figure of Wisdom in the iconography of Novgorod represents the idea of a cosmic reign mirrored on a symbolic microcosm. This seems to be the most re-fined sense that the consecration of any enclosed space, or any circular temple, can assume.

The ritual of the absolution of the dead furnishes us with one of the most curious examples of the ambiguity of a consecration by the drawing of a circle.[23] Today we interpret the triple circle des-cribed about the coffin by the lit candles, the sprinkling of holy water, and the incensation as an expression of our prayer for the deceased that he may enter into "the place of refreshment, of light, and of peace." But such symbolism is neither natural nor primitive. It is rather a Christian interpretation which has been superimposed on a rite found among most primitive peoples, and which must have been adopted with other elements in the funeral ceremonies at a time when paganism had lost its vitality and these rites had ceased to be offensive. But the primary meaning of this triple circle was certainly apotropaic: care was taken to erect a triple barrier about the corpse so that the soul, forced to renounce its stay in its familiar haunts, which could be distressing to the living, is con-strained to quit the earth.

In connection with the liturgy of the consecration of churches, we shall return to the meaning given to the perambulatory rites of consecration in Christianity. But we have already said enough to explain the instinctive aversion of the Hebrew prophets for any attempt to introduce a temple into Israel, that is to say, a space permanently consecrated to God and finding its concrete expres-sion in a cult-edifice more or less like that of the Canaanites. The basic idea which they saw behind such a building was an idolatrous and magical attempt to lay hands on the sacred. The Canaanite Baalim caught in the ritual prison of such a sanctuary appeared to be gods that man had incorporated into his own city. They seemed to be reduced to nothing more than a docile means for furthering

---

[23] See H. R. Philippeau, "Origine et évolution des rites funéraires" in *Le mystère de la mort et sa célébration* (Paris, 1951).

any kind of human activity in return for a cult where no bargaining
was made with the fat of victims, the smoke of incense, or extended prayers, but where extravagant praise concealed demands
that were thought to be infallible.[24]

Here again, however, just as in the case of the acceptance of
kingly rule and wisdom, the prophets finally had to consecrate
what they had been unable to proscribe. But nothing is more interesting than to see how the prophetic mentality transformed its
meaning and import. Here we touch upon the decisive metamorphosis of natural sacredness which was to prepare the way for its
final adoption by the Gospel.

In opposition to the temple of stones in which man believed that
he had confined his God, the prophets set up the tabernacle, that
is to say, the mobile tent where God in the desert freely dwelt with
His people, but as a traveler, always retaining His freedom to
leave, and never belonging to the land through which He was
passing.[25] In fact, the temple at Jerusalem was later distinguished
from the Canaanite temple by the retention of a number of features
of the nomadic tent in the fixed structure. These are not always
easily discernible, for the descriptions which we have of the Mosaic
tent were only put in final form at a late date and contain certain
anachronisms borrowed from the temple itself. In other words,
many details which could hardly have been found in a mobile tabernacle are projected into the past. But these literary contamina-
tions that have crept into the descriptions of the tabernacle from
the temple cannot obscure the essential features of the former.[26]

The question of temple or tabernacle, however, was only symbolically important. The prophets aligned themselves with the opposition to a temple for the very purpose of contrasting the divine
liberty with the fixation, the incorporation of gods who dwelt in
"a house built by the hands of men" into the city of men. This
does not mean that they did not know that other gods than Yah-

[24] See *II Samuel* 7.

[25] *Ibid.*, 7:6.

[26] See Yves M. J. Congar, *The Mystery of the Temple,* trans. R. F.
Trevett (Westminster, Md., 1962),* pp. 49 ff., for the whole theology of
the Temple; for its archaeology, see André Parrot, *The Temple of Jerusalem,* trans. B. E. Hooke (New York, 1955).

weh had been served under a tent, like that of the Sakkout, for which the Israelites had been blamed by Amos.[27]

The decisive element, here as elsewhere, is not the acceptance or rejection of any ritualistic detail but the economy of the whole, which, as we shall see, is manifested by the arrangement of the ritual space.

At first sight, in the Jewish temple this is not very much different from what must have been found in the Canaanite sanctuaries, or even in the places of worship more or less common to all the Indo-European peoples. The first thing that strikes us is the sharp distinction made between the temple proper (the *debhir,* or *naos* in Greek, with its *pronaos,* or *hekhal*), which was regarded as the dwelling of God, and the whole cult-precinct (the Greek *hieron*) surrounding it. The *naos* stood in the farthest area of the *hieron,* at the end of the last court, which the priests alone could enter. This inner court was itself preceded by the Court of Israel, reserved exclusively to male Israelites. From this, one descended by means of a flight of fifteen steps to the lower court, which was open also to women. The singers who accompanied the sacrifices with their music seem to have been stationed on these steps. Entrance to the Court of the Women was through the single gate of the inner precinct known as the "Beautiful Gate." At some distance from this, a balustrade with plaques bearing inscriptions in three languages, one of which has been recovered by archaeological investigations, forbade all uncircumcised to enter further under pain of death.

The Court of the Gentiles, which was itself enclosed by a huge four-sided portico, extended all around the *hieron.*

If we return to the Court of the Priests, we shall note that its center was occupied by an altar of great size which was used for the holocausts. On its side, and a little before coming to it, was the famous brass basin, the vessel used for the priestly ablutions prescribed by Leviticus.

The only entrance to the holy place (the *hekhal*) was probably closed by a first curtain. This hid from view the second altar which was reserved for the sacrifice of incense offered morning and evening by a priest who served for a week, as we see from the history of Zachary, the father of St. John the Baptist.[28] There also were

[27] *Amos* 5:25.
[28] *Luke* 1:5-22.

found the tablet of the twelve loaves of proposition and the *menorah,* the seven-branched candlestick.

Behind this candlestick, a second veil concealed the entrance to the *debhir,* the Holy of Holies. Only the high priest could enter it, and that only once a year, to offer there the blood of the atonement according to the ritual of Yom Kippur. At the time of Christ, ever since the first rebuilding of the temple after the exile under the Macchabees, the "Holy of Holies" was completely empty.[29] According to the rabbis, so much care was taken to preserve the sanctity of this site that when the high priest entered it for a few moments he had to be girt with a long cord, one end of which remained outside the veil. Thus if some highly improbable accident occurred to him at this time he could be dragged out without profaning the sanctuary.

Before the exile, the Holy of Holies had contained the ark, but this had disappeared in the destruction of Jerusalem in 596 B.C., and it was deemed impossible to replace.

It did not matter that this cult, in which everything was centered about a divine dwelling that was paradoxically empty and known to be so, was composed of elements similar to those of other cults, even to the general arrangement of the sanctuary. But there was one difference that sufficed to place an abyss between it and the others: instead of a statue or the more or less shapeless *xoanon* found everywhere else, there was nothing in the *naos* of the Jewish temple.

This state of affairs could at first seem to be accidental. Was not the void simply consequent to the disappearance of the ark? But, as a matter of fact, even when there had been an ark in the Holy of Holies, it had only emphasized the emptiness inherent to it. What exactly was this ark which the Hebrews had brought out of Egypt as their palladium? It was a highly mysterious object, but one which could be compared with the coffin of Osiris: a kind of oblong chest furnished with rings through which long poles were passed for carrying it.[30] Once placed within the Holy of Holies, it was prescribed that the poles should be left in place in such a way

[29] See, in the *Mishnah,* the tractate *Yoma* 5:2, trans. Danby, p. 167.

[30] I have treated this question at greater length in *The Meaning of Sacred Scripture,* pp. 103 ff.

that their ends protruded beyond the veil.[31] The meaning of this prescription is obvious: the presence of the poles indicated that the presence of the ark, no matter how long it might be prolonged in fact, was never more than provisional. In the temple of stones as in the tent, the Lord resided only as long as His good pleasure willed. From one moment to the other, He could, as in the time of the exodus, give the signal for departure.[32]

But what was in the ark? Different objects were added to it in turn: perhaps the *urim* and *thummin* early used for inspired divinations, the tables of the law given to Moses on Sinai, the rod of Aaron, the vessel of manna. But these are objects of only secondary importance. There is no reason for believing that it could have earlier contained, if not a statue of Yahweh, at least some crude *xoanon* like those in Greek temples before they were replaced by the statues of anthropomorphized gods. Above all, it is obvious that it was not what was within the ark that attracted attention but what was outside it. More precisely, it was the empty space on the lid (the *kapporeth,* which had to be sprinkled with the blood of the atonement and which the Septuagint translates as the propitiatory) between the two statues of the cherubim facing each other.[33] We are thus brought back again to the emptiness of the Holy of Holies that is only emphasized by the whole structure of the ark itself. Speaking properly, it is less a chest than a throne, the throne of an invisible presence, but one which is attested by the cherubim prostrate before it.[34] We should recall the fact that these cherubim in the Assyro-Babylonian mythologies were the cosmic forces. The meaning is clear: the God adored by Israel, who is believed to be present with it, is the invisible God whom the powers adored by the other people are the first, or should be the first, to adore.

Even though this presence of the God of heaven with Israel in His sanctuary is invisible and unrepresented, it will still be conceived as being very real, living and active. It had been manifested in the light and the cloud which brought Israel out of Egypt, and which, after descending on the tabernacle, had entered the Temple

[31] *Exodus* 25:15, and *I Kings* 8:8.
[32] See again the vision of Ezechiel.
[33] *Exodus* 25:22.
[34] *Isaias* 6, and *Ezechiel* 1.

of Solomon at the time of its dedication. It was from the empty space between the cherubim that this luminous cloud was diffused whenever it deigned to appear. And it was from this same place that the voice issued that spoke to Moses and Aaron; and the later prophets like Isaias and Ezechiel will still be convinced that the God who has called them and sent them forth speaks to them from it.

This presence, very definitely localized though imperceptible, conceived as an unspeakable and profoundly mysterious condescension on the part of the God of heaven for his people, was called the *Shekinah* by the rabbis, a term derived from *shakan*, that is, "to live under a tent." The Greek σκηνὴ is derived from this, not by way of translation but through transliteration. And it is quite remarkable that the term used by St. John in the prologue of his Gospel to explain the Incarnation refers specifically to it: "The Word was made flesh and dwelt amongst us"—literally, "has pitched his tent (ἐσκήνωσεν) amongst us."[35]

The supreme invocation used by Israel in addressing its God was: "You who sittest between the cherubim." [36]

Singular, therefore, as is the presence in the *naos* at Jerusalem, it is no less remarkable in that it did not abolish the ancient modes of determining a sacred place but validated them in a completely new way.

In the first place, Israel never forgot that the hill of Sion had been a Canaanite high place. The history of Melchisedech, king of Salem, priest of the Most High God, coming to Abraham with an offering of bread and wine and receiving a tithe from him, seems even to indicate an express awareness of an absorption of the primitive sacredness of the Jebusean sanctuary into that of the Mosaic alliance renewed with David.[37]

The second kind of local sacredness that we have considered is no less connected with the establishment of the temple at Jerusalem. Was not the setting up of the ark on Sion justified by the appearance of the Angel of the Lord on the threshing floor of Ornan?[38]

[35] See my study "La Schekinah: Dieu avec nous," *Bible et vie chrétienne*, XX (1957), 7 ff.

[36] Cf. *Psalms* 18:11; 99:11; etc.

[37] *Genesis* 14:17-20.

[38] *I Samuel* 24:16-25.

Finally, with Solomon's ritual consecration of the temple by means of a highly purified form of prayer, "that God should cause His Name to dwell permanently there where the sacrifices which he had prescribed would be offered to Him," [39] the three types of natural sacredness attached to a particular place are found taken up within the special sacredness of the *Shekinah*.

But we should also consider the transformation which this was to undergo through the teachings of the later prophets.

The vision of Isaias in the Temple does not merely renew the theophanies of Horeb-Sinai by its fiery character and its affirmation of the unapproachable transcendence of Yahweh. The cry of the prophet, "Unhappy man that I am, for my eyes have seen the Lord, since I am a man with unclean lips and live in the midst of a people with unclean lips," [40] will be developed throughout his book by identifying the divine sanctity with a demand for justice. This identification was, it is true, already latent in the Mosaic law, but it had never before been stated so explicitly.

This new drawing of moral lessons from the divine sanctity can be compared with Greek rationalism, and especially with the moral teaching of Socrates in as far as this was developed from the "Know thyself" and the "Nothing too much" of the Delphic oracle. But the difference, which is too often neglected, is that in Israel we have a consecration of the moral law rather than a moralization of religion, which would tend to dissolve the divine personality in an abstract moral principle. [41]

To this principal trait of Isaias's teaching should be added its counterpart, which the later prophetic tradition extended to the point of providing the background for the New Testament. It is that which was derived from the vision of the seraphim purfiying by means of a coal from the altar the lips of the prophet (that is to say, his thoughts expressed in action and not merely by words). The consummate sanctity of the God of Israel is precisely that which will make a sinful people holy as He is Himself holy. Ezechiel takes up and develops this theme before the Second Isaias, when he speaks of the purifying waters springing from the sanctuary, [42] while the disciple of the great prophet of Jerusalem

[39] *I Kings* 8:22-52.
[40] *Isaias* 6:5.
[41] See *The Meaning of Sacred Scripture*, pp. 70 ff.
[42] *Ezechiel* 36:25 and 47:1-12.

will himself announce as imminent the intervention through which the most scarlet sins will be made white as snow.[43]

Even before this, Jeremias in the Temple itself had denounced the folly of those who imagined that they had God at their own disposal.[44] It is not that the prophet opposes the religion of the word to all ritual religion — and on this point the Scandinavian school is certainly right — but that he upholds and more closely defines the sovereignty of God in His alliance, for want of which His presence will now leave the profaned sanctuary.

This is precisely what Ezechiel sees in the great visions that open his book.[45] He not only foretells the glorious return of a presence that will be manifest from the time that it has wrought the necessary purification of the people and inspired the rebuilding of the eternal sanctuary,[46] but he announces that even before this is brought about, in the time of trial, the presence, however veiled it may be, will accompany the people in their exile and will become for them a kind of temporary sanctuary.[47] This assertion, akin to the promise made by Jeremias of an alliance engraved on hearts of flesh and no longer on tables of stone,[48] will be the seed of the last developments of Jewish piety that were to be an immediate preparation for the newness of Christianity.

These developments may be summed up in two rabbinical sayings, both of which were very popular and echoes of which are found in the Gospels. The first is the saying of *Pirke Aboth* that where there are ten Jews gathered together to listen to the reading of the Torah, the *Shekinah* is in the midst of them.[49] We are immediately reminded of the saying of Christ: "There where two or three are united in my name, I am in the midst of them.[50] The comparison is revealing since it shows that the Jesus of the synoptics looks upon Himself as the living Word of God and as the living site of the *Shekinah*. This is also what St. John in the prologue to his gospel states explicitly. But the text is no less interesting in the

---

[43] *Isaias* 43:20-25; cf. 1:18.
[44] *Jeremias* 8.
[45] *Ezechiel* 1-11.
[46] *Ezechiel* 43.
[47] *Ezechiel* 11:14-16.
[48] *Jeremias* 31:31.
[49] *Pirke Aboth* 3.8 (cf. 2b, which is nearer to the saying of Jesus).
[50] *Matthew* 18:20.

way it reveals the meaning which the Jews gave to the forms of worship in the synagogue and how they connected it with the worship in the temple.

No less important is the other saying of the rabbis[51] according to which the pious Jew who recites all the *berakoth* prescribed by Jewish liturgical tradition prepares a dwelling for the *Shekinah* in everything. In this saying, we have in germ the Christian theology of the Eucharistic consecration which was to transform the very concept of consecratory prayer.

These last two texts, however, invite us to pass from the sacred place of the temple to the new sacred place that came into being with the exile, the synagogue.

The origins of the cult of the synagogue are more complex than was imagined in the nineteenth century.[52] It did not simply come into being at the time of the Babylonian captivity as a kind of expedient which favored the substitution of a cult of the word for a sacrificial cult because worship in the temple was no longer possible. We should again insist that the worship in the temple (or in the other sanctuaries of Israel that had preceded it, like that of Silo, not to mention the mobile sanctuary of the exodus) was not only aware of such a cult of the word but had employed it from the beginning in the *toroth* which always accompanied the sacrifices.[53] The cult of the synagogue at the time of the exile was therefore plucked like a ripened fruit from the cult of the temple rather than substituted for it.[54] It was, moreover, as we shall soon see, always organically connected with it. Reciprocally, on the return from the exile, the porticoes of the temple became the place for a cult of regular readings like that of the synagogues and developed along with the sacrificial cult on the same site.[55] Nothing was easier than this juxtaposition, for the cult of the synagogue had been from the first organized with reference to the sacrificial cult of

[51] Cf. the words of Rabbi Simeon cited by the *Zohar* and the commentary on them in L. Gillet, *Communion in the Messiah* (London, 1942), pp. 138-139. Some sayings along this line may be found already in *Mishnah*. See for example, *Sanhedrin* 6.5.

[52] See I. Elbogen, *Der Jüdische Gottesdienst in seiner geschichtlicher Entwicklung*, 3rd ed. (Leipzig, 1913).

[53] See the works of Haldar and Engnell mentioned above.

[54] *II Kings* 23.

[55] See Eric Werner, *The Sacred Bridge* (New York, 1959), pp. 22 ff.

Jerusalem, at the very time when the exile forced the suspension of the latter.

Nothing shows this better than the archaeological studies made of the synagogues in the Near East and especially in Palestine during the last few decades. The discoveries have been set forth in a fascinating work by Sukenik which we can only summarize here.[56]

Even before its adaptation by the Christians for their churches, the Jews used for their synagogues the basilical type of building, which had been spread by the Romans throughout the empire. This public building, employed for all kinds of assemblies, had nothing religious about it. Both the synagogue and the church, however, took over this type of building since it was essential to both religions that worship should not be restricted to the clergy, even though this were done in the name of the people, but rather that it should be an act of the people themselves. The primitive opposition between the *naos* and the *hieron* was thus effaced, so that the *naos* now embraced in some way the whole priestly people. At the same time the sanctuary, without ceasing to be the house of God, became the house of the assembled people, or, as the Christians described it, the *domus ecclesiae*.

A different interpretation can, it is true, be given to this transformation. Indeed, the synagogue at first seems rather to be a *hieron* without a *naos,* if we remember that the cult of the synagogue was expressly referred to the cult of the temple instead of being substituted for it, since it was still dedicated to the presence found in a very special way in the temple. But, as we shall see, in accordance with the teaching of the last prophets and the rabbis, a new concept of the divine presence was developed in the synagogue which would be perfected in the Christian church.

As is well known, the basilica was simply an oblong building with two rows of parallel columns which so divided it that there were two passages on the sides and a central nave where the group assembled. The rear wall usually included an apse of some sort or other. In public basilicas this usually contained the chair of the magistrate who presided over the assembly.

But this was not the case when the basilica was used as a synagogue. The apse, at least in the beginnnig, remained empty. The

[56] E. L. Sukenik, *Ancient Synagogues in Palestine and Greece* (London, 1934).

rabbi who presided over the assembly with the assistance of the "ancients," the *presbyteroi,* was seated near the center of the nave on a platform known in Greek as a *bema.* His seat, which was called the "chair of Moses," was placed at the center of the *bema.* About this "chair of Moses," to which Jesus refers in the Gospels in a literal and not simply metaphorical sense, were benches arranged in a semi-circle for the presbyters. When praying, all, including the people, faced the empty apse. In all the ancient synagogues, the building was so constructed that the apse marked the direction of Jerusalem. Thus in the prayer of the liturgy, the people and the rulers were found turned toward the sole *naos* in which the presence was believed to dwell with Israel.

Between the *bema* and the apse was placed a chest, which soon was called the "ark." This chest contained the scrolls of the law and the prophets, which were solemnly taken out by the *chazzan,* or "minister," the prototype of the Christian deacon. He then handed them over to the presbyters or to the rabbi himself for reading. A lectern placed on the *bema* must have been reserved for this function. Later, but apparently not before the beginning of the Christian era, the ark was built of stonework and was gradually pushed back into the apse itself, where it may be seen in modern synagogues.

But even before this was done, a veil had been introduced, concealing this ark as it had that in Jerusalem. To complete the resemblance, the *menorah,* or seven-branched candlestick, was placed between it and the lectern.

This arrangement is highly interesting in the way it materializes the saying of Ezechiel that the *Shekinah* is invisibly present to those who remain faithful to it, and more precisely in the way it illustrates the conviction of the rabbis that this presence is there where the minimal number for a synagogical meeting is found united for reading the Torah. The liturgical reading is thus found assimilated to the direct utterance of the divine voice which was thought to come forth from the presence established on Sion. The *menorah* and the veil before the new ark and the entire orientation on the *debhir* of Jerusalem are a striking indication of these parallels.

It should also be noted here that the synagogues already included adjoining rooms, which must have been used, as they are today, for the celebration of the *Kiddousch,* the sacred meal which was the occasion of the great *berakah,* and which brought together groups of faithful around a rabbi, as well as the members of a pious family, to meditate on the Scriptures while waiting for the Messias.

The assemblies of the primitive Church were chiefly distinguished from those of the synagogue in that this private addition was made to pass over into public worship, where it became the central factor. This is how the Church was separated from the synagogue after having had its origins there as one among the numerous *habouroth,* or Messianic communities. The Eucharistic celebration was then brought into the basilica.[57]

As a matter of fact, the earliest Christian churches known to us, the still Semitic churches of Syria, in the details of their arrangement, are exactly like the ancient synagogue, except that the table for the Eucharistic banquet now occupies the hitherto empty apse, the table itself being concealed by a second veil as was the Holy of Holies at Jerusalem. But the ark for the sacred books with its own veil and the *menorah* is still in place. So too is the *bema.* The "chair of Moses" is now occupied by the bishop. The benches around it have become the seats of the Christian presbyters. Apart from this, the first part of the celebration is exactly like that in the synagogue. But after the reading of the Epistle and Gospel, which was added to the reading of the Torah and the prophets, the bishop and priests go to the apse where the Eucharistic banquet is held in the presence of all the people who take part in it, just as they have already shared in the readings and prayers.[58]

[57] Gregory Dix has ably traced the adaptation of what was originally a private service in the synagogue for public use in the liturgy of the Church. See *The Shape of the Liturgy* (London, 1945), pp. 16 ff. But he tends to take public worship as something open to all, whereas Christian worship, like that of the synagogue before it, though "public" was restricted to God's people.

[58] See J. Lassus, *Sanctuaires chrétiens de Syrie* (Paris, 1947), and, by the same author, "Liturgies nestoriennes médiévales et églises syriennes antiques," *Revue d'Histoire des Religions* (1950), pp. 236 ff.; J. Lassus and G. Tchaleuko, "Ambons syriens," *Cahiers Archéologiques,* V (1951). Mme. N. Maurice-Denis Boulet has a résumé of the finding of these works in her article "L'autel dans l'antiquité chrétienne," *La Maison-Dieu,* XXIX (1952). See also J. Dauvillier, "L'ambon ou bêma dans les textes de l'Église chaldéenne et de l'Église syrienne au moyen-âge," *Cahiers Archéologiques,* VI (1952).

An important qualification, however, must be made here. The Christian church, like the Jewish synagogue, is carefully oriented. But it is no longer directed toward Jerusalem but toward the geographical east. This is so true that contrary to the synagogues, Christian churches to the east of the Holy City did not hesitate to turn their backs on it.

This gives us the exact meaning of the orientation in prayer to which the early Christians clung so tenaciously but which is a bit disconcerting to us.[59] It indicates that they had definitely substituted for the earthly Jerusalem the heavenly Jerusalem that is our mother, of which the Apostle speaks. And they were waiting to see it descend from heaven with Christ in His Parousia, which had become symbolized for them by the East, in accordance with the Gospel formulas.[60]

We should insist, therefore, that this instinctive return to one of the most natural religious symbols took on a fully supernatural meaning from the very first. In the context in which it appears and in which we are going to describe it, the Christian orientation for prayer does not seem to owe anything to the forms of solar syncretism being propagated at the same time as Christianity. It may well be, however, that it had its antecedents in a practice already spread among certain Jewish groups such as the Essenes.[61] But with them, as with the Christians, the immediate reason for this orientation must have been eschatological. It was the expectation of the Messias as the New Orient, which will be that of the Day of Yahweh *par excellence,* that determined this symbolism.

Will not Christ Himself say that His coming will be like the lightning which comes out of the east and shines even unto the west?

This shows how Christian universalism, which replaced Jewish particularism, had nothing to do with an abstraction which would subtract man from his humanity. The "city whose foundations are

[59] See F. Dölger, *Sol salutis,* 2nd ed. (Munster, 1925).
[60] See the *Benedictus,* in *Luke* 1:78; cf. *Matthew* 24:27 (also the short conclusion of *Mark*). For the heavenly Jerusalem, see *Galatians* 4:26; cf. *Apocalypse* 21.
[61] On the Essenes, see Josephus, *Jewish War* 2.8.5. This perhaps simply means that they prayed at sunrise. But the fact that they were thought to worship the rising sun doubtlessly means that they prayed facing it.

eternal,"[62] awaited by the Christians, that is, is in no wise a *civitas Platonica*. It is one with Jesus of Nazareth, a man of our flesh and blood, who has become a part of our history, but who has freed Himself from it, drawing us entirely after Him, body and soul, to the right hand of the Father, from whence He will return to take us with Him.[63]

This gives the clue for the new organization of sacred space within the church. The presence on which the cult is oriented no longer pertains to the earth: the symbolism of the orientation turns us toward the new heaven and the new earth where justice will dwell.[64] This eschatological presence is, however, anticipated in time: it is revealed in the table of the Eucharistic Supper which now occupies the apse that had till then remained empty. In the commemorative banquet of the Cross, the faithful can anticipate the parousia each time they assemble. The presence of the risen Christ not only with, but also in, them brings them there beforehand. Nevertheless, it is still the Word, in the fullness of the Gospel that orients them toward the *parousia,* through the eucharist of the Cross. And this has brought about the rearrangement of sacred space along an ecclesiastical axis, Word-Eucharist-East, that replaces the synagogical axis, Word-Jerusalem.

The spread of Christianity through different countries brought about more or less substantial changes in this arrangement of space, eloquent and effective as it had been. In this regard, it is first necessary to consider the new use made of the basilical structure in the churches of Rome.[65] It seems that the Romans were unacquainted with, or ignored, the use which the synagogue had made of the basilica, and, as a consequence, the churches of Rome represent an original and free use of this type of structure. The freedom employed seems at first to be quite happy, for it has its own logic, simple and severe, like everything Roman. But on closer examination, numerous defects may be seen, which explain

[62] *Hebrews* 11:10.
[63] *John* 14:2-3.
[64] *II Peter* 3:13.
[65] See again the article by Mme. Maurice-Denis Boulet, cited in note 58, as well as her other article, "La leçon des églises de l'antiquité," *La Maison-Dieu,* LXIII (1960) pp. 24 ff. See also P. Testini, *Archeologia cristiana* (Rome, 1953), and R. Vielliard, *Recherches sur les origines de la Rome chrétienne,* 2nd ed. (Rome, 1959).

why this new use was never universal even in Rome, why it never took root elsewhere except in proconsular Africa, and, finally, why Rome never showed much enthusiasm in propagating it. The popularity which it was to enjoy in modern times, as we shall see, has only been the result of a misunderstanding.

When they took over the basilica, the Roman Christians undoubtedly made a more functional liturgical use of it, but with little regard for symbolism. It manifests that prosaic utilitarianism which Edmund Bishop maintained was one of the essential characteristics of the Roman rite.[66] Everything depended upon using the basilica for religious functions in a way that resembled as closely as possible the earlier secular uses made of it. The apse, for instance, instead of remaining empty or being converted into a place for the altar of the Eucharistic celebration, retained its original function: the seat of the magistrate became the bishop's throne, his priests being seated about him just as counselors had once sat about the magistrate. On the other hand, since the symbolism of the ark containing the Scriptures was doubtless forgotten, it disappeared from the sanctuary. Simple, practical considerations led to the preservation of the sacred books like other cult objects (including the Blessed Sacrament) in some secondary spot in the *domus ecclesiae*.[67] The *bema* did not actually disappear, but was altered. Since it was no longer the place for the bishop and priests, it lost its original function. It was used for other, secondary purposes, which anticipated later developments. It was now reserved for the singers. It had already been a duty of the *chazzan,* or minister (ὑπηρέτης) of the synagogue, to sing psalms and other hymns either alone or in unison with the people, whose singing he directed.[68] The development of the peculiarly Roman liturgy partly coincided with the development of this office which was assigned to lesser ministers, especially the subdeacon, who soon assumed the secondary duties of the deacon. From this time on, the *bema* was closely associated with the *schola cantorum,* and

---

[66] Edmund Bishop, *Liturgica Historica: Papers on the Liturgy and Religious Life of the Eastern Church* (Oxford, 1918), p. 12.

[67] This was the *conditorium* mentioned in the *Ordo Romanus* with reference to the preservation of the *sancta,* that is to say, the consecrated species.

[68] See Eric Werner, *The Sacred Bridge* (New York, 1959), pp. 23 ff.

even borrowed its new name from it.[69] For this reason it was kept at the center of the Christian assembly. Corresponding to the disappearance of the ark was the addition to the *bema* of two appendages, the *ambos*. One, raised several steps, was to the right of the bishop as he presided from his throne in the apse. Near it was placed a lampstand. It was to this *ambo* that the deacon went to announce the Gospel. From its steps the subdeacon chanted or led the singing. The other *ambo,* symmetrical but raised slightly over the rest of the *schola,* was used for the other readings.

Moreover, it does not seem that this latter usage was primitive even in Rome. The so-called Ambrosian liturgy, which seems to be a development of an archaic form of the Roman rite, has never had more than one raised *ambo*. This is still located to the right of the presiding prelate, and all the readings are made from it.

This arrangement of the *schola,* even if it obviously originated with the ancient *bema,* also had some connection with the original secular usage of the basilica. At a trial, the lawyers had occupied a reserved place in the front rows of the assembly immediately before the *cancelli,* that is to say the slight barrier which separated the assembly from the area about the apse reserved for the assistants of the magistrates such as the lictors, torchbearers, and those in charge of the firebox used to light the torches. These last were now replaced by the tapers and censer.

There is only one thing which obviously had no parallel in the earlier use made of the basilica. This was the table which the Christians soon called the altar.[70] Where was it to be placed? The Roman answer to this problem is quite typical of the economy, some would say indigence, that for a long time characterized Roman practice. Since it could not be placed in the apse, it was simply set up between it and the *schola*. But here again, rather than create anything new, the Romans simply made the best possible use of what was already at hand. One of the features of the large basilicas was a fairly large intervening space in front of the apse where the rows of lateral columns were broken off. The

[69] The word *schola,* in fact, was used already before by pagan authors like Vitruvius to designate the *bema* or *exedra.*

[70] It should be noted that even today the Orientals when speaking of the "altar" mean by this not only the "table" but the surrounding space as well.

transverse quadrilateral area that was thus created became almost universal in the Christian basilicas. It was reserved for the altar and the ministers who surrounded it, and it provided an easy access not only for them but also for the faithful, especially for the reception of the Eucharist.

We thus have a complete picture of the typically Roman basilica: the pope and his priests in the apse, the *schola* (or choir) replacing the *bema* in front of the assembly — which stands outside the barrier formed by the chancel across from the altar — while the *schola* on this side extends into the *ambos*.

At first, all this seems to be a marked secularization of the liturgical setting inherited from Judaism by the primitive Church. But, as a matter of fact, the traditional symbolism, which had been brought over from Judaism, was not suppressed as much as it might seem. The principal feature to be retained was the orientation of the whole structure for prayer. Since the Church at Rome at this period was little concerned with such matters, the fact that this was retained is evidence of the importance of this detail (or what we are inclined to regard as simply a detail) for primitive Christianity.[71] But since the place for the bishop and his clergy had been reversed, some modification had to be made to observe the proper orientation. In most of the Roman basilicas, therefore, the apse was turned not toward the east but toward the west for the greater convenience of the bishop and his clergy. Thus, whenever the bishop prayed, at his throne or at the altar, he did not have to turn around. But if the apse faced the east as in the Syrian churches he had to turn around to pray in both instances.

We know, as a matter of fact, that even at Rome the new custom was never universal. In St. Mary Major's, even at the time of Pope St. Pascal, the *bema* was still placed in the middle of the church and the altar in the rear.[72] At this time the women, according to the Jewish custom followed in many Christian churches, were kept in the tribunes while the men occupied the nave. But in some

---

[71] See what St. Leo, *Sermo* 7.4, says about those who salute the rising sun when entering the church. Nevertheless, the importance of this text should not be exaggerated, as is sometimes done: all the ancient Roman basilicas are oriented.

[72] The *Liber pontificalis* expressly states this in its notice on Pope St. Paschal.

churches, and perhaps soon in the majority of them, the men were stationed between the *bema* and the altar, and the women behind the *bema*. Pope Pascal, however, was disturbed by the fact that the women behind his back could hear what he told his deacons. He therefore decided to transfer his throne to the apse.

Much can be learned from the various details. The first is that all the discussion in recent years about the altar "facing the people" is based on a misunderstanding. If the altar of the Roman basilicas was turned toward the people (*versus populum*) as seen from the episcopal throne in the apse, this could never mean that the celebrant faced the people when he celebrated the Eucharist, if by this is understood that he was face to face with them. There were only two possibilities: either the throne of the celebrant in the apse was turned east or not. If it faced the east, the bishop or the priest substituting for him did not have to turn around when he came to the altar. But as soon as the congregation began to pray with him, it also turned its back to the altar to face the east. If the throne did not face the east, when the celebrant prayed at his throne, he had to turn around, and when he came to the altar he had to go around it. In this case, priest and people prayed facing the altar together, as was customary in Syrian churches and in the great majority of other Christian churches also, as we shall see. This is also why even today the *Ceremoniale episcoporum* considers it perfectly natural for the clergy to pray with their faces toward the rear of their stalls and their backs turned to the rest of the congregation.

In other words, the notion that the arrangement of the Roman basilica is ideal for a Christian church because it enables priests and faithful to face each other during the celebration of Mass is really a misconstruction. It is certainly the last thing which the early Christians would have considered, and is actually contrary to the way in which the sacred functions were carried out in connection with this arrangement.

More should be said. The notion that the Roman basilica and its altar *versus populum* would provide a better view of the ceremonies is not even true when one is stationed facing the celebrant in defiance of the traditional orientation. Today, when a papal Mass is regarded as an interesting spectacle, the place in front of the altar is so poorly adapted for seeing what is going on that those

who are experienced in such matters always ask for tickets for
places on the side of the apse!

Moreover, even if this had not been so, it is quite doubtful
whether the faithful, even if turned toward the altar, could have
seen anything particularly interesting during the celebration. The
date of the first *ciboria* to cover the Roman altars is difficult to
ascertain. But it seems that from the very beginning they served to
maintain, despite all their subsequent transformations, another
element of the primitive symbolism besides that of orientation.
This was the veil, which in Syrian churches hid the holy table as it
had earlier hidden the Holy of Holies. We may even wonder
whether the *ciborium,* as found in the Roman basilicas, was not
the successor to a close imitation of the ancient Jewish tabernacle,
in other words, to a real tent completely surrounding the altar. As
a matter of fact, in the Ambrosian rite, this tent, the *padiglione,*
has survived down to our own time. This may well be a further example of what the Roman rite embraced in its primitive form.[73]

Our age, however, has not been the first to interpret details of
the Roman rite in a sense opposite to that which was originally
intended. The fact that the larger ambo was placed to the left of
the apse as viewed from the nave meant that the deacon to face the
people had to look north when he mounted it to read the Gospel.
This provision, which was carried over with the Roman liturgy into
churches with an opposite orientation, brought about the incongruity that still persists today of having the most important Biblical
passages sung by a reader facing the wall! Little attention can be
here paid to the artificial symbolism that grew up about such purely utilitarian details once their original meaning was lost. During
the Middle Ages it was thought that this reading facing the north
was a challenge hurled at the powers of darkness, despite the fact
that in antiquity, by reversing the symbolism of the basic orientation on the east,[74] it had always been the west that had been assigned to them.

These errors, however, should not make us forget that the
typical arrangement of the Roman basilicas was never taken up

---

[73] See Pietro Borella, "Cortine d'altare: Padiglione-conopeo," *Arte
cristiana,* XXX (1942), pp. 173 ff.

[74] Jungmann, *The Mass of the Roman Rite,* I, 413.

as such outside of Rome except in proconsular Africa.[75] This fact
is all the more remarkable considering the wide diffusion of the
Roman liturgy itself. But it should be remembered that this liturgy
was never adopted in other areas without absorbing many elements
of the local liturgies which it supplanted. The result is that what
we are accustomed today to call "the Roman liturgy" has since
the early Middle Ages been a mixture of widely different customs
framed, more or less conveniently, in a Roman setting, which has
itself not remained free from major alterations.[76]

Be this as it may, if the basilical style of church was introduced
almost everywhere in the West, its arrangement owed more to
Syria than to Rome. The Western church, as we know it, with its
altar in the apse at the east, its choir still linking the chanters with
the clergy, though now close to the altar, is in fact merely a
Syrian church in which the *bema* has been pushed forward so that
it meets the apse.[77]

The reason behind this basic alteration, from which all the rest
flow, was quite simple. Monasticism everywhere complicated what
had been the earlier modes of Christian worship. The consequent
reaction was that the people no longer assisted at all the services
as they had in earlier times. Since it seemed abnormal to the more
or less monastic clergy to celebrate most of the liturgical functions
lost in the center of an empty church, the *bema* was brought up to
the altar. This arrangement was later so perfected that it constituted a veritable *ecclesiola in ecclesia*. The choir and sanctuary,
which was now no more than a prolongation of the choir, were enclosed in walls which separated them from the rest of the building.
The only concession made to the possible assistance of the faithful
was a central gate which, if it did not permit them to see the altar,
something which does not seem to have been a matter of much

[75] See F. van der Meer, *Augustine the Bishop: The Life and Work of a
Father of the Church,* trans. Brian Battershaw and G. R. Lamb (New
York, 1962).* On the other hand, J. Braun, *Der christliche Altar,* 2nd ed.
(Munich, 1932), knows of only two Carolingian altars north of the Alps
turned toward the nave.

[76] See particularly the study of A. Chavasse, *Le sacramentaire gélasien*
(Paris, 1958).

[77] See the first chapter of G. W. O. Addleshaw and Frederick Etchells,
The Architectural Setting of Anglican Worship (London, 1948), for everything that follows.

concern until modern times, at least enabled them to follow the progress of the sacred functions (two things too easily confused today). This led to changing the place for the episcopal throne. It was now no longer located at the center but to the right of the entrance to the choir.

The opposite practice of placing the episcopal throne close to the altar on the other side (which has tended to be more common after the adoption outside of Rome of the modern *Ceremoniale episcoporum*) is a compromise. It is an attempt to adapt Roman usage, which presupposed a throne behind the altar, to non-Roman churches with the altar in the apse.[78]

The typical Roman usage not only suppressed almost entirely the ancient symbolism, but it had, it must be confessed, another serious defect, that of separating the action of the clergy from, and contrasting it with, that of the faithful in the liturgy. The ancient Syrian usage distinguished them perfectly, but made the bishops and priests appear as the head and heart of the Church, leading the latter along in the sacred action as a truly sacerdotal people. By force of circumstances, the Roman usage already tended to give the faithful the impression that the liturgy was something for the clergy, and, in fact, exclusively theirs. The remote foundations were thus laid for our present mentality, which looks upon the celebration of Mass as a kind of spectacle at which one assists, but in which one has only a little share, if any at all.

As the *schola cantorum* gradually abandoned its primitive role of leading the faithful in singing, it introduced compositions that were further and further removed from popular songs.[79] For some time the faithful retained a share in the Eucharistic celebration by listening to the readings and singing, and by taking part in the two processions, one for the offering of the elements for the Eucharistic meal and the other for the Communion. Because the lessons were read in a dead language, listening soon became a mere formality except where preaching in the vernacular to a certain extent repaired the breach. Yet it seems that even at Rome this disappeared quite early. At the beginning of the Middle Ages the offertory procession also disappeared. And finally, except in some

[78] See Léon Gromier, *Commentaire du Ceremoniale episcoporum* (Paris, 1959), pp. 125 ff.
[79] See Jungmann, *op. cit.*, I, 124.

exceptional instances, the Communion also disappeared. The priestly people of the new alliance were not only reduced to a merely passive role, they were now simply spectators of ceremonies which no longer concerned them and which they little understood, or not at all.[80]

In the churches of France and Germany the joining of choir, sanctuary, and altar did not leave even this minor advantage. The people had nothing to do but keep themselves busy while the Mass was celebrated on the other side of a wall. If their occupations were pious, which was not always the case, they consisted in practices of piety with little or no connection with what transpired beyond the wall.

Spain was the sole exception.[81] Either the primitive *bema,* even when developed into a choir surrounded by walls, remained in the center of the nave, being open on the side facing the altar, or, if it was displaced, in contrast to that of churches in other areas, it was moved back to the end of the nave opposite the altar. As a consequence, the faithful were not in the least separated from the altar, but were, on the contrary, placed between the choir and the sanctuary (the *capella mayor,* as it is called in the cathedrals where this disposition has been retained). In more modern times, there are even instances, as in the church of the Escorial, where the whole choir has been extended along a vast tribune to the west so that the faithful remain in complete possession of the church.

This development had as its counterpart the total absorption of the readings into the ritual, the altar of the rite drawing to itself the sacredness of the word, which had now become reduced by its incomprehensibility to a simple rite. However, the evolution has been on the whole less harmful in the Spanish churches than in other churches in the West.

We must now consider another historic arrangement of Christian churches. It bears some resemblance to the last mentioned, and is quite similar to the arrangement found in early Syrian churches, though it has completely outgrown the basilica system. It is that of the Byzantine church with circular cupola on a square base.[82] At a single stroke the building is freed from the division

---

[80] *Ibid.*

[81] See Addleshaw, *op. cit.,* pp. 19 ff.

[82] See Charles Diehl, *Manuel d'Art byzantin,* 2nd ed. (Paris, 1925).

into three bays, which the synagogue had taken over from the
basilica, and which the Church in the West seems now so re-
luctant to abandon.

As a matter of fact, this new type of church flows immediately
from the primitive Syrian church, and through it from the synagogue. It was, moreover, the work of the Syrian architects, Igna-
tius and Isidore, who designed Sancta Sophia in Constantinople.
It may be regarded as a happy solution to the peculiar needs of
Christian worship, set free from the limitations of the basilica
which had been its first shelter. The basilica, once it had been
adapted for entirely new functions, simply shed the reminders of
its former use. Similarly the new type of building, evolving along
new lines, developed according to its own proper logic.

The circular design on a square base easily brought about a
cult-assembly centered about the heralding of the divine Word
by the apostolic hierarchy which had become its heart. The apse
at the east, preserved and enlarged, maintained and even magni-
fied the movement of this assembly toward the Eucharistic celebration seen in its eschatological perspectives. At the same time
the old cosmic symbolism of the cupola arose anew in a Pauline
vision of Christ Pantocrator, recapitulating and reconciling all
things with His Father in His sacrifice. The appearance on the
dome and on the walls of a progressively systematized iconography, following the line of Byzantine theologico-liturgical speculation, gave concrete expression to what existed already as an
idea in the primary concept of the building, namely, to celebrate
the Christian mystery as explicitly as possible.[83]

Under the cupola, at the exact center of the building, was the
bema. We know that at Sancta Sophia it was a raised structure
with the episcopal throne, the seats for the priests, the ark for
the sacred books, and the ambo for the Scriptural readings and
the patriarchal homily. A half-cupola to the east, facing the
bishop's throne, rose over the altar. The enlarged area assured the
perfect participation of the faithful in both the liturgy of the
word and the Eucharistic liturgy. On either side, to the north
and south, two other half-cupolas sheltered the two halves of the
choir which could, as a consequence, be easily engaged in anti-

[83] See L. Ouspensky, *Essai sur la théologie de l'icône dans l'Église
orthodoxe* (Paris, 1960), pp. 19 ff.

phonal singing, while at the same time they could without difficulty lead the assembly in choral singing.

The cupola soon received the image of Christ in glory, holding
in his hand the book of the Gospels as angelic hierarchies as-
cended toward Him in adoration. On the half-cupola of the apse,
the Virgin in prayer, surrounded by the apostles, represented the
Church of the earth rising up to meet that of heaven. Between
the two, above the altar, the empty throne of the *etimasia* (expectation) expressed the eschatological meaning of the Eucharist, prefiguring the union of heaven and earth in the *parousia*.

Below the Virgin and the apostles, in a double register, were
represented the celestial liturgy, that is, the angels carrying the
instruments of the passion, and the Last Supper. These were a
reminder of the historical passion and the sacrifice of heaven,
between which is inserted the Eucharistic celebration. At the four
corners of the building, in the horns, or pendentives, of the cupola
were the four prophets, the four evangelists, as the leaders of
the procession of hierarchs and martyrs, bringing the living assembly toward the Messianic feast.

Later, a twofold change was made in this type of church, without however effacing its primitive lines. Copying the arrangement of the Roman basilicas, the episcopal throne was set up in
the apse behind the altar along with the crown of presbyterial
benches which was its necessary complement. Likewise, the *solea,*
a semi-circular projection of the floor of the altar, was gradually
substituted for the *bema* as the place for reading the Gospel, and
later for the prayers of the deacon.

Without completely disappearing, the central *bema* thus gradually lost its importance. It remained the place for all the readings prior to the Gospel, and, at least in the pontifical liturgy, the
clergy still occupied it in the midst of the people for the liturgy
of the word, even after it had ceased to be the place for their
permanent seats.

The monastic office, however, or an office of this type, here,
as in the West, introduced stalls for the use of a large "religious"
or clerical gathering. But instead of creating a choir separated
from the church of the people, these stalls simply surrounded it,
the bishop's stall being the first to the right of the entrance, a

corresponding one on the other side being reserved for the religious superior or archpriest.[84]

It is hardly necessary to stress the fact that this last type of church, especially as it was originally conceived, embraces and interprets the meaning of the Christian ceremonies better than any other. The transformations that were later introduced never altered the arrangement nor obscured its meaning so seriously as those in the West.

An important detail should be added to this description of the different classical styles of Christian churches. They all originally included an annex, only a relic of which exists today. It was of capital importance, however, as an intermediary space between the holy place and the world. Catechumens and penitents had their place in this narthex, as it was called. It is still used today in the East for all the functions of a penitential character such as the nocturnal vigils.[85]

This brings us to the problem of the specific character of the Christian initiation.

In the mysteries of pagan antiquity, the concept and practice of initiation had already occupied a highly important place. This is because the mysteries were the first religions of the West which at least provided for the beginning of a conversion, for an approach of men to a "sacred" which was not innate to him. However, except for some secondary lustrations, the mysteries do not seem generally to have included separate initiatory rites. More exactly, the initiation was only the first (if not the sole) participation in the rite of the mystery itself.

In this connection, it is necessary to note the confusion that has been created by many modern historians of religion who draw a parallel between the mysteries and the puberty rites practiced by most primitives.[86] The confusion is only a decal of the situation that actually arose in Christianity when the rites of conversion to

[84] See F. Mercenier, *La liturgie des Églises de rite byzantin,* I (Paris, 1937), xv ff.

[85] *Ibid.* It should be noted that at Montserrat, Matins are always said in the great tribune of the narthex.

[86] This is the fundamental error which vitiates a work like that of O. E. Briem, *Les sociétés secrètes de mystères.* Mircea Eliade's work, *Naissances mystiques* (Paris, 1959), is not entirely free from it.

Christianity became *de facto* the initiatory rites of children into the religion of their fathers. But it is impossible to see in the mysteries of the Hellenistic Age anything to match the pedagogical rites which constitute the initiations through which the adults of primitive tribes receive into their ranks children who have reached the age of puberty. Such rites, moreover, were actually to be found among the Greeks and Romans; but it must be admitted that they had undergone an almost complete secularization, as we would say today, correlative to the rationalism inherent in Greco-Roman humanism.[87]

By substituting baptism for the primitive initiatory rite of circumcision, Christianity formally introduced the idea of a new, completely supernatural birth.[88] Baptism was necessary for participation in the Christian mystery because, as we have seen, it was the first mystery to have an effectively supernatural content in the strict sense of the word. For it is the only mystery which, in place of an association with the natural powers, effects a really redemptive alliance with the Sovereign God come to free us from these rebellious powers.

This is the reason for the unique importance of the intermediary space in the Christian church where the catechumens received instruction in the Word without being as yet able to advance further and partake in the sacramental mystery.

In one way or another, the narthex became centered about the baptistry. In many churches, as can still be seen in Italy, this developed into an autonomous building, circular or octagonal in shape, with the baptismal font at its center.[89] Normally it had two doors or, at least, two approaches to the font, one on the west, through which the neophyte came as he left the world of darkness, and one on the east, through which he passed on to the luminous world of the Church assembled for the Eucharist.

[87] See J. Bayet, *Histoire politique et psychologique de la religion romaine* (Paris, 1957), pp. 67 ff.

[88] This does not mean that there was no idea of a rebirth before baptism (see the work of Eliade cited in note 86), but there was no concept of a rebirth that would make us children of the transcendent God.

[89] See F. Dölger, "Zur Symbolik de altchristlichen Taufhauses," *Antike und Christentum,* IV (1934), 153 ff., and L. de Bruyne, "La décoration des baptistères paléochrétiens," *Miscellanea Liturgica in Honorem L. C. Mohlberg,* I (Rome, 1948), 189 ff.

The font itself was as a rule supplied with running water, a symbol of the new Red Sea, or the new Jordan, which had to be crossed with Christ in the exodus through His death toward His resurrection. The neophyte was stripped of everything to descend into the font. Dead with Christ, he was there reborn with Him to the new life of the new man, which was represented by the white robe and the lighted candle which were given to him immediately after he had been anointed with the royal and priestly chrism of the Spirit.

The deadly struggle with the powers from which one was snatched through Christ's victory was expressed in the exorcism which marked the preparatory phases of the initiation, and finally in the anointing with the oil of the catechumens at the very moment of renouncing Satan and confessing the Saviour.[90]

The introductory procession into the church after baptism signified how acceptance of the faith and acceptance of Christ are one in the admission of the newly baptized into the priestly assembly of the Church celebrating the Eucharist.[91]

Thus the polarization of the church on the altar to the east was completed by a second polarization on the baptistry in the west, where the passage from the world of darkness to the world of light was accomplished. The precise meaning of sacred space in Christianity received from it a kind of final touch. This is the sacralization of the place where the Eucharist is carried out in the Church, but it could be said equally well of the place where the Church itself takes shape in the Eucharist. The basic feature is still the convocation of the faithful assembled by the Word of God. This Word, by its own dynamism, unites the Church, and then consecrates it in the Eucharistic celebration. But the symbolic orientation of the Church (the community in prayer and the building that shelters it) expresses the incompleteness on earth of every Eucharist tending towards its fulfillment in the *parousia*. At the same time, it is the whole cosmos that is reconstituted, centered on the Lordship of the Risen Christ, leading the whole universe, human and angelic, material and spiritual, toward the Father. The approach to the church through the narthex, and more exactly across the sea or the Jordan symbolized by the baptistry, manifests this dynam-

[90] See my *Paschal Mystery* (Chicago, 1950), pp. 156 ff.
[91] See my *Liturgical Piety* (Notre Dame, 1955), p. 168.

ism inherent in the Christian celebration. It implies the passage from this world to another, or, rather, the passage of the world, with man and about him, from this aeon, that is, the present age, to the aeon of judgment and of the eternal Kingdom.

The Christian rites of ordination must be viewed in these same perspectives if they are to be understood. The Church is built up through the preaching of the Word, in the Eucharist which responds to it. But this Word is God Himself made flesh, and this Eucharist is that of the Man-God. It therefore needs as instruments for this preaching and this celebration members of the Body of Christ who should be representative of their Head, of their unique Master. Ordination will grant them access to the *bema* and to the altar, so they can there perform in and for the Church those essential functions through which Christ remains present to, and acts in, the assembly of His own people.

The imposition of hands, to be understood as a taking possession, rather than as a transmission of powers, is the essential consecratory rite of this accession. By this it is affirmed that there is no ministry in the Church except through association with the Head of the Church, whose Headship is the source of the efficacy of His own service of the Father. In the following chapter, we shall return to this point: the apostolicity essential to the Christian ministry. Suffice it to say here that what we have stated with respect to every participation in the life of the Church is doubly true of the priestly offices: there is need of a recreative intervention on the part of the Saviour God, which is first asserted by the passage from the profane world of the first creation to the sacredness of the new, and which is consummated in the introduction of a man at the center of the sacred action, where it can no longer be he who acts but God, laying hold of him in Christ, in the interest of all the members of Christ.[92]

These considerations lead us to conclude this section of our study with some remarks on the consecration of the sacred place itself. A transition to this final problem may be found in an examination of the new way in which the primitive expressions of the sacred are to be understood in the initiatory rites which we have described above.

The material element of the Christian initiation, from which is derived its value as a symbol, lies in the approach to a sacred

[92] *Ibid.,* pp. 143 ff.

place. But it is now clear that this place is sacred only because it is the place for the Eucharistic celebration, toward which the preaching of the Word leads, inviting us at the same time to advance toward the east, that is, to the *parousia* of the glorious Christ. Though it is of an entirely new type, the holy place that is the Christian church still realizes in a supereminent way that toward which the ancient sacred mountain of the alliance between heaven and earth had tended. But the church is above all the new cosmos of which Christ Pantocrator is the Lord and Prince, the sovereign Archon. It is the place of the ineffable light which is only reached by turning away from darkness. For this reason there is need of a decisive passage through the waters of death — which brings in the negative symbolism of the waters of the flood. But they are also revealed as the waters of life through the Resurrection. Here we find the second symbolic meaning of waters, that of the source, the maternal waters of the new creation. The royal unction at last introduces the holy people to the Kingdom, in order to present to, and in, the King of Ages the pure offering, the offering of His vivifying death, the Eucharist of the people believing in His reconciling and regenerating Word.

All this should make it clearer than ever that the essential consecration of the holy place is in the Eucharistic celebration itself. This celebration is at the same time that which secures the divine presence and consecrates, along with the new humanity which is there dedicated, the whole universe restored to conformity with the design of its Creator.

The principal rite, therefore, and at first the only rite, for the consecration of a church as we see it in the ancient Roman liturgy, was simply the first celebration of the Eucharist in a building planned and built for it. All that the Gregorian Sacramentary provides for this are prayers and a special preface for this Mass.

A first addition to the rite was made by the churches of Africa and southern Italy.[93] The practice of celebrating Mass at the tombs of the martyrs on their anniversaries, by a kind of reflex action, brought it about that relics of the martyrs were introduced into all the churches, where they were placed in recesses cut into the altar for this purpose. This accretion to the rite only emphasized the

---

[93] See M. Andrieu, *Les "Ordines romani" du haut moyen age,* IV (Louvain, 1931), 361 ff.

prolongation through the Christian Eucharist of the sacrifice of Christ as the Head into an oblation of the whole body of the Church. For the martyrs exemplify the perfect union with Christ of those members of the Church who have been fully united with the Cross of her glorified Head.[94]

Later, as a third element of the rite, a custom was added which seems to have been first introduced for the consecration of ancient pagan temples for Christian worship, like the Pantheon, for example, which became St. Mary of the Martyrs. This was a ritual made up of exorcisms and purifications. It suggested the idea of a kind of baptism of the stone structure that enclosed the living Church.[95] Among the Germanic nations, particularly sensible to the reality of a world alienated by the demons which must be reconquered by and for the Saviour God, this aspect of eviction and reconquest soon predominated. There were processions outside and inside the church along with sprinklings of a special kind of holy water. The latter, known as "Gregorian water," was a mixture of water, wine, and ashes blessed by the bishop. A fully apotropaic ritual evolved which easily took on the appearance of white magic, but in which the victory of the Cross over the powers was ceaselessly reaffirmed. In Gaul, on the other hand, an analogy of the more positive aspects of the baptismal rite was retained and developed with the anointing of the main stones of the church and altar.[96] But, it must be admitted, there was some degradation of the idea of baptism in such a literal extension of the concept of man's regeneration to his external dwelling. The artificial, pedantic renewal of the ancient rituals followed by the patriarchs could only accentuate the same regression toward elementary forms of the sacred that was already latent in the lustrations.[97]

The most serious error in this juxtaposition of three secondary rites of consecration (transfer of relics, lustrations, and anointings) of kindred but somewhat discordant inspiration, was the eventual reduction to the status of an appendage of that which had been fundamental in the Christian ritual: the celebration of

[94] See my *Spiritualité du Nouveau Testament et des Pères,* pp. 238 ff.
[95] Cf. *Missale francorum,* ed. L. C. Mohlberg, pp. 57-58. On the primitive rite, see Vigilius, *Ad Profuturum* 4 (*Patrologia Latina* 84:832).
[96] See A. Chavasse, *Le sacramentaire gélasien* (Tournai, 1958), p. 42.
[97] See Andrieu, *op. cit.,* 319 ff.

the first Mass in the place prepared for it. And yet we have said nothing about other additions to the rite, such as, for example, the taking possession of the site by the cross of ashes on which the bishop had to write the alphabet.

The consecration of the altar, the central rite of the consecration of a church, nevertheless recalls the basic and central part which the Eucharistic sacrifice has in the consecration of a place for Christian worship. The two great prayers, eucharistic in character, of the present Pontifical, concluding both the consecration of the church and that of the altar (the latter being simply the Preface of the ancient Gregorian Mass), also tend to reabsorb into the Eucharist all the ritual of the consecration, elaborate as this had become. They formulate in a most expressive manner the renovation of all the earlier forms of consecration, whether natural, or whether borrowed from the Old Testament, and their assumption into the unique consecration of the Christian sacrifice.[98]

[98] The recent simplification of the ritual has reduced the phase preparatory to the celebration of the first Mass.

CHAPTER X

Sacred Time

I F OUR concept of space, abstracted from the objects which occupy it, has developed slowly, this is even more true of the concept of uniform time, mechanically measured. Even today among peoples of a low cultural state such a concept is hardly known. If a question is asked them about the age of a group or of an individual, the answer will likely be an avowal of utter ignorance or some fantastic number. It is under an entirely different aspect that time, and its divine correlative, eternity, affect the primitive. In some way it is for him the mark of creation and of its fall. Or, more accurately, since the two have never been clearly distinguished outside the Judaeo-Christian revelation, this draining away, or consumption, of our existence inseparably connected with its development is the very sign of the profane, non-divine character of man and the world. Conversely, the same time which excludes us from the sphere of the sacred is a constant reminder of our strict dependence upon the gods in whatever we do. This time in which we are immersed, but which still escapes us, is the absolute and unfailing proof of their sovereignty.

Nevertheless, in a certain way, time cuts across divine eternity, or rather, it is eternity that touches time and is constantly being called to mind by the rhythms of time. Through these rhythms and

[1] On sacred time in general, see G. van der Leeuw, *Religion in Essence and Manifestation,* pp. 384 ff., and Mircea Eliade, *Patterns in Comparative Religion,* pp. 388 ff.

their unfailing recurrences, the powers of this world, which are, as
it were, the support of the hierophanies, constantly remind us of
their mastery over our existence and that of the world, both of
which are constantly changing. The day alternating with the night
is the hierophany of the powers of the sun and of the darknesses
which form the warp and woof of the dualism that under one form
or other lies beneath all the great myths. But it is the solar year
which generally provides the essential framework for the ritual
celebrations. For the return of the year, with the rebirth of plant
life which it occasions, has the appearance of a genuine repetition
of the creative act where the divine intervention is to be seen again
in every new birth. The new year literally produces a new world,
or, what amounts to the same, it produces the world anew.

The first advanced civilizations, particularly those of the Semites, superimposed upon this annual rhythm a larger stellar
rhythm corresponding to the real or imagined return of certain
astral configurations. The concept of a cosmic year, a much more
radical reintegration of all things than that affected by the solar
year, led to a belief in a final conflagration and rebirth of the
world that was later developed by the Stoics and was to furnish
Nietzsche with his idea of an eternal return.

On a lesser scale, beneath the great solar rhythm, the rhythms
of the moon with its succession of months brought about a completely different hierophany, one that was maternal rather than
paternal, and intimately connected with what were, or what appeared to be, the regular changes in female fertility.[3] To these
lunar gestations, whose relation with the shiftings of the tides was
soon perceived, correspond the hierophanies of water, just as
those of light or fire accompany the solar fecundations, or the
more mysterious influences of the stars.

The final step seems to have been first taken by the Babylonians.
Their astronomical observations led them to introduce the week,
which was connected with the alchemic sympathies that were believed to exist between the planets and the elements of the world.[4]

Across these different systems, which are found more or less
the same in all mythologies, may be seen the primary meaning of

[2] Eliade, *op. cit.,* pp. 400 ff.
[3] *Ibid.,* pp. 165 ff.
[4] See F. Cumont, *Oriental Religions,* pp. 162 ff.

a feast.[5] The lucky day (*dies festus*), like the unlucky day (*dies nefastus*), is like a node in the celebration of the ritual, or, to change the simile, like a *tempo forte*. In the course of human or cosmic events, it is marked by a manifestation of the powers which support, preserve, and even renew the world. The day designated as that of the new year especially appears as that of a new creation. The ritual is therefore carried out as a human activity in sympathy with the epiphany in this world of the divine energies upon which the very existence of man himself depends. It may be said that he acts in such a manner in order that these energies may be revealed in him under their most benevolent aspect.

The gods who are thus thought to be reached in the celebration of the rites are above time. That is to say, they do not share in its ebb and flow, which is for us inevitable and even irremediable. But their eternity does not simply remove them from it. It is revealed in time itself by the rhythms it imposes upon time. In this respect, eternity, rather than being timeless, can be said to be the time of the gods. It is distinguished from our time, although it envelops and contains it, because it is a strictly cyclic time. The alternations which it undergoes are regularly balanced off.[6]

With respect to these unchangeable rhythms, the time of man takes on the appearance of an ever-contracting spiral. It is connected with eternity because it unfolds on a plane regularly intercepted by the sacred rhythms. But while these are invariable, the time of man, even when it appears to pass again through the same periods, does not cease to be contracted as it tends towards the final immobility of death. Viewed in this way, the ritual celebration appears to be a hope and an attempt to enlarge the human or cosmic spiral, to make it coincide with the unbreakable circle of the eternal powers.

Only when this is taken into account can the meaning of the myths be fully perceived. At first sight, and this explains at least in part the pejorative connotation that clings to the word, a myth is seen as a history in which the gods are described in completely human terms. This is due to the fact that the myth appears at a moment in man's spiritual and intellectual development when he has gained a new consciousness of himself, and, more precisely, a

[5] See G. van der Leeuw, *op. cit.,* pp. 388 ff.
[6] See M. Eliade, *op. cit.,* pp. 392 ff.

certain consciousness of his own transcendence with respect to the world. But to see only this in a myth would be to miss what is essential. To repeat what has been mentioned several times before, a myth actually reflects a religious reaction of man as he is becoming more civilized and is faced with the temptation of magic which is inseparably connected with this development. The myth rises at the very time when man is tempted to believe that he can dominate all reality, including that of the gods, through his use of ritual. Consequently, in the same terms in which man explains to himself his own relative superiority to the world, the myth comes to reaffirm the absolute superiority of the gods. In this stage of man's spiritual development, the gods appear to be spiritual beings *par excellence,* that is to say, not disembodied but complete masters of this bodily reality where the spirit is necessarily manifested or runs the risk of evaporating into a pure abstraction. The transcendence of the gods is, therefore, reaffirmed, together with this immanence, apart from which they would become inaccessible, and, in fact, quite simply unreal to man.

Divine history, that is, the myth, is not actually a history such as ours despite appearances. As Mircea Eliade has shown, it is necessary that a myth takes place in that primordial time which escapes the defects inherent in our own.[7] But still, it is not outside of time, since then it would evidently be of no concern to us. Rather, this divine history stamps the impress of eternity upon our own time as being that which is the foundation and support of time itself. Sharing in our vicissitudes but surmounting them, the essentially cyclic history of the myths, which imperturbably subsists beneath the spiral of our own constantly contracting history, bears witness to a presence in time that cannot be reduced to time.

In this way the myth, while still maintaining the sovereign elevation of the sacred, reopens to us in the rite a hope of reaching it, not as something which man can attain through his own resources by some Promethean effort, but as something which he can only receive. Doubtless, too, in this way, the myth, as the most religious pages of Plato attest, preserved among men a hope for grace, a foreshadowing of faith, but in a sense which these terms would never attain outside of Judaism or Christianity.

[7] See again, Mircea Eliade, *Mythes, rêves, et mystères,** pp. 9 ff.

Actually, it was only a bare outline. The proliferation of myths, so characteristic of the Hellenistic Age, like some persistent uneasiness, bears witness to the radical dissatisfaction which man finds in all the purely natural manifestations of the sacred.

This purely cyclic time, which is a kind of temporal image of eternity in the myth, is really never more than an ideal which constantly recedes as one attempts to approach it. The superimposition of the various cycles, of the planetary week, the lunar month, the solar year, and the great stellar year, is a tacit avowal of the fact that none of them is conceived as being perfect. The desired reintegration must therefore constantly pursue its quest without ever being able to reach its complete realization, unless perhaps in those areas which surpass human experience, as for example in Stoic eschatology. As a matter of fact, the indefatigable pursuit of a conjunction of the converging spiral of human evolution with the ideal circles of the supposedly immutable powers is nothing more than a chimera.

At the same time, a spirituality such as that of late Stoicism, while striving for this integration, reveals the existence of an even more serious source of dissatisfaction which must sooner or later weigh down upon the naturally religious man. How can man's liberation through an identification with the immutability attributed to the cosmic powers be distinguished from a real enslavement? Are not these endless circles, like that of a snake devouring its tail, for the gods themselves, and *a fortiori* for man who strives to align himself with them, simply an indication of the subservience of the universe even under its divine aspect to the rule of blind fate?[8]

In short, neither the transcendence nor the immanence which the myth attributes to the divine can satisfy man's aspirations. The gods remain above men. They impinge upon their actions, but they really never share their lot since they are guaranteed a kind of automatic victory over our essential decline. And when their transcendence ceases to be doubtful, it becomes oppressive. Either the perfect circles which one strives to attain have no real existence, or, if they have, they are no more than lofty prisons in which the gods have been the first to be chained.

To state the problem more simply and concretely, the death of the gods is never more than an appearance. Compassion for such a

[8] Cf. the *amor fati* to which Marcus Aurelius constantly strove to return.

death can never console us for our own death, since at their departure the gods are assured of an inevitable rebirth. And conversely, such a rebirth can never stir up in us the hope of a true resurrection. For the gods are reborn only to die again. They are actually never reborn except to the perpetual cycles of descents and ascents, which in turn are only the prelude to further descents.

In this connection, as has been observed by Vladimir Soloviev, the criticism which Buddha made of the myths of Brahmanism is applicable to all myths, and the denial of their ability to save man is much nearer to the Christian concept of salvation than the false hopes of salvation held out by all the various forms of paganism. What actually would be a real salvation would be an escape from the wheel of deaths and rebirths.[9] But it must be confessed that until the advent of the Judaeo-Christian revelation the only possible escape from this wheel took the form of a withdrawal from existence itself.

Greek rationalism pointed out the folly of these eternities that are nothing more than idealized cyclic times. But it only broke through the circle by postulating an abstract eternity which existed in the mind alone and which man could not enter except by subscribing to a false idealism. Plato's world of ideas is a pure, intangible, eternal world, a world of essences. But it is a world that has no existence like our own.

Entirely different from this Platonic world is the divine world which invades our own through the prophetic word and the saving event as found in Judaism.

The God speaking on Sinai can be described as the God of heaven in opposition to the gods dwelling in temples built by the hands of men, just as their existence is incorporated into that of the universe. Actually, His transcendence is something entirely different from that of a sidereal sphere, of a prime, immovable mover that embraces and sustains all other things without sharing in their decline. It is rather that of the Sovereign, wholly Other, who is also everywhere present, who is above all, and from whom all proceeds without His having need of anything.

His intervention in the world at a particular moment of history, recognized as unique and forever decisive, does not at all involve

---

[9] See Vladimir Soloviev, *The Justification of the Good: An Essay on Moral Philosophy*, trans. N. A. Duddington (London, 1918).

Him in the inevitable decay of the things of this world. He freely intervenes, and, having come down to us, He remains free as ever. Yet He is really committed: Israel knows that the divine immutability is not simply reflected in a typical event destined to be everlastingly repeated. His omnipotence is introduced once for all into the course of earthly events in such a way that it stamps the history of mankind and of the universe with an irreversible intervention.

The Pasch as it was celebrated annually by the Semites was nothing more than the feast of the eternal, and eternally provisional, renewal of vegetation. The Pasch of Israel was the eternal reminder of a decisive act of God through which He had once and for all taken in hand the cause of His people.[10] More explicitly, He has created forever a new people, one that belongs to Him because He has made it His in a sense quite apart and because the decision He has made is final.

Through this unique intervention, the history of man ceases to be a string of interchangeable events. It has acquired a new meaning once and for all, since God, the Lord of the powers of the world, has engaged Himself with it.

Though it is unique, the event ceaselessly commemorated by the Jewish Pasch is not an isolated fact like a meteor that falls to the earth without a past or future. In its own way it is also typical of the manner in which God intervenes in the world, not to keep it within the closed circle of a finite eternity that constantly repeats itself, but to lead it step by step towards a design whose realization is both progressive and continuous.

In the center of history, which becomes oriented upon it, the day of the Pasch, the passage of God among His people, signifying for them their definitive passage from slavery to freedom, reverberates like a double echo into a primordial day — that of creation, and into a final day, the Day of Yahweh *par excellence* —the day of judgment.

These first and last days, as has been noted by others, were originally, in Israel, not much different from the great cosmolog-

---

[10] The central importance of this notion of the ἐφάπαξ is the fundamental theme of Oscar Cullmann's work, *Christ and Time: The Primitive Christian Conception of Time and History,* trans. F. V. Filson (Philadelphia, 1950).

ical days of the Babylonians, where all things received together both their end and their renewal.[11] But what is of real interest is to see how the radical transformation, or "historization," of the Pasch was soon to effect a general metamorphosis of the first and the last days through the teachings of the prophets.

The beginning described by the cosmology of Genesis no longer has anything to do with the countless new beginnings of the other cosmologies. It is the absolute beginning, having nothing prior to it except the eternal design and the eternal wisdom of God. For it is not a simple reflection on our world of those perpetual rebirths to which the gods themselves are subjected. It is the free and sovereign effect of the sole Word, that is to say, of the sole expression of the holy will of the Creator Who Himself has no beginning, no birth, in whatever way this may be understood.

Similarly, the Day of Yahweh, the day of judgment, is not simply a final catastrophe, after which all things would have nothing to do except to take up again their usual cycle. It is the final intervention through which the Eternal will make our time approach His eternity. It is the judgment without appeal, which causes those who accept God's known design to enter into His kingdom, to reign there with Him in eternal life, to share in his life; while it hurls into the abyss, or encloses definitively in the circle of eternal death, those who will have rejected this same design.

Between those two great days, the central saving event of the Pasch discloses its full meaning. It is the opportunity offered to our created liberties to detach themselves from their mortal opposition to the creative liberty of God. Thus, in the end, they will be both freed from the perverted powers which had made them captive, and will participate, through filial adoption, in that sovereign liberty which is the glory of the Creator.

Human history — once it has thus been saved — becomes something entirely different from a simple decal on our lives of a fate enclosed upon itself, in contrast to the mythical history reproduced by the *dromenon* of the mysteries, which humanized only in an image borrowed from us the ever impersonal figure of

[11] This is what Hugo Gressmann emphasized in *Der Ursprung der Israelitischjüdischen Eschatologie* (Göttingen, 1905). Mowinckel, on the other hand, sees it as being something *sui generis* from the very first in Israel. See his *Psalmenstudien,* II′ (Kristiania, 1921), pp. 506 ff.

the cosmic processes. This history of men and of the world, which only discovers its true character inasmuch as it is revealed to be a part of sacred history, is now the drama of created liberties, all preceded by a single uncreated liberty, all remaining in His hand when they seem to be withdrawn from it, but returning to it not to be extinguished but to be perfected.

This did not prevent the historic Pasch of Israel from becoming the object of an annual representation, of a periodic renewal in the celebration of the cult, like the cosmic Pasch of the worship of nature. But how should this be understood? Only within an essentially progressive, irreversible movement which was no longer cyclic in any sense, though the cosmic cycles were themselves taken up in it. This movement was that of the historical dialectic, by means of which creative liberty, after it has been separated from created liberties through sin, managed to take them up again within itself. But, to repeat again, this does not destroy the created liberties any more than their alienation from uncreated liberty had meant a real enfranchisement. This is their salvation, their fulfillment despite their own failure, that is to say, despite themselves; but these liberties are still not to be saved without their own concurrence.

This movement can be described as being both an interiorization and a universalization of the redemptive process. But it is necessary to stress the fact that this interiorization is not at all a timeless spiritualization of salvation, as in Buddhism. Nor should the universalization be understood in the sense of an abstraction, an uprooting like that of Hellenic humanism. It must rather be explained as man's participation in the divine saving event through a communion that grows in depth as it expands, and which at least virtually should embrace all men.

We should note at once how the passage of the Red Sea with Moses will undergo a first renewal, not ritual but real, in the crossing of the Jordan with Joshua.[12] And yet this is not merely a renewal of the saving event. It is an Israel shaken through the sieve, purified of rebels and doubters, that is engaged in this new liberating passage. Accordingly, it is no longer the people going out of the land of bondage into the desert, but going into the Promised Land.

[12] *Joshua* 3.

Later, with Josias, the renewal of the Paschal rite came to mean a heightened awareness of the alliance made on Sinai. It signified submissive faith clarified by the teachings of the prophets after the renunciation of the idolatrous worship of golden calves.[13]

Taking their stand on these already creative renewals, the faith of the later prophets soars upwards to represent to Israel the trial of the exile as a new exodus.[14] If instead of gaining an easy victory over its foreign enemies, Israel is now delivered to them, it is in order that it may itself be purified in passing through the crucible of suffering. The new deliverance which follows is thus described by Ezechiel not only as a new exodus but as a real resurrection of the people.[15] Reassembled from all over the world by the divine Word, it is reanimated to a new life by God's own Spirit that is poured into it.

In this way, the celebration of the Pasch in the time of Christ came to mean not so much a recollection of the past as a preparation for the future. This was the basic pattern behind the great liturgical *berakoth* which in the Jewish celebrations recalled the high creative and redemptive acts of old as a promise and a sketch of the desired, definitive event that was expected to come with the Messias King. Thus, as we know from St. Luke, when Christ went up to Jerusalem to celebrate the Pasch for the last time, he could tell his disciples, in words deliberately chosen by the evangelist, "of His exodus that He was to accomplish at Jerusalem."[16]

But what is this exodus if it is not His death and resurrection? The resurrection of one who has remained faithful unto death and whom trials have separated from the faithless mass, which in Ezechiel was still only an image, becomes now absolute reality. And in the resurrection of the only faithful Servant, from the vista opened up by the songs in the second part of the Book of Isaias, it is not simply the gathering of the dispersed children of God of the house of Israel that is to be accomplished:[17] the elect

[13] *II Kings* 23.
[14] For instance *Isaias* 43:16-21.
[15] *Ezechiel* 37.
[16] *Luke* 9:31.
[17] *John* 11:52.

of all the nations are to be found there reconciled, with the Father and among themselves, in the very body of His only Son.[18]

Accordingly, by renewing for a last time the ritual Pasch and its historic reality at the Supper and on the Cross, Christ brings it to its perfect fulfillment.

But instead of bringing to a close the ritual renewals, this fulfillment, once again, gives a new and final sense to them. What has been now accomplished in the only Son, Himself gradually prepared for and ultimately segregated from the multitude, is to be extended to a new and far greater multitude so as to gather and renew it in His own personal unity.[19]

The passage of God over the land had first drawn out of Egypt, out of a profane and sinful world, a people destined for the alliance. Then from this people, by means of trials and the light of His word, He had picked out a remnant for whom the alliance was no longer a mere external reality inscribed on its flesh through circumcision and the observance of the ceremonial prescriptions, but an inner reality, one that was graven on the heart. From this remnant He at last has drawn forth the Elect, the faithful Servant, the new Man who really passed through death and returned to life, a life no longer that of the earth but of heaven, one of justice, of holiness, and of divine love.

In the Elect, in His only Son who sanctifies Himself for all of them, He now wishes to gather in His countless children, sanctified in the truth of the one definitive sacrifice which He alone could accomplish.[20]

It can now be said that the Paschal celebration, inasfar as it concerns the Leader, has all its perfectly achieved reality behind it. On the other hand, for the whole body and for each of its members, the Paschal celebration still anticipates, awaits, and begs for it. With a wholly new clarity, this celebration is, and remains, what it became for the Jews of the last stage of the old alliance: the expectation of the new and eternal alliance, of the coming of the King and of His Eternal Kingdom in the *parousia*. But what

[18] *Colossians* 1:20; cf. *Ephesians* 2:16.

[19] See O. Cullmann, *La royauté du Christ et l'Église dans le Nouveau Testament* (Paris, 1941), pp. 35 ff.

[20] This is the sense of St. Paul's description of Christ as the "last Adam," that is to say the final man, in *I Corinthians* 15.

the body expects for itself in the imminent and eternal future, it finds it already fully realized in the work fully accomplished, in the fully revealed person of its glorious Leader.

We are here brought, as it were, to a focal point from which can be recapitulated all the different aspects of our study.

We are now in a position to define the reality that makes up the content of the Christian rites and the way in which it is present in them.

It can be said that in the Jewish ritual the saving event was present to the extent that it pursued its own development in the people of the preparation. The fact of the Pasch, of the creative deliverance of the people of God, was there prolonged and deepened. It there became the object of an increasing understanding, both qualitatively and quantitatively, for the holy people themselves. In their celebration of the renewed Paschs, the people gradually became aware of all that was virtually contained in the first and fundamental saving act. In this way the people were prepared for further developments.

It is there that we see the dialectic of word and event at play, where the divine presence is given in proportion to the accomplishment of its work. The rite already appears there as the juncture of these two inseparable and irreducible aspects of the divine intervention. In the celebration of the ritual, the people enlightened by the word assimilate the contents of the saving act as it progresses, and in this way are disposed for this progress. Through submissive faith, actively expressed in the ritual celebration, they recognize the meaning of the events toward which God is moving them. Thus God, in His turn, takes possession of the people in the rite to advance them further in carrying out His saving design.

When Christ comes, His own celebration of the rite at the Supper leads this design to its complete fulfillment, the Word of God made flesh. He is also, in His humanity taken from the holy people that reaches its full sanctification in Him, the perfect answer to this Word. Therefore, at this instant, He is in Himself and achieves in His work the fullness and fulfillment of the Word of God to man. And thus, just as the ritual Pasch extended and developed the realities hidden in the historic Pasch of the exodus, so the Paschal Supper of the Saviour foreshadows their accomplishment at the height of history on the Cross of salvation.

Now all is accomplished. The future ritual celebrations of the new Pasch no longer tend toward the fulfillment of the saving act, since this has been consummated. They tend to assimilate us to it, and this can only be accomplished through our integration with the person of the Saviour-God. This integration, with our participation in the Cross essential to it, is at once both the work of the Church and its own edification. For the work of the Church in the world is nothing but its own self-edification upon the foundation and cornerstone that is Christ.[21]

This is the same as saying that the liturgical celebration of the Christian mystery, which is the mystery of Christ and of His Cross, if conceived in its full spiritual dimensions, is the realization of the apostolate of the Church. Indeed, the term, "apostolate," at once designates the mode of the Church's existence and its function in the world, with reference to Christ considered as both the fulfiller and the fulfillment of the divine plan. The apostolate, actually, is defined by the word of Christ as He sends His disciples, whom He has made His cooperators, into the world: "As the Father has sent me, I also send you. Whoever receives you, receives me, and whoever receives me, receives Him who sent me."[22] In other words, the Eucharist of the Supper and of the Cross which the Church celebrates is Christ's own Eucharist celebrated by Himself in her. And in this celebration, God is in Christ "reconciling the world with Himself," as Christ has reconciled it on the Cross. For this continuous celebration in the Church extends the Cross of her Head to the whole body, just as the Cross, with all its meaning and reality, at once fully human and fully divine, had gone forth from the Eucharist of Jesus at the Last Supper.[23]

This shows us the way in which the divine Word with its salvific action tends toward its accomplishment. And, as a consequence, it further shows us how this Word should be understood in the Church celebrating the Eucharist, in the light of the definitive Pasch, that had been foreshadowed and prepared by the Pasch of the transitory alliance. The key is there given to us of that full exegesis of the divine Word which the Church has always considered to be her own exclusive possession. This is the spiritual

[21] *I Corinthians* 3:10 ff.
[22] *John* 20:21 and *Matthew* 10:40.
[23] See *Liturgical Piety,* pp. 132 ff.

exegesis, that is to say, the exegesis by means of which the divine Spirit communicated by Christ to all His body reveals all the potentialities of the letter while producing them. By the word, "letter," we mean the first, but only figurative and preparatory, realization of the divine design.[24]

This exegesis, as found in St. Paul, and before him in the rabbis and even in the later prophets, is set forth under the form of an allegory.[25] But such a description is quite inadequate. The special kind of allegory found in Jewish and Christian exegesis, which has its origins in the intrinsic development of the Word and its realization in sacred history, is completely *sui generis*.

In itself, an allegory is only a transposed meaning of a text in which one finds another meaning than that which it has when taken in its narrowest and most immediate sense. As a reaction to the traditional rationalism of Greek thought, Hellenistic speculation, deprived of, and therefore, obsessed with, a longing for mystery, tended to find an allegorical meaning, which often degenerated into pure fantasy, in all the traditional texts. More than once, both among the rabbis and among the Fathers of the Church who came after them, allegory took the same turn. Victims of rationalism in antirationalism itself, as is usually the case, they too created allegories no longer justified by the trends found in the literal meaning of the texts but *in spite of* them. To fasten onto this aspect of the matter, however, would be to see only the failures in Jewish and Christian allegory, passing over what is proper and substantial.[26]

On the contrary, what is specific in the traditional Christian teaching about the triple spiritual sense of Scripture can be preserved, if only the theory outlined by Origen and developed by the whole of the Middle Ages is carefully taken into account.[27]

[24] This is the meaning of the opposition of the letter to the spirit, for example, in *II Corinthians* 3:6.

[25] This is what St. Paul says in *Galatians* 4:24.

[26] This is the error of such a work as E. Pépin, *L'exégèse allégorique* (Paris, 1959).

[27] See on this subject the work of Father H. de Lubac, *Histoire et esprit,* and the three volumes of his immense work, *L'éxègese mediévale,* that have thus far been published.

The basic allegorical meaning of Scripture is in its most intimate and profound sense, through which the Scriptures are seen in their entirety as an outline in the texts and a preparation in the facts for Christ and His work, for the mystery of His redeeming Cross. Therefore the Messianic images of the Priest-King who reconciles man with God and introduces him into the divine Kingdom, of the unique faithful Servant gathering together and saving in Himself the multitude, and of the Son of man who is the heavenly Man restoring in man the perfect image of God, find their allegorical meaning *par excellence* in the crucified and glorified Christ, in the God who was made Man to adopt man and make of him a child of God.

Since we must all be recapitulated in Christ and made His living members and temples of the Holy Ghost, "in order to make up in our flesh that which is wanting to the sufferings of Christ for His body, which is the Church," [28] that which has had its fulfillment in Christ should be shared by us through faith and the sacraments in which faith meets its object. The essential allegorical sense, therefore, continues in each of us through that which is called the tropological, or moral, sense. This is not a mere application of the teachings and narratives of Scripture to each of the faithful in turn. It is the realization of all the meaning that the Scriptures have for inspiring us with faith "in Christ Jesus," according to the expression of St. Paul, and for defining from the viewpoint of Christ and the Church the "life of the Spirit" which should replace in us the life "according to the flesh."

Finally, what Christ living in us through the Spirit works in us today should find its ultimate fulfillment in eternity, at the *parousia* of the Saviour. The ultimate understanding of the Scriptures is therefore directed toward a dawning realization of this term, when "Christ in us, our hope of glory" will be fully revealed, and when, because of this, God will be all in all. This is what is called the anagogical sense of Scripture, according to which it leads us toward the plenitude of Christ, which is our completion in the plenitude of God.

Therefore, the Church, celebrating in its Eucharistic liturgy the mystery of Christ as that of the new Pasch, which is also the Pasch of eternity, ceaselessly nourishes this celebration through a medita-

[28] Cf. *Colossians* 1:24.

tion on the Scriptures pursued along the lines of this triple meaning. Far from denying or doing away with the literal sense, this vital interpretation only reveals all the potentialities which remained latent in it and are made manifest in "the Lord who is the Spirit."[29] In this way, moved by the understanding that it alone may get of the mystery of Christ, the Church sets out toward the realization of the fullness of Him who fulfills Himself in all, which is, as it were, the definition of the Church given in the Epistle to the Ephesians.[30] Here it is seen how the rite, even more so in Christianity than in Judaism, is nothing other than our entrance through faith into the reality announced by the Word. This Word there offers us, and there effectively confers upon us when we thus accept it, the participation in the divine event which saves us in making us the adopted sons of the Father in His Son made man of our flesh.

From this it follows that the sacred time *par excellence* for Christianity is the time of the celebration of the Eucharist, just as the sacred place, as we have seen, is the place of its celebration. It is the "today" of salvation, when the mystery of Christ in us, our hope of glory, is presented to our faith and can be acknowledged.[31]

The taking up again of the cycle of annual feasts will therefore have no other meaning than to point out the complementary aspects of the mystery. More precisely, this renewal expands the dynamism of the mystery in a way that enables us to adapt ourselves to it. For the law of physical biology is still true at the level of supernatural life: ontogenesis should reproduce phylogenesis. The development of each one of us in Christ should follow the course of Christ's own development, to the point that we all, as the Apostle again says, reach the plenitude of His adult age.[32]

In this process, we find the opposite of that to which the celebrations of the pagan mysteries tended in their claim to associate man with the avatars of the cosmic powers. They tended, as we have said, to match the decreasing spiral of human life with the supposedly perfect circles of those apparent gods, who were the elements of the world. But from these elements and from the prison

[29] *II Corinthians* 3:17.
[30] *Ephesians* 1:23.
[31] *Colossians* 1:27.
[32] *Ephesians* 4:13.

of their usurped kingdom, the Cross of Christ has delivered us for the liberty of the glory of the children of God,[33] freeing the world itself from the false gods that had enslaved it. As a result, the annual celebration of the Christian Pasch, with all the train of added feasts, breaks through this closed circle. Across the seemingly unchanged circle of the cosmic years, the expanding spiral of the Christian mystery tending towards its eschatological fulfillment prepares our faith for the tangential escape toward the infinity of the divine Kingdom.[34]

The same happens to the lower circles. The place of the monthly cycles is taken by the maternal wreath of the feasts of the Virgin and the saints, through which the Church-Spouse of Christ is revealed as bringing us forth through the trials of holy martyrdom and heroic faith.[35] The elementary cycles of the weeks, which constantly remind us of our enslavement to the cosmic elements, have yielded to the cycle of the Sundays, that is to say, of the celebrations of the Resurrection, which makes a "feast" of all our days, a perpetual festival in which is prolonged the eighth day of the new and immortal creation.[36]

Finally, in the lives of each of us, the sacraments of Christian initiation, which cannot be repeated, bring us into the ἐφάπαξ, the association consummated once and for all of our individual destinies with the unique destiny of Him in whom all the divine design has found its completion.[37]

Inversely, each day of our lives, like an image of our entire existence and of each single day of shared eternity, makes us pass, across the praise of all the hours, from the memory of creation at the hour of Lauds, through the memory of the history of salvation at the hour of Vespers, to the vigil ceaselessly renewed in the anticipation of the *parousia, ut in omnibus glorificetur Deus.*[38]

---

[33] *Romans* 8:21.

[34] For more details, see *Liturgical Piety*, pp. 259 ff.

[35] *Ibid.,* pp. 257 ff.

[36] On the theme of the eighth day in the Fathers, see J. Daniélou, *Sacramentum futuri* (Paris, 1950).

[37] *Ibid.,* pp. 241-242.

[38] See my *Introduction to Spirituality,* trans. Mary Perkins Ryan (New York, 1961).

Conclusion

THE PURPOSE of this study has been to show how the combined resources of the history of comparative religion and depth psychology can furnish us today with a better understanding of the Christian ritual. If we had aimed at anything more than a survey of the field, we would have had to write not only a much longer work, but one that would have run into many volumes, especially since many of the chapter headings would require several volumes for adequate treatment.

It should also be noted that there are other areas for investigation which we did not take up. One of these, for example, from the area of psychology, would be the "second phase" of Szondy's researches on the analysis of destiny, so brilliantly expounded by Père Niel. This could serve as a point of departure for more profound studies of the problems discussed in the last chapter.[1] Similarly, the existential analysis of Binswanger,[2] and the cosmological studies of Minkowski,[3] could considerably enhance the definition of the hierophanies so ably identified by Mircea Eliade. And the same psychological methods could certainly be used to develop the phenomenology of the various rituals as outlined by Gerard van der Leeuw.

[1] Henri Niel, *L'analyse du destin* (Paris, 1960).
[2] See the collection of essays edited by H. Ellenberger, *Existence* (New York, 1960).
[3] E. Minkowski, *Vers une cosmologie* (Paris, 1936).

206

Instead of trying to exhaust the topics we have touched upon, we have simply attempted to point out to other scholars the rich possibilities that are opening up today along these lines. Those who explore them will obviously find much to complete and to correct in our own rough draft, and it is our hope that they do so.

Pure science, however, has certainly not been the primary object of this work. We wished at least to begin to gather materials for some necessary reconstructions. Because of the renewed interest that has been taken in it, the liturgy has made much progress in recent decades, even though this has been somewhat uneven. Many things have been cast aside — not always too happily — and they have frequently been replaced by others of doubtful value. It is not always easy to maintain the proper balance, to be found somewhere between a timid conservatism that would tie itself to false traditions, and fearless reforms that would discard some of the most permanent realities of human nature and Christian belief as having only an antiquarian interest. But in the long run neither excessive conservatism nor baseless innovations will prove to be acceptable. The sacred rites are realities which cannot be known, much less reshaped, if their roots in human nature and Christian tradition are never really understood.

More penetrating studies will make our own work obsolete, but as a conclusion to it, we would like to point out three things which should have been somewhat clarified by what has already been said and which are of special importance for the future of the liturgical movement. The first of these is the place which the word should have in our worship. The second deals with the principles that should guide the inevitable adaptations and reforms that must always be made in the liturgy. The third aims at the concrete realization of these adaptations and deals especially with the setting in which the liturgy is to be carried out.

In earlier studies dealing with the liturgy and the ecumenical movement, we have stressed the importance of a truly biblical and traditional theology of the word. But, as we have discovered on numerous occasions, not everybody agrees with us in this. We have been accused of trying to Protestantize Catholicism. When we have asked for a clarification, those who have taken the trouble to give their reasons say that we reabsorb supernatural facts and saving events into the word, which they understand only as an expressed thought, even though it is one that is divine. The complaint is quite naive since it shows that those who see Protestantism lurking behind every theology of the word suffer themselves from a peculiarly Protestant inability, the inability to see in the word in general, and in the divine word in particular, anything more than an idea expressed by a sound. But if there is anything foreign to the Jewish and Christian biblical tradition, it is just such a notion of the word.

It is our hope that the present book will show how the divine Word, whose importance we have stressed, instead of minimizing or excluding the supreme importance of the facts and events in the history of salvation, actually stresses them. To pretend to separate the events of sacred history from the divine Word, or to dissociate it in the least from them, whether in the redemptive Incarnation itself or in the way in which it is mysteriously brought to bear on our lives through the sacraments, is to mutilate the Word itself and to pervert its interpretation.

But the necessary connection of the word with the facts, and therefore with the sacramental rites, of Christianity implies a reciprocal relationship. No Christian event or Christian rite can become an object of faith independently of the divine Word which gives it its meaning. We must even go so far as to say that the very substance of the Christian fact would dissolve if we strove to separate it from the Christian word. When St. John says that Christ is the Word made flesh, he is saying something that he intends to be taken literally and is not simply using a figure of speech. If the worship of Christ is in no way idolatrous, it is precisely because Christ manifests the Father and is His living manifestation not only in what He says but in what He does and in what He is.

This has necessary consequences in sacramental theology, which in turn should affect pastoral liturgy. St. Thomas perceived these consequences and defined them with remarkable clarity and depth. But our theological textbooks and actual practice fall far short of doing justice to them.

First of all, this means that the sacraments and the whole complex of Christian rites can in no way be conceived and discussed as if they were a kind of white magic superimposed on the preaching of the Gospel without any intrinsic connection with it. In fact, as we have already seen, this was a common tendency in the Middle Ages. And, what is worse, this is what many current practices only tend to accentuate. A threatening negation of true Christian sacramentalism, for example, may be found in the commentary sometimes given as Mass is being celebrated. Here an naively rationalistic explanation is superimposed upon a rubrical Mass that has become unintelligible, and even inaudible, in its formulas, and increasingly foreign in its rites to those who assist at it. To juxtapose the rite to the word, and, behind the rite, the saving event to the intelligible teaching, as if they were two different realities, associated but foreign to each other, is to destroy the Christian rite. For, as St. Thomas has clearly demonstrated, the sacraments are not efficacious apart from their meaning but in virtue of it.⁴ This is the whole meaning of the theology of matter and form in the sacraments. Their form, which gives them their efficacy, is the divine Word which defines their meaning for us.

But contrary to what Protestants and many contemporary Catholics, who have succumbed to the same rationalistic tendencies, believe, this is of no less consequence for the word itself than it is for the sacraments.

What actually is this meaning which the word confers upon them so that they become charged with reality? Or, again, how does it happen that the word itself only reaches its final expression in the sacraments? We should recall the saying of St. Paul about the death of the Lord which we "announce" each time we celebrate the Eucharist.

This is because the divine Word, which we are here discussing, has something to tell us that is completely different from a dull truth of common sense. It proclaims a mystery to us, that is to say, according to the excellent formula of Gabriel Marcel, a truth which cannot be comprehended, in a strict sense, since it is rather we that are comprehended in it. This truth is Christ, the Christ known only to Christian faith, that is to say, according to the expression of St. Paul to which we must always return: "Christ in us, our hope of glory."

What this word tells us, is not therefore simply an idea which we can file away with others. It is a fact that cannot be reduced to any kind of abstraction, a fact rich in meaning, so rich indeed as

⁴ Following a good formula due to Söhngen, they signify what they do, and they do it because they signify it.

to be inexhaustible. For this fact, the fact of Jesus Christ, and Him crucified, has on the one hand the unique power of laying hold of our whole life, of penetrating, dominating and assimilating it; and it has on the other the power of opening up to us an approach to God's life, to what is most unfathomable and inexplicable in it.

This is why, as St. Thomas has so clearly taught, we can only have an analogical knowledge of this fact, without which it would remain utterly foreign to us.[5] But it can in no way be reduced by any intellectual analysis to a univocal application of the categories through which we obtain a conceptual knowledge of the realities which our mind can reach and embrace. And this is also why the living presentation of this fact in the divine Word, however much the use of reason may help us to appreciate it, has no substitute for it in the reasoning process itself. Just as theology, if it is not confused about its own proper object, must begin with revelation if it is to be valid, so it must always return to revelation. When at the end of his life St. Thomas declared that the work he had done on his *Summa* was no more than straw to him, this was precisely what he meant to say. When he was about to pass from time into eternity, he knew what his own thought had been able to contribute to the enrichment of his own interior life and to his own understanding of essential truth. But this understanding, because it was so genuine, assured him the more that the supreme apprehension of the Truth, as well as its elementary apprehension, was not a matter of pure thought but of faith in the divine Word nourished by the sacraments.

True theology, as a consequence, should be a help rather than a hindrance in understanding the exact intent of the word whose spontaneous expression is of another order than that of abstract concepts, for its effective apprehension demands of us, over and above acts of reason, the assent of faith, which takes place at the sacramental level, where sacred history becomes our own. Attempts to expound the mystery should not tend to dissolve it, but rather to place it in a better light so that it can be more easily accepted in its own way.

[5] The exact nature of this doctrine of the *analogia entis,* completely caricatured by Karl Barth, has recently been illuminated by Père Bouillard and Hans Urs von Balthasar.

This brings us directly to our second problem, that of the adaptations to be made in the liturgy. These can in no way be resolved in the abstract but must be considered in their concrete reality. Before any adaptations can be made, it is first of all necessary to know their aim. The liturgy today must be adapted to modern man with his technical and rational outlook, and to civilizations other than our own, which has developed from the Greco-Roman tradition.

The two problems at first seem to be so different that they might seem to be independent. Actually, their conjunction in the present state of missionary activity is quite happy. It enables us to grasp the problem at its roots under its complementary aspects. The problem of liturgical adaptation is in reality at the center of the larger problem of the connection between the preaching of Christianity and the myth. The preaching of Christianity can no more free itself completely from the mythic expression of reality than it can immerse itself in it. The fact that Christianity cannot be divorced from such an expression should help us in adapting the liturgy to contemporary Western civilization. The fact that it cannot be immersed in myth should help us to adapt it to other civilizations than our own.

By means of a few examples we shall strive to show how such an adaptation can be made in the performance of the rite. There can never be a question of discarding rites so intimately connected with the substance of Christianity and with the fundamental hierophanies of every religious experience as those of the baptismal ablution and the Eucharistic meal. But if they are to regain all their living meaning, it will be first necessary that they regain their reality. The less suggestive the hierophanies of water and eating are for modern man, the more necessary it is that the saving bath should become again a real bath, that the sacred species should be recognized as those of true bread and true wine.

But it is no less necessary that a culture directly inspired by Scripture should restore to water and eating, along with the naturally religious meaning they have for man, their supernatural meaning which sacred history gradually imposed upon these primitive hierophanies.

When both of these goals will have been pursued to their own mutual clarification, the liturgy will again become for modern man something living and significant. On the other hand, trite and impoverished signs added to abstract explanations can only complete the divorce between the liturgy and modern man.

When we pass from the essential sacramental signs to those which are secondary and whose whole purpose is to prolong and perfect the insertion of the ritual into the whole of human life, the problem of adaptation becomes more complex. It may well be that one or other of these ancillary rites is too closely connected with a passing phase of civilization to survive. Again it is essential to know precisely what one is doing when he deals with them. Frequent anointings and complicated ablutions are certainly rites which should be restricted and even suppressed in the present Roman liturgy. But if the symbolism of the anointing with olive oil and balm, which cures and strengthens and at the same time creates a new atmosphere, is less direct than the symbolism of water or bread, and less easy to restore, one should not immediately conclude that it should be completely abandoned.

Even the ultramoderns could rediscover the meaning of the sacred oils if they were actually applied as an embrocation. The same could be said of chrism if it had an obvious fragrance as it does in the East. These examples should suffice to show that, even in the relatively secondary rites, an attempt should first be made to restore the primitive meaning to the rites by insisting upon their reality, before any attempt is made to abolish them on the ground that they have lost their symbolic meaning, when, as a matter of fact, this meaning has only been extenuated by the poor use which we have made of them.

Actually, the only rites whose retention can be seriously questioned are those accretions, more dramatic than symbolic, which aim at explaining the substance of the rites, but which are themselves quite artificial. This is the case with a number of picturesque ceremonies which really do not belong to the liturgy but only encumber it. While attempting to focus the mind on what is essential, they actually distract it. New ceremonies of this type should certainly not be introduced without a good deal of thought, and then only with great moderation. They weaken the liturgy by turning it into living tableaux. These may be useful and instructive for a time, but they become wearisome as soon as their novelty wears off. And they constantly run the risk of obscuring the true nature of sacramental symbolism by actually concealing what they attempt to clarify.

In fine, shortsighted rationalism is the temptation that must be resisted in the adaptation of the liturgy to our contemporaries. Such an approach would readily dissolve whatever is mysterious under the pretext of explaining it, or of rescuing it from the twilight of mythic thought which advances more by way of suggestion than by definition.

On the other hand, when there is a question of adapting Christian forms to civilizations that do not share in our Western tradition, one must guard against the temptation of absorbing the originality of the Christian mystery into pre-Christian mythologies. Here two things must always be kept in mind: the first is the unity, or homology, of man's religious consciousness, which explains the striking structural resemblances in myths peculiar to different civilizations; the second is that this natural, basically unchangeable substance of man's religiously oriented soul has already been assumed, first by the Jewish, and later by the early Christian, rites.

Here again, before any modification or transformation of the rites is made, it would be well first to revive the original reality of the Christian ritual symbols. Once this has been done, it is often surprising to discover how completely the primitives of today, or those whom we consider to be such in comparison with our own hyper-intellectualization, find themselves at home in our rites, even more so perhaps than we do ourselves. For the same reason, the same should be said of the scriptural presentation of the Christian message. This does not beget the same prejudices in them as it does in us. On the other hand, the presentation of Christianity under a more intellectual guise, as has become common with us, is frequently for them only an obstacle.

The object of a transforming adaptation must obviously not be so much the substance of the essential rites as their secondary trappings, and especially the rather late symbolic meanings that have been given to them. Here also, what was helpful to our ancestors, if not to us, can be a hindrance to others. This is true with respect to the shape or color of the liturgical vestments, of signs of respect (such as kissing, prostrating, having the head or feet covered or not), and also of the modes of sacred chant and the posture for prayer, whether it be one of standing, sitting, or kneeling. When something new seems desirable in such matters, guidance may be found in the prudence shown in similar circumstances by the Fathers of the Church. They never permitted the use of symbols connected with the pagan cults as long as the special character of Christian worship had not yet been clearly defined in the Greco-Roman civilization, so that the borrowing of such symbolism would not be misunderstood. If this is kept in mind, one can perhaps conclude that such a question as that of the admission of certain Chinese rites into Christianity, which in the past were the source of so much controversy, cannot be answered in the abstract. Something which could not be admitted as long as there was the possibility of its being understood in a pre-Christian sense becomes acceptable as soon as it is clear that the earlier meaning attached to it has disappeared.

At such a time, however, it may be asked if the revitalizing of a rite that has in some way lost its primitive meaning does not needlessly entangle us in forms already dead. This danger should always be kept in mind when an attempt is made to express Christianity in the setting of cultures in a state of rapid evolution. It is important not to burden oneself with empty archaisms, but rather always to distinguish what deserves to be preserved and transformed in the culture of a people that is undergoing a process of civilization as well as Christianization from what cannot survive.

In such an adaptation, however, we should, above all, never separate the ritual from the sacred word. Our ritual adaptations will be something more than a mere disguise, only insofar as they go hand in hand with a fine translation, not only verbal but also notional, of the divine word. Here more than anywhere else we should pay attention to the essential metamorphosis of the mythic themes, without which they will never become expressive of the sacred word. We should be on our guard against translations which are only a search for abstract equivalents. Like the extension of the Incarnation, the communication of the word is a vital and continuous historical process. It has never been extracted from a Jewish mould to be recast into a Greek one. The body of Jewish thought, which was fashioned after the development of revelation itself, is to be prolonged in other forms of thought, which in turn will be greatly modified, as were the forms of Greco-Roman thought.

The whole experience of the Church, while it has to be again and again decanted in the process, is also to be preserved. In the first expression of faith, there is something permanent, which will ever make of us spiritual Semites. However, in all the later attempts of understanding and expressing the truth, there is also something which cannot be bypassed. All this has become incorporated into the message of the Church, which is inseparable from its history.

Such a claim, of course, does no injury to the originality of the cultures which the Church must assimilate. An error common to all manifestations of excessive nationalism or racism is to believe that a culture can only maintain its originality and vigor by growing in a hothouse. On the contrary, a culture only reveals its potentialities by opening itself to its fullest extent to all other forms of human experience in order to make its own proper contribution to the whole. A culture proves its own worth insofar as it thus extends its own riches to the full dimensions of humanity.

This leads us to the last problem we wish to discuss in this work, that of the installation of Christian worship in its proper place: the Christian church.

Perhaps the consequences of what we have already said about sacred space can now be seen in a clearer light. Architects, artists, and craftsmen who work together to provide a material shelter for the ritual should have a clearer notion of the freedom they possess and of the limitations to which they are necessarily subject. Instead, however, we still see churches whose arrangement misconstrues and positively violates the most elementary rules of a liturgical function because it has been enslaved by the false exigencies of a tradition that has no other existence than that of an erroneous imagination.

A cruciform plan for a Christian church, for example, is absolutely unnecessary. It is only an artificial interpretation that was later imposed upon the basilica with its apse and transept. Such a plan, like the building from which it was derived, probably has more disadvantages than advantages for a liturgical celebration that is true to its own intrinsic demands.

On the contrary, the renewed attempt to employ a structure with a central, more or less circular plan, is all to the good. We have seen the excellent use made of it by Byzantine architects. But the relation of this plan to the organization of the Christian assembly should not be misunderstood. To center the church about the altar, as is sometimes done today, is to commit a

grievous error. It betrays, first of all, an ignorance of the hierarchical ordering of the ecclesiastical assembly, flowing down
from the celebrant, its source. The gathering of the Church about
the Eucharist is not, and never can be, a kind of round-table con-
ference. Secondly, and no less important, it is not a static gathering about a center belonging to this earth and, as it were, fixed
on it. It is rather a dynamic gathering, where the divine word in-
vites us to proceed together toward the Eucharistic banquet,
which in its turn has no end in itself, but should orientate us
towards the final uprooting of the *parousia*. This is what has given
rise to the basic axis, the orientation of the primitive *bema* upon
the altar, and of the altar upon the symbolic East, which always
lifts the earthly celebration above this earth.

On the other hand, the hierarchical arrangement of the Eucharistic assembly does not at all demand that singers, readers, offi-
cers, and choir should be closely packed about the altar. Is there
any architect who would dare to draw his inspiration freely from
the arrangement of the ancient Syrian, the medieval Spanish, or
the early Byzantine churches? The first fruits of such a borrowing would be a greater unification of the Christian assembly and
a more effective participation in the singing and hearing of the
divine word. And to these practical considerations would be
added the advantage of greater solemnity.

This would certainly be a more fruitful innovation, and one
more securely founded on tradition, than the chimera of an altar
facing the people. The latter, as we noted before, is based on a
misunderstanding, and sanctions the idea that the liturgy is a kind
of spectacle.

It will perhaps be well to end this chapter and this book with a
brief observation on the proper orientation of a church. We have
here an example of one of those symbols deeply rooted in human
nature and Christian tradition, but which are said, often rather
frivolously, to be of no concern to modern man. This is perfectly
true of an abstract orientation, only ascertainable by means of a
compass. But is this the case with an orientation on which the
whole economy of the church visibly depends, its lighting, both
natural and artificial, and its decoration? A church whose orientation is thus manifested would permit the morning celebration to
unfold in an increasing light, which each time would reveal anew
the dynamism of an iconography adapted to the structure of the

church, as it was in ancient times. Thus our churches would become a permanent *verbum visible,* which would ceaselessly interpret the mysterious "announcement" of the Eucharistic rite.

In all the questions which we have considered, we find the same problem. It is one which Rudolf Bultmann has sought to reduce with a brilliant but facile solution. This has had a peculiar fascination not only for Protestants but also for a number of Catholics as well. The solution has been defined by its author as a process of "demythologization" — *Entmythologisierung.* It is based on the twofold idea that Christian ritual and every formulation of the Christian message in the word of God, particularly in the New Testament, is of a mythic nature, and that the myth represents a mode of thought that is radically outmoded and repugnant to our contemporaries.

What, then, according to Bultmann, is mythic in the New Testament? It is the idea of an intervention on the part of God in the events of this world, whether it is a question of the Incarnation, of the Redemption, or of their consequences in the effusion of the Holy Spirit on man. He thinks that in all that there is something repugnant to a scientific concept of the world, according to which the course of phenomena is governed by a fixed order so rigidly determined that it is completely opposed to the possibility of any such interventions, and, as a consequence, they are for us simply unthinkable.

Bultmann then asks how, in such circumstances, the teaching of the Gospel can be interpreted to modern man. The concepts, or rather the images contained in the Gospel, should be recognized as a simple outmoded façade covering a timeless and ever valid truth, for they give expression to man's permanent status in the universe. This is equivalent to saying that man's self-expression, apart from God, amounts to nothing, and cannot escape from the desperate dialectic which flows from the Heideggerian analysis of existence. On the other hand, "faith," interpreted as a renunciation on the part of man of all hope of founding his existence on himself, with its positive counterpart of an absolute confidence in the transcendent reality of the universe, despite all the phenomenological evidence that seems to deny it, will save us from despair by saving us from ourselves.

This new interpretation of Christianity could be the object of endless discussion, but we shall limit ourselves here to two observations that are pertinent to our own theme.

The first of these has been formulated with rare appropriateness by the philosopher Jaspers, who is even less suspect than Bultmann of being inordinately attached to traditional dogma.[6] He has shown that the opposition which Bultmann places between a scientific and a mythic view of the world is an oversimplification that has already been left behind by the progress of science. On the one hand, we have given up defining the universe purely in terms of scientific determinism, which could perhaps be defended by the physics of the nineteenth century, but which cannot satisfy the vision of the world suggested by the science of the twentieth. And, on the other hand, we cannot retain the nineteenth-century definiton, or rather vague pejorative concept, of a myth, conceived as a childish and outmoded representation of the universe. It is just such a concept of the myth, as Jaspers has shown, which recent progress in the history of comparative religions and depth psychology has completely routed. From this it follows that a vision of the world that is both religious and contemporary cannot be conceived as simply bypassing the myth, but it must be conceived as a necessary dialectical integration of a scientific concept, which has itself become far more subtle than the one proposed by Bultmann in the name of an outmoded rationalism, and of a mythic concept whose permanent value can no longer be doubted. We should add that the dialectical acceptance and reconciling of such patterns of thought, which at first appear to be contradictory, is quite in keeping with recent developments in science. This kind of dialectic actually finds its own proper place and development in modern science. It can even be said, for example, that modern physics has come to postulate it. Only in such a way can the corpuscular and undulatory conceptions of sensible reality be reconciled.

The study which we have just made enables us to add a necessary complement to these observations of Jaspers, whose force would be undiminished even if the Gospel had been expressed purely and simply in mythic formulas. If the Christian message,

[6] See Jasper's criticism and the response, hardly convincing, of Bultmann, in *Études Théologiques et Religieuses,* XXVIII (1954).

like every other religious message, finds its natural and necessary expression in concepts that are of mythic origin (in the true sense of the word as defined by historians of contemporary religions, and which has nothing to do with fable, which is unreal in its very definition), it does not do so without making a radical split in the natural structure of myth itself. And how did the faith of the Jews and later that of the Christians break up and remake what was till then most constant and universal in the mythic vision of the universe? It did this by substituting for the cyclic vision of the universe, in which the same powers ceaselessly reproduce the same invariable order of phenomena, a really transcendent intervention which, by means of a unique saving event, effected a definitive modification in reality. In other words, in the Christian message as formulated in the Scriptures, Bultmann attributes to the myth the very thing through which both Jews and Christians transcended the earlier mythic formulas.[7]

Conversely, the timeless truth which Bultmann aims at substituting for the saving event is the exact analogue of the rationalizations of the mythic view of things which is the substance of the Greek philosophical interpretations of the natural mysteries. In other words, it is the Gospel in its pristine tenor that really surpasses the myth, while integrating whatever it contained of lasting value. An endeavor such as that of Bultmann's, on the other hand, unwittingly ends up in the same impasse that confronted Greek rationalism in its comprehension of reality: it devitalized the myth without being able to transcend it.[8]

The bearing which this analysis has on our problem is perhaps already apparent. If the mind of modern man had actually become utterly irresponsive to every form of expression connected with the primitive myth, it would be necessary to conclude that it had become impervious to any religious faith whatever, including that of Christianity. For if there is one thing which the history of comparative religion and depth psychology have succeeded in bringing to the fore, it is the fact that, through a process of integration

[7] For a critical study on the theses of Bultmann, see L. Malevez, S. J., *The Christian Message and Myth: The Theology of Rudolf Bultmann*, trans. Olive Wyon, D.D. (Westminster, Md., 1953).

[8] See on this point J. A. Cuttat, *The Encounter of Religions* (New York, 1958).

and elaboration, the myth can be surpassed, as has been done in Christianity, but it can in no wise be nullified. To empty it of its content would be to remove from man his natural ability to give a religious interpretation of any sort to his own life and to the world.

If, on the other hand, a technological mentality tends to produce such a state of affairs, we are assured by depth psychology that it will never actually achieve it. And the closer it comes to such an achievement, the more will it corrupt and upset our whole psyche. Even apart from all positive religion, the dreams of modern man, his poetry, and a whole complex of compensatory attitudes tend to restore to him the mythic universe which the technological civilization in which he lives threatens to suppress. And if these attitudes were not at least somewhat effective, men would lapse into a neurotic state.

If this is so, there is all the more reason that our adaptations of the liturgy should not attempt to rationalize it, to empty it not only of its mystery but also of all its expressions that are not strictly rational. They should, on the contrary, seize again upon the chords in the heart of modern man which respond to these eternal expressions in order to restore to them their maximum efficacy. At the same time, we must do everything in our power to revive man's atrophied faculties. It will be necessary to restore to the essential liturgical symbols their living richness which has been sadly weakened by our own rationalism. But it will be equally necessary to strive to bring back to our contemporaries a religious culture that will be human to the extent that it is also biblical. Here, of course, as in every age, theology, if it is both realistic and traditional, must carry out its essential task of rejoining a religious view of the world with the rational view of it which we cannot give up. But it would exceed its proper function if it attempted to achieve an artificial, unthinkable reduction of the mystery to pure rationality.